Days to Remember

Bahá'í Holy Days

Compiled by Dr Baher Forghani

Bahá'í Publications Australia

© Bahá'í Publications Australia

First Edition 1983
Second Revised Edition 2000

ISBN 0 909991 26 X

Bahá'í Publications Australia
173 Mona Vale Road
Ingleside NSW 2101
Australia

Telephone: 61 2 9913 1554
Fax: 61 2 9970 6710
Email: bpa@bahai.org.au
Website: www.bahaibooks.com

Printed in Australia

Introduction

The main aim of this compilation is to provide available information and some relevant readings on Bahá'í Holy Days and Anniversaries. It is obvious that such a collection cannot be free of imperfection. This is especially true for parts two and three which provide only some suggested readings on celebration or commemoration of the Bahá'í Holy Days and Anniversaries. There are some Tablets revealed by Bahá'u'lláh Persian and Arabic, in celebrating certain anniversaries, which are not, at present time, available in English. There are also many other passages in the Bahá'í literature in relation to Holy Days and Anniversaries that are not, for the sake of brevity, included in this production. Materials provided in this compilation therefore should be taken as suggested readings rather than fixed and inflexible programmes.

Texts used in this compilation are, with a few exceptions, taken from the writings of Baha'u'llah, the Báb, 'Abdu'l-Bahá, Shoghi Effendi and the Universal House of Justice. *The Dawn-Breakers* is also used to illustrate the historical events related to Holy Days and Anniversaries. The few exceptions are the information taken from the *Bahá'í World* vol. XV, *Baha'u'llah, the King of Glory* and *'Abdu'l-Bahá* both by Mr H. M. Balyuzi.

There are few quotations taken from early publications in which the Persian and Arabic names are not in accordance with the transliteration system adopted for Bahá'í books. For the sake of accuracy however they have been quoted in their original form.

It should also be mentioned that in parts two and three of this compilation materials are arranged in the form of suggested programmes for the celebration or commemoration of the Bahá'í Holy Days and Anniversaries. For this reason, in some occasions the historical or introductory information precede the writings of Baha'u'llah.

It is hoped that this compilation will help the individuals as well as Bahá'í communities to observe the Holy Days and Anniversaries befittingly, to study the glorious and inspiring life of the Central Figures of the Faith deeply, and to arise and serve the beloved Cause with more joy and confidence. B.F.

Foreword to the Revised Edition

Since the publication of the last edition of this compilation, a few Tablets and talks of 'Abdu'l-Bahá pertinent to Naw-Rúz have been retranslated. These new translations, kindly provided by the Universal House of Justice, are published for the first time here in this edition. A few communications from the Universal House of Justice pertaining to Holy Days and anniversaries, issued in recent years ,have also been added to relevant parts of the book.

This new edition is further enriched by the addition of more passages from the Writings of the Faith and by the inclusion of several photographs of some of the Holy Places related to historic events of Holy Days.

Baher Forghani

Contents

Contents

PART ONE

General Information on
Bahá'í Holy Days and Anniversaries

1.1 General Information on Bahá'í Holy Days and Anniversaries

1.1.1 Bahá'í Holy Days Established in *The Kitáb-i-Aqdas*

In *The Kitáb-i-Aqdas* Bahá'u'lláh established the festivals of Riḍván (on the first, ninth and twelfth days of which work is to be suspended), the Declaration of the Báb, the Birthday of the Báb the Birthday of Bahá'u'lláh, and Naw-Rúz. The Martyrdom of the Báb, in the days of Bahá'u'lláh, was commemorated and 'Abdu'l- Bahá added the observance of the Ascension of Bahá'u'lláh as a corollary to these Holy Days, making nine in all. In addition to these nine days, the Day of the Covenant and the Anniversary of the Passing of 'Abdu'l-Bahá' are commemorated, but work is not suspended on these last two days.[1]

1.1.2 Bahá'í Feasts and Anniversaries

- Feast of Riḍván (Declaration of Bahá'u'lláh), 21 April -2 May
- Feast of Naw-Rúz (New Year), 21 March
- Declaration of the Báb, 23 May, 1844
- The Day of the Covenant, 26 November
- Birth of Bahá'u'lláh, 12 November, 1817
- Birth of the Báb, 20 October 20, 1819
- Birth of 'Abdu'l-Bahá, 23 May 23, 1844
- Ascension of Bahá'u'lláh, 29 May 29, 1892
- Martyrdom of the Báb, 9 July, 1850
- Ascension of 'Abdu'l-Bahá, 28 November, 1921.[2]

1.1.3 Bahá'í Holy Days on Which Work Should be Suspended

- The first day of Riḍván.
- The ninth day of Riḍván.
- The twelfth day of Riḍván.
- The anniversary of the declaration of the Báb.
- The anniversary of the birth of Bahá'u'lláh.
- The anniversary of the birth of the Báb.
- The anniversary of the ascension of Bahá'u'lláh.
- The anniversary of the martyrdom of the Báb.
- The feast of Naw-Rúz.[3]

---

1. The *Kitáb-i-Aqdas*, Notes, p. 225.

2. *The Bahá'í World*, vol. XV, 1968-1973, p.688.

3. Ibid., p.689

Nine days in the year have been appointed on which work is forbidden. Some of these days have been specifically mentioned in the Book. The rest follow as corollaries to the Text ... Work on the Day of the Covenant (Fete Day of 'Abdu'l-Bahá), however, is not prohibited. Celebration of that day is left to the discretion of the friends. Its observation is not obligatory. The days pertaining to the Abhá Beauty (Bahá'u'lláh) and the Primal Point (the Báb) that is to say these nine days, are the only ones on which work connected with trade, commerce, industry and agriculture is not allowed. In like manner, work connected with any form of employment, whether governmental or otherwise should be suspended. [4]

He wishes also to stress the fact that, according to our Bahá'í laws, work is forbidden on our Nine Holy Days. Believers who have independent businesses or shops should refrain from working on these days. Those who are in government employ should, on religious grounds, make an effort to be excused from work; all believers, whoever their employers, should do likewise. If the government, or other employers, refuse to grant them these days off, they are not required to forfeit their employment, but they should make every effort to have the independent status of their Faith recognized and their right to hold their own religious Holy Days acknowledged. [5]

1.1.4   Unity of Action in the Observance of Bahá'í Holy Days is Essential

The Guardian... feels truly delighted at the news of the splendid meetings that were held in Bombay in honour of the anniversary of the birthday of His Holiness Bahá'u'lláh. This fresh evidence of the loyalty and devotion with which the Bombay friends are upholding the institutions of the Faith is highly gratifying and encouraging to him, indeed.

But he cannot but deplore the fact that some of the believers are reluctant to observe, as strictly as they should, the Feasts and anniversaries prescribed by the Cause. This attitude, which may be justified in certain exceptional circumstances, is fraught with incalculable dangers and harm to the community, and will, if allowed to persist, seriously endanger its influence and prestige in the public eye. Unity of action, in matters of so vital an importance as the observance of

---

4. 'Abdu'l-Bahá, quoted in *The Bahá'í World*, vol. XV, 1968-1973, p. 689.
5. Shoghi Effendi, quoted in *Principles of the Bahá'í Administration*, 1976, p. 55.

Bahá'í holidays, is essential. It is the responsibility of the NSA* to remind and urge the friends to faithfully carry out all such laws and precepts of the Cause, the enforcement of which does not constitute an open violation of the laws of their country. [6]

1.1.5 On Recitation of the Tablet of Visitation

The Universal House of Justice has received your letter expressing concern about the appropriateness of using the *Tablet of Visitation* at a commemoration held in a public restaurant, at which time those present were asked to stand and face the Qiblih.

The development of programmes for the observance of Holy Days is a matter left to the discretion of the appropriate National and Local Spiritual Assemblies, which are entrusted with the responsibility of ensuring that such observances are conducted in a manner in keeping with the spirit of the divine Teachings and Ordinances. Nothing is found in the Writings to prevent the use of the *Tablet of Visitation* as described in your letter; however, Assemblies are to be guided by dignity and propriety in arranging Holy Day observances in public places.

● ● ●

Far more important than the details of the programme and whether the particular decision was a wise one, is the preservation of unity and amity... . [7]

The Universal House of Justice has received your letter... asking whether the *Tablets of Visitation* must be read when commemorating the birth or passing of Bahá'u'lláh, the Báb, and 'Abdu'l-Bahá. While it is only natural for the friends to recite these Tablets on the anniversaries associated with the Central Figures of our Faith, no texts have been located by the Research Department of the House of Justice which make the use of these Tablets obligatory.

You have also requested guidelines regarding recitation of these Tablets. Some friends have asked in the past about the necessity of standing when reciting these Tablets and whether the friends should face the Qiblih on such occasions. Nothing has been found in the Writings concerning these matters. The House of Justice has stated that it is of utmost importance that the friends should not

___

* National Spiritual Assembly, the national administrative body of the Bahá'í Faith.

6. Shoghi Effendi, *Dawn of A New Day*, p. 56.

7. Universal House of Justice, letter to an individual believer, 31 December 1992.

allow secondary matters, such as these, to be a cause of argument and disagreement, and that they should try to safeguard the unity of the Bahá'í community.[8]

1.1.6 The Sale of Tea, Other Refreshments, and Bread by Bahá'ís on Bahá'í Holy Days

Regarding the sale of tea and other refreshments in a cinema under non-Bahá'í ownership; those friends who have hired from the owner of the cinema a stall for the sale of such refreshments should make every effort to obtain permission to close on Bahá'í holidays. In case, however, the non-Bahá'í owner or partner refuses to grant their request their only alternative is to obey.

The case is different with a bread bakery owned by a believer. In this case there can be no excuse whatever why the shop should not be closed during Bahá'í holidays, as there are always non-Bahá'í bakers from whom the public can buy.[9]

1.1.7 Bahá'í Doctors and Suspension of Work on Bahá'í Holy Days

He thinks it is better for Bahá'í doctors not to work on our 9 Holy Days—but, of course, that does not mean they should not attend to very sick people and emergencies on these days.[10]

1.1.8 Believers Who Have Independent Businesses Should Refrain from Working on Bahá'í Holy Days

From time to time questions have arisen about the application of the law of the *Kitáb-i-Aqdas* on the observance of Bahá'í Holy Days. As you know, the recognition of Bahá'í Holy Days in at least ninety-five countries of the world is an important and highly significant objective of the Nine Year Plan, and is directly linked with the recognition of the Faith of Bahá'u'lláh by the civil authorities as an independent religion enjoying its own rights and privileges.

The attainment of this objective will be facilitated and enhanced if the friends, motivated by their own realization of the importance of the laws of Bahá'u'lláh, are obedient to them. For the guidance of believers we repeat the instructions of the beloved Guardian:

8. Universal House of Justice, letter to an individual believer, 10 August 1994.

9. Shoghi Effendi, *Dawn of a New Day*, p. 65.

10. Ibid, p. 116.

He wishes also to stress the fact that, according to our Bahá'í laws, work is forbidden on our nine Holy Days. Believers who have independent businesses or shops should refrain from working on these days. Those who are in government employ should, on religious grounds, make an effort to be excused from work; all believers, whoever their employers, should do likewise. If the government, or other employers, refuse to grant them these days off, they are not required to forfeit their employment, but they should make every effort to have the independent status of their Faith recognized and their right to hold their own religious Holy Days acknowledged.[11]

This distinction between institutions that are under full or partial Bahá'í control is of a fundamental importance. Institutions that are entirely managed by Bahá'ís are, for reasons that are only too obvious, under the obligation of enforcing all the laws and ordinances of the Faith, especially those whose observance constitutes a matter of conscience. There is no reason, no justification whatever, that they should act otherwise ... The point which should be always remembered is that the issue in question is essentially a matter of conscience, and as such is of a binding effect upon all believers.[12]

In addition, steps should be taken to have Bahá'í children excused, on religious grounds, from attending school on Bahá'í holy days wherever possible. The Guardian has said:

Regarding children: at fifteen a Bahá'í is of age as far as keeping the laws of the *Aqdas* is concerned—prayer, fasting, etc. But children under fifteen should certainly observe the Bahá'í holy days, and not go to school, if this can be arranged on these nine days.[13]

National Assemblies should give this subject their careful consideration, and should provide ways and means for bringing this matter to the attention of the believers under their jurisdiction so that, as a matter of conscience, the mass of believers will uphold these laws and observe them.[14]

---

11. Shoghi Effendi, *Directives of the Guardian*, pp. 37-8.
12. From a letter written on behalf of the Guardian to the American National Spiritual Assembly, 2 October 1935, *Bahá'í News*, No. 97, p. 9.
13. *Lights of Guidance*, No. 517, pp. 154-5.
14. Universal House of Justice, *Messages from the Universal House of Justice: 1963-1986*, pp. 70-1.

1.1.9 Bahá'í Administrative Institutions and Suspension of Work on Bahá'í Holy Days

The Universal House of Justice has asked us to convey the following response to your letter of 21 July 1977 asking whether National Spiritual Assemblies, Local Spiritual Assemblies or Bahá'í committees should meet on Bahá'í Holy Days.

In a letter written on behalf of the beloved Guardian by his secretary to an individual, dated 3 January 1929, it is said:

On Bahá'í festivals and the sad commemorative occasions (among the Bahá'í Anniversaries) it would be preferable for Assemblies, Committees and Bahá'í institutions to suspend their activities. However, final decision in these matters rests with the Universal House of Justice.

The House of Justice has not yet made any decision about this matter, and therefore you should be guided by the above directive from the beloved Guardian.[15]

• • •

With reference to your email ... about the holding of National Assembly meetings on a Bahá'í Holy Day, the Universal House of Justice has directed us to share with you an excerpt from the translation of a Persian letter from the beloved Guardian dated 3 January 1929 in response to a similar question from an individual believer:

On the Bahá'í festivals and solemn commemorations it is preferable for Assemblies, Committees and Baha'i Institutions to suspend their activities. However, final decision in these matters rests with the Universal House of Justice.

The House of Justice feels that the above directive of the Guardian is adequate for the time being. It should be clear, however, that in the event of an emergency which requires the holding of a meeting of a Bahá'í institution on any of the nine Holy Days of the Faith, this would be permissible.[16]

15. Universal House of Justice, letter to the National Spiritual Assembly of the Bahá'ís of Australia, 11 August 1977.
16. Universal House of Justice, letter to a National Spiritual Assembly, 6 October 1994.

1.1.10   Bahá'í Holy Days on Which Suspension of Work is not Obligatory

You quote from page 537 *"Bahá'í World"* * words written by 'Abdu'l-Bahá— further down on the same page you will find the following *"As a corollary of this Tablet (above) it follows that the anniversaries of the birth and the ascension of 'Abdu'l-Bahá are not to be regarded as days on which work is prohibited. The celebration of these days is however obligatory"*.—These are the words of the Guardian. We really have eleven Holy Days but as stated, work is only prohibited on the first nine mentioned in the Tablet.[17]

The Day of the Covenant, 26 November , and the Day of the Ascension, 28 November, anniversaries of the birth and the Ascension of 'Abdu'l- Bahá must be observed by the friends coming together, but work is not prohibited. In other words the friends must regard observance of these two anniversaries as obligatory—but suspension of work not to be regarded as Obligatory.[18]

1.1.11   Proper Time to Celebrate

The Guardian would advise that, if feasible, the Friends should commemorate certain of the feasts and anniversaries at the following time:

* The anniversary of the Declaration of the Báb on 22 May, at about two hours after sunset.
* The first day of Riḍván, at about 3 p.m. on 21 April.
* The anniversary of the Martyrdom of the Báb on 9 July, at about noon.
* The anniversary of the Ascension of Bahá'u'lláh on 29 May, at 3 a.m.
* The Ascension of 'Abdu'l-Bahá on 28 November, at 1 a.m.

The other anniversaries the believers are free to gather at any time during the day which they find convenient.

Regarding your question of the proper time to celebrate or hold our meetings of commemoration, the time should be fixed by counting after sunset; the Master passed away one hour after midnight, which falls a certain number of hours after sunset; so His passing should be commemorated according to the sun and regardless of daylight saving time.

---

* *The Bahá'í World* Vol. XV, page 689.

17. Shoghi Effendi, *Letters to Australia and New Zealand*, p. 94.

18. Ibid, p. 89.

The same applies to the ascension of Bahá'u'lláh who passed away about eight hours after sunset.[19]

He would like to point out that if the believers gather before sundown on a certain date it does not matter if the meeting continues after sunset; it may still be considered as being held on the day they gathered. [20]

1.1.12 Observance of Bahá'í Holy Days and Anniversaries According to Standard Time

A number of questions have been asked concerning the exact times at which certain Bahá'í Holy Days should, if possible, be observed in view of the different times of sunset in various localities and also the use by some countries of such devices as daylight saving time. Since this matter will be of particular importance to the friends during the Holy Year, the Universal House of Justice has asked us to share the following advice with you.

As the Guardian indicated, the commemoration of the Ascension of Bahá'u'lláh should be held, if feasible, at 3 a.m. on 29 May, and that of the Ascension of 'Abdul-Bahá at 1 a.m. on 28 November. These times should be measured according to standard time in each area. If daylight saving time is being used in the country, the commemorations should continue to be observed according to standard time.

It will be noted that, in accordance with this schedule, the observances held on each Holy Day succeed one another for an entire twenty-four hours, as the earth turns on its axis.[21]

1.1.13 Definition of the Bahá'í Day

With reference to your question in connection with the observance of Bahá'í Holy Days; the Bahá'í day begins and ends at sunset. The night preceding a Holy day is therefore included in the day, and consequently work during that period is forbidden.[22]

---

19. Shoghi Effendi, *Unfolding Destiny*, p. 170.
20. *Lights of Guidance*, No. 1026, p. 302.
21. Universal House of Justice, from a letter to all National Spiritual Assemblies, dated 15 March 1992.
22. Shoghi Effendi, *Dawn of A New Day*, p. 68.

1.1.14 Use of Vocal or Instrumental Music in Holy Day Observances

Vocal or instrumental music befitting the dignity or solemnity of the occasion may be used during the readings and prayers in a Holy Day observance. Although instrumental music should not be used in Houses of Worship, in other places there is no objection to its use. [17]

1.1.15 Exchange of Presents on Bahá'í Holy Days

The exchanging of presents among believers or the giving of gifts to children is not an integral part of any of our nine Bahá'í Holy Days. There is no prohibition against it, and it is, as you mention, a custom among some Persian believers to exchange gifts at Naw-Rúz. In *The Kitáb-i-Aqdas* Bahá'u'lláh established the Intercalary Days. In *The Bahá'í World* vol. XV, p. 691, we read: *"Bahá'u'lláh designated those days as the 'Ayyám-i-Há and ordained that they should immediately precede the month of 'Alá, which is the month of fasting. He enjoined upon His followers to devote these days to feasting, rejoicing, and charity."*

The beloved Guardian's secretary, writing on his behalf to a National Spiritual Assembly on 26 December 1941, made this statement: *"The intercalary days are specially set aside for hospitality, the giving of gifts, etc. Bahá'u'lláh Himself specified that they be used this way, but gave no explanation for it."* [18]

• • •

The passage from a letter written on behalf of the Guardian... clearly associates the observance of the Intercalary Days with *"the giving of gifts"*. It should be left to the discretion of the believers to decide whether they wish to give gifts to each other, or whether to choose to restrict their gift giving to the poor and needy...

The fact that the practice of gift giving is subject to possible commercialization does not constitute a sufficient reason to discourage it in the Bahá'í community. The giving of gifts may also be regarded as a demonstration of friendship or gratitude, or may well be motivated solely by the desire to bring pleasure to others. As the believers grow in their understanding of the Bahá'í teachings, and as Bahá'í community life more fully embodies the ennobling

---

23. Universal House of Justice, from a message to a National Spiritual Assembly, 4 September 1990.

24. Universal House of Justice, from a letter to an individual believer, 25 March 1985.

values conveyed in the teachings, the practice of gift giving will be restored to its position as a worthy element of a society whose members wish to strengthen the bonds of amity and concord and to foster its unity and harmony.[25]

1.1.16   Observance of Former Holidays

As regards the celebration of the Christian Holidays by the believers, it is surely preferable and even highly advisable that the friends should in their relation to each other discontinue observing such holidays as Christmas and New Years, and to have their festival gatherings of this nature instead during the intercalary days and Naw- Rúz.[26]

1.1.17   Non-Bahá'ís May Be Invited to Holy Day Celebrations

As with other Holy Days of the Faith, the Riḍván celebration is not necessarily for Bahá'ís only, and non-Bahá'ís may be invited to participate. Regarding inviting non-Bahá'ís to attend the annual election meeting, no statement has been found in the Writings or in the letters of the Guardian on this particular question. This is a matter for the National Spiritual Assembly to consider, bearing in mind the private and sensitive character of this meeting.[27]

---

25. Universal House of Justice, from a letter to a Local Spiritual Assembly, 17 August 1989.

26. Shoghi Effendi, *Principles of Bahá'í Administration*, p. 57.

27. Universal House of Justice, letter to a National Spiritual Assembly, 19 February 1998.

PART TWO

Suggested Readings for Celebration or
Commemoration of Bahá'í Holy Days and
Anniversaries on Which Work Should be
Suspended

Bahá'í Holy Days and Anniversaries on Which Work Should be Suspended

2.1   Feast of Naw-Rúz—Bahá'í New Year
2.2   Feast of Riḍván—Declaration of Bahá'u'lláh (1st, 9th and 12th).
2.3   Declaration of the Báb
2.4   Ascension of Bahá'u'lláh
2.5   Martyrdom of the Báb
2.6   Birth of the Báb
2.7   Birth of Bahá'u'lláh

2.1
Feast of Naw-Rúz
Bahá'í New Year, 21 March

"Now is the beginning of a cycle of Reality, a New Cycle, a New Age, a New Century, a New Time and a New Year. Therefore, it is very blessed..."[28]

Suggested Readings:

2.1.1   A Meditation Revealed by Bahá'u'lláh for Naw-Rúz
2.1.2   Prayer Revealed by Bahá'u'lláh
2.1.3   Prayer Revealed by 'Abdu'l-Bahá
2.1.4   *It is New Year*, from the Writings of 'Abdu'l-Bahá
2.1.5   *This Cause is Progressive*, from the Writings of 'Abdu'l-Bahá
2.1.6   *This is the Time for Growing*, from the Writings of 'Abdu'l-Bahá
2.1.7   *Spirit of Life*, from the Writings of 'Abdu'l-Bahá
2.1.8   *A Blessed Day*, A Talk Given by 'Abdu'l-Bahá,
2.1.9   *The Symbol of Life*, A Talk Given by 'Abdu'l-Bahá in Paris, 21 March 1913
2.1.10   Proper Time to Celebrate
2.1.11   The Beginning of the Naw-Rúz
2.1.12   Sending Naw-Rúz Cards

---

28. 'Abdu'l-Bahá, quoted in Star of the West, vol. IX, no. 1, p. 1.

2.1.1 A Meditation, Revealed by Bahá'u'lláh, for Naw-Rúz

Praised be Thou, O my God, that Thou has ordained Naw-Rúz as a festival unto those who have observed the fast for love of Thee and abstained from all that is abhorrent unto Thee, Grant, O my Lord, that the fire of Thy love and the heat produced by the fast enjoined by Thee may inflame them in Thy Cause, and make them to be occupied with Thy praise and with remembrance of Thee.

Since Thou hast adorned them, O my Lord, with the ornament of the fast prescribed by Thee, do Thou adorn them also with the ornament of Thine acceptance, through Thy grace and bountiful favour. For the doings of men are all dependent upon Thy good-pleasure, and are conditioned by Thy behest. Shouldst Thou regard him who hath broken the fast as one who hath observed it, such a man would be reckoned among them who from eternity had been keeping the fast. And shouldst Thou decree that he who hath observed the fast hath broken it, that person would be numbered with such as have caused the Robe of Thy Revelation to be stained with dust, and been far removed from the crystal waters of this living Fountain.

Thou art He through Whom the ensign *'Praiseworthy art Thou in Thy works'* hath been lifted up, and the standard *'Obeyed art Thou in Thy behest'* hath been unfurled. Make known this Thy station, O my God, unto Thy servants, that they may be made aware that the excellence of all things is dependent upon Thy bidding and Thy word, and the virtue of every act is conditioned by Thy leave and the good-pleasure of Thy will, and may recognize that the reins of men's doings are within the grasp of Thine acceptance and Thy commandment. Make this known unto them, that nothing whatsoever may shut them out from Thy Beauty, in these days whereon the Christ exclaimeth: *'All dominion is Thine, O Thou the Begetter of the Spirit (Jesus)'*; and Thy Friend (Muḥammad) crieth out: *'Glory be to Thee, O Thou the Best-Beloved, for that Thou has uncovered Thy Beauty, and written down for Thy chosen ones what will cause them to attain unto the seat of the revelation of Thy Most Great Name, through which all the peoples have lamented except such as have detached themselves from all else except Thee, and set themselves towards Him Who is the Revealer of Thyself and the Manifestation of Thine attributes.'*

He Who is Thy Branch and all Thy company, O my Lord, have broken this day their fast, after having observed it within the precincts of Thy court, and in their eagerness to please Thee. Do Thou ordain for him, and for them, and for all such as have entered Thy presence in those days all the good Thou didst destine in Thy Book. Supply them, then, with that which will profit them, in both this life and in the life beyond. Thou, in truth, art the All-Knowing, the All-Wise.[29]

2.1.2 Prayer Revealed by Bahá'u'lláh

Glory to Thee, O my God! The first stirrings of the spring of Thy grace have appeared and clothed Thine earth with verdure. The clouds of the heaven of Thy bounty have rained their rain on this City within whose walls is imprisoned Him Whose desire is the salvation of Thy creatures. Through it the soil of this City hath been decked forth, and its trees clothed with foliage, and its inhabitants gladdened.

The hearts of Thy dear ones, however, will rejoice only at the Divine Springtime of Thy tender mercies, whereby the hearts are quickened, and the souls are renewed, and the trees of human existence bear their fruits.

The plants that have sprung forth, O my Lord, in the hearts of Thy loved ones have withered away. Send down upon them, from the clouds of Thy spirit, that which will cause the tender herbs of Thy knowledge and wisdom to grow within their breasts. Rejoice, then, their hearts with the proclamation of Thy Cause and the exaltation of Thy sovereignty.

Their eyes, O my Lord, are expectantly turned in the direction of Thy bounty, and their faces are set towards the horizon of Thy grace. Suffer them not, through Thy bounty, to be deprived of Thy grace. Potent art Thou, by Thy sovereign might, over all things. No God is there but Thee, the Almighty, the Help in Peril, the Self-Subsisting.[30]

2.1.3 Prayer Revealed by 'Abdu'l-Bahá

O Lord, my Lord

This is the day which Thy Sacred Tongue and Thy Pen of Glory both have sanctified, and made it a day of heavenly blessings, of divine benediction and favour Thou hast honoured it with Thy bestowals, endued it with Thy Grace, and invested it with Thy Glory, and caused it to be a day of joy and gladness unto them that have turned to the Light of Thy Divine Revelation; that the hearts may thereby be gladdened, that the radiance of happiness may illumine

---

29. Bahá'u'lláh, *Prayers and Meditations*, no. 46, pp. 67-70.
30. Ibid, no. 117, pp. 199-200.

the lives of them that remember the manifestation of Thy Glory upon Thy Sacred Mount.

Hallow it, O Lord, with Thy grace, and make it a day of joy and blessedness for Thy loved ones, that have stood fast and firm in Thy Covenant, Thy friends that have sung Thy Praise, and especially for this servant of Thine that hath turned his face to Thy Holy Kingdom, supplicated the glory of Thy might and power, circled Thy throne of grandeur and fell prostrate at Thy threshold of Divine Mercy.

Thou art the Gracious, the Bountiful the All-Merciful.[31]

2.1.4 *It is New Year*, from the Writings of 'Abdu'l-Bahá

O ye children of the Kingdom! It is New Year, that is to say the rounding of the cycle of the year. A year is the expression of a cycle (of the sun); but now is the beginning of a cycle of Realty, a New Cycle, a New Age, A New Century, a New Time and a New Year. Therefore, it is very blessed.

I wish this blessing to appear and become manifest in the faces and characteristics of the believers, so that they, too, may become a new people, and having found new life and been baptized with fire and spirit, may make the world a new world, to the end that the old earth may disappear and the new earth appear; old ideas depart and new thoughts come; old garments be cast aside and new garments put on; ancient politics whose foundation is war be discarded and modern politics founded on peace raise the standard of victory; the new star shine and gleam and the new sun illumine and radiate; new flowers bloom; the new spring become known; the new breeze blow; the new bounty descent; the new tree give forth new fruit; the new voice become raised and this new sound reach the ears, that the new may follow the new, and all the old furnishings and adornments be cast aside and new decorations put in their places.

I desire for you all that you may have this great assistance and partake of this great bounty, and that in spirit and heart you may strive and endeavour until the world of war become the world of peace; the world of darkness the world of light; satanic conduct be turned into heavenly behaviour; the ruined places become built up; the sword be turned into the olive branch; the flash of hatred become the flame of the love of God and the noise of the gun the voice of

31. 'Abdu'l-Bahá, Star of the West, vol. 14, no. 3, p. 82.

the Kingdom; the soldiers of death the soldiers of life; all the nations of the world one nation; all races as one race; and all national anthems harmonized into one melody.

Then this material realm will be paradise, the earth heaven and the world of Satan become the world of angels.[32]

2.1.5 *This Cause is Progressive*, from the Writings of 'Abdu'l-Bahá

O thou attracted maid-servant of God!

The celebration of the Feast of Naw-Rúz made me glad. Consider how different this meeting was from that of last year. Consider the bounty and the blessing of God. Therefore, know that this Cause is progressive. No obstacles in the world can hinder it. Thou didst realize divine joy and happiness in that meeting. Is it possible for earthly gatherings to give such divine joy? This bounty is itself the greatest evidence of the appearance of the Kingdom. I ask God to increase daily the fire and zeal of the love of God. Thus may that land become a veritable paradise and the heavenly attainments become manifest.

If thou knewest in what [spiritual] state I write this letter thou wouldst surely become like a flame of fire and set aglow the hearts by the fire of the love of God.

Thou hast written concerning *The Most Holy Book [Kitáb-i-Aqdas]*. It is intended that in the future, God willing, means will be provided and with the utmost care it will be translated and sent to those regions.[33]

2.1.6 *This is the Time for Growing*, from the Writings of 'Abdu'l-Bahá

O Friends of God!

Do ye know in what cycle ye are created and in what age ye exist? This is the age of the Blessed Perfection and this is the time of the Greatest Name! This is the century of the Manifestation, the age of the Sun of all horizons and the beautiful springtime of the Eternal One!

The earth is in motion and growth; the mountains, hills and prairies are green and pleasant; bounty is overflowing; mercy universal; rain is descending from the clouds of compassion; the brilliant sun is shining; the full moon adorneth

---

32. 'Abdu'l-Bahá, quoted in *Star of the West*, vol. IX, no. 1, p. 1.

33. 'Abdu'l-Bahá, from a recently translated Tablet.

the ethereal horizon; the great ocean-tide is flooding every little stream; gifts and favours follow one upon the other and a refreshing breeze is blowing, wafting the fragrant perfume of the blossoms.

If we are not happy and joyous at this season, for what other season shall we wait and for what other time shall we look?

Boundless treasure is in the hand of the King of Kings! Lift the hem of thy garment to receive it.

This is the time for growing; the season for joyous gathering! Take the cup of the Testament in thy hand; leap and dance with ecstasy in the triumphal procession of the Covenant! Place your confidence in the everlasting bounty, turn to the presence of the generous God; ask assistance from the Kingdom of Abhá; seek confirmation from the Supreme World; turn thy vision to the horizon of eternal wealth; and pray for help from the Source of Mercy!

Soon shall ye see the friends attaining their longed-for destination and pitching their tents, while we are but in the first day of our journey.[34]

2.1.7 *Spirit of Life*, from the Writings of 'Abdu'l-Bahá

O thou who art turning unto the Kingdom of God!

Thy letter hath been received and perused. It afforded us joy and pleasure, gave us good news and is a token of the wealth of thy love. This period of time is the Promised Age, the assembling of the human race to the Resurrection Day and now is the great Day of Judgement. Soon the whole world, as in springtime, will change its garb. The turning and falling of the autumn leaves is past; the bleakness of the wintertime is over. The new year hath appeared and the spiritual springtime is at hand. The black earth is becoming a verdant garden; the deserts and mountains are teeming with red flowers; from the borders of the wilderness the tall grasses are standing like advance guards before the cypress and jessamine trees; while the birds are singing among the rose branches like the angels in the highest heavens, announcing the glad-tidings of the approach of that spiritual spring, and the sweet music of their voices is causing the real essence of all things to move and quiver.

O my spiritual friend! Dost thou know from what airs emanate the notes sung by those birds? They are from the melodies of peace and reconciliation, of love and unity, of justice and security, of concord and harmony. In a short time this heavenly singing will intoxicate all humanity; the foundations of en-

---

34. 'Abdu'l-Bahá, from a recently translated Tablet.

mity shall be destroyed; unity and affection shall be witnessed in every assembly; and the splendours of the love of God will shine forth in these great festivals.

Therefore, contemplate what a spirit of life God hath given that the body of the whole earth may attain life everlasting! The Abhá Paradise will soon spread a pavilion in the midmost heart of the world, under whose shelter the beloved shall rejoice and the pure hearts shall repose in peace.[35]

2.1.8 *A Blessed Day*, A Talk Given by 'Abdu'l-Bahá,

According to ancient custom, every nation has general holidays when all the people rejoice and are glad. That is, they choose the day of the year whereon a great or glorious event had occurred. On that day they manifest great joy and happiness. They visit one another; if they have any feelings of bitterness towards one another, they become reconciled on that day; hard feelings pass away and they unite in love for each other. As great events occurred on the day of Naw-Rúz for the Persians, that nation therefore made it a national feast and considered it a national holiday.

This is, indeed, a blessed day because it is the beginning of the temperate season and the commencement of springtime in the northern hemisphere. All earthly things, whether trees, animals or humans, become refreshed; they receive power from the life-giving breeze and obtain new life; a resurrection takes place and, because it is the season of springtime, there is a general marvellous activity in all contingent beings.

There was a time when the Persian dynasty died out and no trace remained thereof. On such a day [Naw-Rúz] a new one was founded. Jamshíd* ascended the throne. Persia became happy and at peace. Its power, which had been dissipated, once more returned. Hearts and souls became possessed of wonderful susceptibilities, to such a degree that Persia became more advanced than it had been in former days under the sovereignty of Kayumars and Húshang.** The glory and greatness of the government and the nation of Persia rose higher. Likewise, a great many events occurred upon the day of Naw-Rúz that brought honour and glory to Persia and to the Persians. Therefore, the Persian nation, for the last five or six thousand years, has always considered the Feast of

---

35. 'Abdu'l-Bahá, from a new translation of a Tablet previously published in *Tablets of Abbdul-Baha Abbás* (Chicago: Bahá'í Publishing Society, 1915), vol. 2, pp. 318-19.

* Legendary King of Persia.

** Legendary Kings of Persia.

Naw-Rúz as a day of national happiness, and until now it is sanctified and recognized as a blessed day.

In brief, every nation has a day to mark as a holiday which they celebrate with joy. In the sacred laws of God in every cycle and dispensation, there are blessed feasts, holidays and workless days. On such days no kind of occupation, commerce, industry, agriculture, or the like, is allowed. All work is unlawful. All must enjoy themselves, gather together, hold general meetings, become as one assembly, so that the oneness, unity and harmony of the people may be demonstrated in the eyes of all. As it is a blessed day it should not be neglected or left without results by making it a day limited to the fruits of mere pleasure. During such blessed days institutions should be founded that may be of permanent benefit and value to the people so that in their conversations and in history it may become widely known that such a good work was inaugurated on such a feast day. Therefore, the intelligent must look searchingly into conditions to find out what important affair, what philanthropic institutions are most needed and what foundations should be laid for the community on that particular day, so that they may be established. For example, if they find that the community needs morality, then they may lay down the foundation of good morals on that day. If the community be in need of spreading sciences and widening the circle of knowledge, on that day they should proceed in that direction, that is to say, direct the thoughts of all the people to that philanthropic cause. If, however, the community is in need of widening the circle of commerce or industry or agriculture, they should inaugurate the means of attaining the desired aim. If the community needs protection, proper support and care of orphans, they should act upon the welfare of the orphans, and so forth. Such undertakings as are beneficial to the poor, the weak and the helpless should be pursued in order that, on that day, through the unity of all and through great meetings, results may be obtained, the glory and blessings of that day may be declared and manifest.par

Likewise in this wonderful Dispensation this day [Naw-Rúz] is a blessed day. The friends of God should be confirmed in service and servitude. With one another they must be in the utmost harmony, love and oneness, clasping hands, engaged in the commemoration of the Blessed Beauty and thinking of the great results that may be obtained on such a blessed day.

Today, there is no result or fruit greater than guiding the people, because these helpless creatures, especially the Persians, have remained without a share in the bestowals of God. Undoubtedly, the friends of God, upon such a day, must leave tangible, philanthropic or ideal traces that should reach all mankind and not only pertain to the Bahá'ís.

In all the prophetic Dispensations, philanthropic affairs were confined to their respective peoples only—with the exception of small matters, such as charity, which it was permissible to extend to others. But in this wonderful Dispensation, philanthropic undertakings are for all humanity, without any exception, because this is the manifestation of the mercifulness of God. Therefore, every universal matter—that is, one that belongs to all the world of humanit— is divine; and every matter that is sectarian and private is not universal in character—that is, it is limited. Therefore, my hope is that the friends of God, every one of them, may become as the mercy of God to all mankind.[36]

2.1.9 *The Symbol of Life*, A Talk Given by 'Abdu'l-Bahá in Paris, 21 March 1913

I am extremely glad to see you on this Naw Rúz occasion. This day is considered holy by the Persians … From time immemorial this day has been consecrated for in this there is a symbol.

At this moment the sun appears at the meridian and the day and night are equal. Until today the North Pole has been in darkness. Today the sun appears on the horizon of the North Pole. Today the sun rises and sets at the equator and the two hemispheres are equally illumined. This sacred day, when the sun illumines equally the whole earth, is called the equinox, and the equinox is the symbol of the Manifestation of God. The Sun of Truth rises on the horizon of Divine Mercy and sends forth its rays. This day is consecrated to commemorate it. It is the beginning of spring. When the sun appears at the equinox, it causes a movement in all living things. The mineral world is set in motion, plants begin to shoot, the desert is changed into a prairie, trees bud and every living thing responds, including the bodies of animals and men.

The rising of the sun at the equinox is the symbol of life, and likewise it is the symbol of the Divine Manifestation of God, for the rising of the Sun of Truth in the Heaven of Divine Bounty established the signal of Life for the world. The human reality begins to live, our thoughts are transformed and our intelligence is quickened. The Sun of Truth bestows Eternal Life, just as the solar sun is the cause of terrestrial life.

---

36. 'Abdu'l-Bahá, from a new translation of a talk.

The day of the appearance of God's Manifestations on earth must be a sacred day when man must commemorate God in prayer and praise. Among the ancient Persians this day was looked upon as the holy day of the year and on it hospitals and charitable institutions were founded. Collections for the poor are made on this day and every effort is put forth so that it may not be allowed to pass without leaving some divine traces. Throughout Persia one sees the historical traces of this sacred day by the many good works that have commemorated it.[37]

2.1.10 Proper Time to Celebrate

The Naw-Rúz Feast should be held on 21 March before sunset and has nothing to do with the 19-day Feast. The 19-day Feast is administrative in function whereas the Naw-Rúz is our New Year, a Feast of hospitality and rejoicing.[38]

"Regarding Naw-Rúz: If the vernal equinox falls on the 21st of March before sunset, it is celebrated on that day. If at any time after sunset, Naw-Rúz will then, as stated by Bahá'u'lláh, fall on the 22nd. As to which spot should be regarded as the standard, this is a matter which the Universal House of Justice will have to decide. The American NSA need not therefore take any action in this matter at present.[39]

2.1.11 The Beginning of the Naw-Rúz

The Universal House of Justice referred to the Department of the Secretariat for response your letter of 28 October 1988 in which you request guidance regarding the date and the hour for the beginning of the Naw-Rúz Feast insofar as the equinox is concerned.

Bahá'u'lláh has left the details of many laws to be filled in by the Universal House of Justice. Among these are a number of matters affecting the Bahá'í calendar. For example, Bahá'u'lláh has specified that Naw-Rúz shall be that day (measured from sunset to sunset) on which the spring equinox occurs "even should this occur one minute before sundown". In order to implement this law universally a particular spot on earth must be chosen in relation to which the times of the spring equinox and sunset can be established each year; the choos-

---

37. 'Abdu'l-Bahá, quoted in Star of the West, vol. V, no. 1, p. 4.
38. Shoghi Effendi, Directives of the Guardian, no. 75, p. 30.
39. Ibid, no. 76.

ing of this spot has been left to the decision of the House of Justice.

It is apparent that until this decision is made it is not possible to know the exact correlation of Bahá'í and Gregorian dates, because in some years Naw Rúz will coincide with the 20th of March, in some with the 21st, and in some with the 22nd. Therefore, until such time, the Bahá'ís in most of the world are observing the Bahá'í Holy Days on their anniversaries in the Gregorian calendar. Once the necessary legislation to determine Naw-Rúz has been made, the correspondence between Bahá'í and Gregorian dates will vary from year to year depending upon whether the spring equinox falls on the 20th, 21st or 22nd of March. In fact in Iran the friends have been, over the years, following the spring equinox as observed in Tihrán, to determine Naw-Rúz, and a Bahá'í calendar is issued every year for the guidance of the friends.

The unification of the eastern and western calendars regarding the dates for observance of the Holy Days is a much more complicated matter than appears on the surface, involving the establishment of the original dates themselves. The records found in Nabíl and elsewhere are at times in conflict and irreconcilable with each other. This is due to the fact that the countries of the Middle East do not necessarily follow identical lunar calendars, and it is difficult to ascertain in each case on which country's calendar Nabíl has based his lunar date. Work is being done on this problem but the House of Justice feels that this is not a matter of urgency.

In the meantime, as with other unresolved matters, this must never be a cause of dispute or in harmony among the friends. They must accept, for the time being, the calendar in force in the countries in which they live, and certainly not disturb the spiritual atmosphere with which the observances of the Holy Days should be imbued.[40]

2.1.12 Sending Naw-Rúz Cards

There is no objection to individual Bahá'ís sending Naw-Rúz cards if they want to; also the NSA can send them out occasionally, but it should not become a fixed custom.[41]

---

40. Universal House of Justice, from a letter to a National Spiritual Assembly, 8 December 1988.

41. Shoghi Effendi, *Letters to Australia and New Zealand*, p. 65.

2.2
Feast of Riḍván
Declaration of Bahá'u'lláh
April 21-May 2, 1863

Rejoice with exceeding gladness, O people of Bahá, as ye call to remembrance the Day of supreme felicity.[42]

Suggested Readings:

2.2.1   *The Divine Springtime is Come*, Tablet Revealed by Bahá'u'lláh for the Occasion

2.2.2   *He Who is the Best-Beloved is Come*, Tablet Revealed by Bahá'u'lláh

2.2.3   Prayer Revealed by Bahá'u'lláh

2.2.4   Prayer Revealed by Bahá'u'lláh

2.2.5   Excerpts from the Tablet of Bahá'u'lláh Addressed to Naṣirid-Dín Sháh

2.2.6   *The Day-Star of Truth*, A Tablet from 'Abdu'l-Bahá

2.2.7   Excerpts from A Tablet Revealed by 'Abdu'l-Bahá

2.2.8   Riḍván Festival

2.2.9   Declaration of Bahá'u'lláh

2.2.10 The Station of Bahá'u'lláh

2.2.11 The First, Ninth and Twelfth Days of Riḍván

---

42. Bahá'u'lláh, *Gleanings From the Writings of Bahá'u'lláh*, XIV, p. 35.

2.2.1   *The Divine Springtime is Come*, Tablet Revealed by Bahá'u'lláh for the Occasion.

The Divine Springtime is come, O Most Exalted Pen, for the Festival of the All-Merciful is fast approaching. Bestir thyself, and magnify, before the entire creation, the name of God, and celebrate His praise, in such wise that all created things may be regenerated and made new. Speak, and hold not thy peace. The day star of blissfulness shineth above the horizon of Our name, The Blissful, inasmuch as the kingdom of the name of God hath been adorned with the ornament of the name of thy Lord, the Creator of the heavens. Arise before the nations of the earth, and arm thyself with the power of this Most Great Name, and be not of those who tarry.

Methinks that thou has halted and movest not upon My Tablet. Could the brightness of the Divine Countenance have bewildered thee, or the idle talk of the forward filled thee with grief and paralyzed thy movement? Take heed lest anything deter thee from extolling the greatness of this Day—the Day whereon the Finger of majesty and power hath opened the seal of the Wine of Reunion, and called all who are in the heavens and all who are on the earth. Preferest thou to tarry when the breeze announcing the Day of God hath already breathed over thee, or art thou of them that are shut out as by a veil from Him?

No veil whatever have I allowed, O Lord of all names and Creator of the heavens, to shut me from the recognition of the glories of Thy Day—the Day which is the lamp of guidance unto the whole world, and the sign of the Ancient of Days unto all them that dwell therein. My silence is by reason of the veils that have blinded Thy creatures' eyes to Thee, and my muteness is because of the impediments that have hindered Thy people from recognizing Thy truth. Thou knowest what is in me, but I know not what is in Thee. Thou art the All-Knowing, the All-Informed. By Thy name that excelleth all other names! If Thy overruling and all-compelling behest should ever reach me, it would impower me to revive the souls of all men, through Thy most exalted Word, which I have heard uttered by Thy Tongue of power in Thy Kingdom of glory. It would enable me to announce the revelation of Thy effulgent countenance where through that which lay hidden from the eyes of men hath been manifested in Thy name, the Perspicuous, the sovereign Protector, the Self-Subsisting

Canst thou discover any one but Me, O Pen, in this Day? What hath become of the creation and the manifestations thereof? What of the names and their kingdom? Whither are gone all created things, whether seen or unseen? What of the hidden secrets of the universe and its revelations? Lo, the entire creation hath passed away! Nothing remaineth except My Face, the Ever-Abiding, the Resplendent, the All-Glorious.

This is the Day whereon naught can be seen except the splendours of the Light that shineth from the face of Thy Lord, the Gracious, the Most Bountiful. Verily, We have caused every soul to expire by virtue of Our irresistible and all-subduing sovereignty. We have, then, called into being a new creation, as a token of Our grace unto men. I am, verily, the All-Bountiful, the Ancient of Days.

This is the Day whereon the unseen world crieth out: *"Great is thy blessedness, O earth, for thou has been made the foot-stool of thy God, and been chosen as the seat of His mighty throne."* The realm of glory exclaimeth: *"Would that my life could be sacrificed for thee, for He Who is the Beloved of the All-Merciful hath established His sovereignty upon thee, through the power of His Name that hath been promised unto all things, whether of the past or of the future."* This is the Day whereon every sweet smelling thing hath derived its fragrance from the smell of My garment—a garment that hath shed its perfume upon the whole of creation. This is the Day whereon the rushing waters of everlasting life have gushed out of the Will of the All-Merciful. Haste ye, with your hearts and souls, and quaff your fill, O Concourse of the realms above!

Say: He it is Who is the Manifestation of Him Who is the Unknowable, the Invisible of the Invisibles, could ye but perceive it. He it is Who hath laid bare before you the hidden and treasured Gem, were ye to seek it. He it is Who is the one Beloved of all things, whether of the past or of the future. Would that ye might set your hearts and hopes upon Him!

We have heard the voice of thy pleading, O Pen, and excuse thy silence. What is it that hath so sorely bewildered thee? The inebriation of Thy presence, O Well-Beloved of all worlds, hath seized and possessed me.

Arise, and proclaim unto the entire creation tile tidings that He Who is the All-Merciful hath directed His steps towards the Riḍván and entered it. Guide, then, the people unto the garden of delight which God hath made the Throne of His Paradise. We have chosen thee to be our most mighty Trumpet, whose blast is to signalize the resurrection of all mankind.

Say: This is the Paradise on whose foliage the wine of utterance hath imprinted the testimony: *"He that was hidden from the eyes of men is revealed, girded with sovereignty and power!"* This is the Paradise, the rustling of whose leaves proclaim: *"O ye that inhabit the heavens and the earth! There hath appeared what hath never previously appeared.*

He Who, from everlasting, had concealed His face from the sight of creation is now come." From the whispering breeze that wafteth amidst its branches there cometh the cry: *"He Who is the sovereign Lord of all is made manifest. The Kingdom is God's,"* while from its steaming waters can be heard the murmur: *"All eyes are gladdened, for He Whom none hath beheld, Whose secret no one hath discovered, hath lifted the veil of glory, and uncovered the countenance of Beauty."*

Within this Paradise, and from the heights of its loftiest chambers, the Maids of Heaven have cried out and shouted: *"Rejoice, ye dwellers of the realms above, for the fingers of Him Who is the Ancient of Days are ringing, in the name of the All-Glorious, the Most Great Bell, in the midmost heart of the heavens. The hands of bounty have borne round the cup of everlasting life. Approach, and quaff your fill. Drink with healthy relish, O ye that are the very incarnations of longing, ye who are the embodiments of vehement desire!"*

This is the Day whereon He Who is the Revealer of the names of God hath stepped out of the Tabernacle of glory, and proclaimed unto all who are in the heavens and all who are on the earth: *"Put away the cups of Paradise and all the life-giving waters they contain, for lo, the people of Bahá have entered the blissful abode of the Divine Presence, and quaffed the wine of reunion, from the chalice of the beauty of their Lord, the All-Possessing, the Most High."*

Forget the world of creation, O Pen, and turn thou towards the face of thy Lord, the Lord of all names. Adorn, then, the world with the ornament of the favours of thy Lord, the King of everlasting days. For We perceive the fragrance of the Day whereon He Who is the desire of all nations hath shed upon the kingdoms of the unseen and of the seen the splendour of the light of His most excellent names, and enveloped them with the radiance of the luminaries of His most gracious favours—favours which none can reckon except Him, Who is the omnipotent Protector of the entire creation.

Look not upon the creatures of God except with the eye of kindliness and of mercy, for Our loving providence hath pervaded all created things, and Our grace encompassed the earth and the heavens. This is the Day whereon the true servants of God partake of the life-giving waters of reunion, the Day whereon those that are nigh unto Him are able to drink of the soft-flowing river of immortality, and they who believe in His unity, the wine of His Presence, through their recognition of Him Who is the Highest and Last End of all, in Whom the Tongue of Majesty and Glory voiceth the call: *"The Kingdom is Mine. I, Myself, am, of Mine own right, its Ruler."*

Attract the hearts of men, through the call of Him, the one alone Beloved. Say: This is the Voice of God, if ye do but hearken. This is the Day Spring of the Revelation of God, did ye but know it. This is the Dawning-Place of the Cause of God were ye to recognize it. This is the Source of the commandment of God, did ye but judge it fairly. This is the manifest and hidden Secret; would that ye might perceive it. O peoples of the world! Cast away, in My name that transcendeth all other names, the things ye possess, and immerse yourselves in this Ocean in whose depths lay hidden the pearls of wisdom and of utterance, an ocean that surgeth in My name, the All-Merciful. Thus instructeth you He with Whom is the Mother Book.

The Best-Beloved is come. In His right hand is the sealed Wine of His name. Happy is the man that turneth unto Him, and drinketh his fill, and exclaimeth: *"Praise be to Thee, O Revealer of the signs of God!"* By the righteousness of the Almighty! Every hidden thing hath been manifested through the power of truth. All the favours of God have been sent down, as a token of His grace. The waters of everlasting life have, in their fullness, been proffered unto men. Every single cup hath been borne round by the hand of the Well-Beloved. Draw near, and tarry not, though it be for one short moment.

Blessed are they that have soared on the wings of detachment and attained the station which, as ordained by God, overshadoweth the entire creation, whom neither the vain imaginations of the learned, nor the multitude of the hosts of the earth have succeeded in deflecting from His Cause. Who is there among you, O people, who will renounce the world, and draw nigh unto God, the Lord of all names? Where is he to be found who, through the power of My name that transcendeth all created things, will cast away the things that men possess, and cling, with all his might, to the things which God, the Knower of the unseen and of the seen, hath bidden him observe? Thus hath His bounty been sent down unto men. His testimony fulfilled and His proof shone forth above the Horizon of mercy. Rich is the prize that shall be won by him who hath believed and exclaimed: *"Lauded art Thou, O Beloved of all worlds! Magnified by Thy name, O Thou the Desire of every understanding heart!"*

Rejoice with exceeding gladness, O people of Bahá, as ye call to remembrance the Day of supreme felicity, the Day whereon the Tongue of the Ancient of the Days hath spoken, as He departed from His house, proceeding to the Spot from which He shed upon the whole of creation the splendours of His name, the All-Merciful. God is Our witness. Were We to reveal the hidden secrets of that Day, all they that dwell on earth and in the heavens would swoon away and die, except such as will be preserved by God, the Almighty, the All-Knowing, the All-Wise.

Such is the inebriating effect of the words of God upon Him Who is the Revealer of His undoubted proofs, that His Pen can move no longer. With these words He concludeth His Tablet: *"No God is there but Me, the Most Exalted, the Most Powerful, the Most Excellent, the All-Knowing."* [43]

2.2.2 *He Who is Best Beloved is Come*, Tablet Revealed by Bahá'u'lláh

Release yourselves, O nightingales of God, from the thorns and brambles of wretchedness and misery, and wing your flight to the rose-garden of unfading splendour. O My friends that dwell upon the dust! Haste forth unto your celestial habitation. Announce unto yourselves the joyful tidings: *"He Who is the Best-Beloved is come! He hath crowned Himself with the glory of God's Revelation, and hath unlocked to the face of men the doors of His ancient Paradise."* Let all eyes rejoice, and let every ear be gladdened, for now is the time to gaze on His beauty, now is the fit time to hearken to His voice. Proclaim unto every longing lover: *"Behold, your Well-Beloved hath come among men!"* and to the messengers of the Monarch of love impart the tidings: *"Lo, the Adored One hath appeared arrayed in the fullness of His glory!"* O lovers of His beauty! Turn the anguish of your separation from Him into the joy of an everlasting reunion, and let the sweetness of His presence dissolve the bitterness of your remoteness from His court.

Behold how the manifold grace of God, which is being showered from the clouds of Divine glory, hash, in this day, encompassed the world. For whereas in days past every lover besought and searched after his Beloved, it is the Beloved Himself Who now is calling His lovers and is inviting them to attain His presence

Take heed lest ye forfeit so precious a favour; beware lest ye belittle so remarkable a token of His grace. Abandon not the incorruptible benefits, and be not content with that which perisheth. Lift up the veil that obscureth your vision, and dispel the darkness with which it is enveloped, that ye may gaze on the naked beauty of the Beloved's face, may behold that which no eye hath beheld, and hear that which no ear hath heard.

Hear Me, ye mortal birds! In the Rose Garden of changeless splendour a Flower hath begun to bloom, compared to which every other flower is but a thorn, and before the brightness of Whose glory the very essence of beauty must pale and wither. Arise, therefore, and, with the whole enthusiasm of your

---

43. Bahá'u'lláh, *Gleanings From the Writings of Bahá'u'lláh*, XIV, pp. 27-35.

hearts, with all the eagerness of your souls, the full fervour of your will, and the concentrated efforts of your entire being, strive to attain the paradise of His presence, and endeavour to inhale the fragrance of the incorruptible Flower, to breathe the sweet savours of holiness and to obtain a portion of this perfume of celestial glory. Who-so followeth this counsel will break his chains asunder, will taste the abandonment of enraptured love, will attain unto his heart's desire, and will surrender his soul into the hands of his Beloved. Bursting through his cage, he will, even as the bird of the spirit wing his flight to his holy and ever-lasting nest.

Night hath succeeded day, and day hath succeeded night, and the hours and moments of your lives have come and gone, and yet none of you hath, for one instant, consented to detach himself from that which perisheth. Bestir your-selves, that the brief moments that are still yours may not be dissipated and lost Even as the swiftness of lightning your days shall pass, and your bodies shall be laid to rest beneath a canopy of dust. What can ye then achieve? How can ye atone for your past failure?

The everlasting Candle shineth in its naked glory. Behold how it hath con-sumed every mortal veil. O ye moth-like lovers of His light! Brave every danger, and consecrate your souls to its consuming flame. O ye that thirst after Him! Strip yourselves of every earthly affection, and hasten to embrace your Be-loved. With a zest that none can equal make haste to attain unto Him. The Flower, thus far hidden from the sight of men, is unveiled to your eyes. In the open radiance of His glory He standeth before you. His voice summoneth all the holy and sanctified beings to come and be united with Him. Happy is he that turneth thereunto; well is it with him that hath attained, and gazed on the light of so wondrous a countenance.[44]

2.2.3   Prayer Revealed by Bahá'u'lláh

Since Thou hast, O my God, established Thyself upon the throne of Thy transcendent unity, and ascended the mercy seat of Thy oneness, it befitteth Thee to blot out from the hearts of all beings whatsoever may keep them back from gaining admittance into the sanctuary of Thy Divine mysteries, and may shut them out from the tabernacle of Thy Divinity, that all hearts may mirror Thy beauty, and may reveal Thee, and speak of Thee, and that all created things may show forth the tokens of Thy most august sovereignty, and shed the splen-

---

44. Bahá'u'lláh, *Gleanings From the Writings of Bahá'u'lláh*, CLI, pp. 319-322.

dours of the light of Thy most holy governance, and that all who are in heaven and on earth may laud and magnify Thy unity, and give Thee glory, for having manifested Thy Self unto them through Him Who is the Revealer of Thy oneness.

Divest, then, Thy servants, O my God, of the garments of self and desire, or grant that the eyes of Thy people may be lifted up to such heights that they will discern in their desires naught except the stirring of the gentle winds of Thine eternal glory, and may recognize in their own selves nothing but the revelation of Thine own merciful Self, that the earth and all that is therein may be cleansed of whatever is alien to Thee, or anything that manifesteth aught save Thy Self. All this can be fulfilled throughout Thy dominion by Thy word of command, *"Be,"* and it is! Nay, even swifter than this, and yet the people understand not.

Glorified immeasurably glorified art Thou, O my Beloved! I swear by Thy glory! I recognize this very moment that Thou hast granted all for which I have supplicated Thee, in this blessed night which, as decreed by Thee, calleth to remembrance Him Who was the Companion of Thy beauty and the Beholder of Thy face, ere I had been mentioned by thee, or called into being within the court of Thy holiness. I perceive that Thou hast made all things to be the manifestations of Thy behest, and the revelations of Thy handiwork, and the repositories of Thy knowledge, and the treasuries of Thy wisdom. I recognize, moreover, that were any of the revelations of Thy names and Thine attributes to be withheld, though it be the weight of a grain of mustard seed, from whatsoever hath been created by Thy power and begotten by Thy might, the foundations of Thine everlasting handiwork would thereby be made incomplete, and the gems of Thy Divine wisdom would become imperfect. For the letters of negation, no matter how far they may be removed from the holy fragrances of Thy knowledge, and however forgetful they may become of the wondrous splendours of the dawning light of Thy beauty, which are shed from the heaven of Thy majesty, must needs exist in Thy realm, so that the words which affirm Thee may thereby be exalted.

Thy might beareth me witness, O my Well-Beloved! The entire creation hath been called into being to exalt Thy triumph and to establish Thine ascendancy, and all the bounds that have been set by Thee are but the signs of Thy sovereignty, and proclaim the power of Thy might. How great, how very great, are the revelations of Thy wondrous power in all things! They are such that the lowliest among Thy creatures hath been made by Thee a manifestation of Thy most august attribute, and the most contemptible token of Thy handiwork hath been chosen as a recipient of Thy most mighty name. Poverty, as decreed by Thee, hath been made the means for the revelation of Thy riches, and abasement a path leading to Thy glory, and sinfulness a cause for the exercise of Thy forgiveness. By them Thou hast demonstrated that to Thee belong Thy most excellent titles, and unto Thee pertain the wonders of Thy most exalted attributes.

Since Thou hast purposed, O my God, to cause all created things to enter into the tabernacle of Thy transcendent grace and favour, and to waft over the entire creation the fragrances of the raiment of Thy glorious unity, and to look upon all things with the eyes of Thy bounty and Thy oneness, I beseech thee, therefore, by Thy love, which Thou hast made to be the mainspring of the revelations of Thine eternal holiness, and the flame that gloweth within the hearts of such of Thy creatures as yearn towards Thee, to create, this very moment, for those of Thy people who are wholly devoted to Thee, and for such of Thy loved ones as love Thee, out of the essence of Thy bounty and Thy generosity, and from the inmost spirit of Thy grace and Thy glory, Thy Paradise of transcendent holiness, and to exalt it above everything except Thee, and to sanctify in from aught else save Thyself. Create moreover, within it, O my God, out of the lights shed by Thy throne, handmaidens who will intone the melodies of Thy wondrous andmost sweet invention, that they may magnify Thy name with such words as have not been heard by any of Thy creatures, be they the inmates of Thy heaven or the dwellers of Thine earth, nor been comprehended by any of Thy people. Unlock, then, the gates of this Paradise to the faces of Thy loved ones, that haply they may enter them in Thy name, and by the power of Thy sovereignty, that thereby the sovereign bounties vouchsafed by Thee unto Thy chosen ones and the transcendent gifts granted unto Thy trusted ones be perfected, that they may extol Thy virtues with such melodies as none can either intone or describe, and that none of Thy people may conceive the design of appearing in the guise of any of Thy chosen ones, or of emulating the example of Thy loved ones, and that none may fail to discern between Thy friends and Thine enemies, or to distinguish them that are devoted to Thee from such as stubbornly oppose Thee. Potent art Thou to do what Thou wiliest, and powerful and supreme art Thou over all things.

Exalted, immeasurably exalted art Thou, O my Beloved, above the strivings of any of Thy creatures, however learned, to know Thee; exalted, immensely exalted art Thou above every human attempt, no matter how searching, to describe Thee! For the highest thought of men, however deep their contemplation, can never hope to outsoar the limitations imposed upon Thy creation, nor ascend beyond the state of the contingent world, nor break the bounds irrevocably set for it by Thee. How can, then, a thing that hath been created by Thy will that overruleth the whole of creation, a thing that is itself a part of the contingent world, have the power to soar into the holy atmosphere of Thy knowledge, or reach unto the seat of Thy transcendent power?

High, immeasurably high art Thou above the endeavours of the evanescent creature to soar unto the throne of Thine eternity, or of the poor and wretched to attain the summit of Thine all-sufficing glory! From eternity Thou didst Thyself describe Thine own Self unto Thy Self, and extol, in Thine own Essence, Thine Essence unto Thine Essence. I swear by Thy glory, O my Best-Beloved! Who is there besides Thee that can claim to know Thee, and who save Thyself can make fitting mention of Thee? Thou art He Who, from eternity, abode in His realm, in the glory of His transcendent unity, and the splendours of His holy grandeur. Were any one except Thee to be deemed worthy of mention, in all the kingdoms of Thy creation, from the highest realms of immortality down to the level of this nether world, how could it, then, be demonstrated that Thou art established upon the throne of Thy unity, and how could the wondrous virtues of Thy oneness and Thy singleness be glorified?

I bear witness, this very moment, to what Thou hast testified for Thine own Self, ere Thou hadst created the heavens and the earth, that Thou art God, and that there is none other God besides Thee. Thou hast from everlasting been potent, through the Manifestations of Thy might, to reveal the signs of Thy power, and Thou hast ever known, through the Day Springs of Thy knowledge, the words of Thy wisdom. No one besides Thee hath ever been found worthy to be mentioned before the Tabernacle of Thy unity, and none except Thyself hath proved himself capable of being praised within the hallowed court of Thy oneness.

Praise be to Thee, O my God, that Thou hast revealed Thy favours and Thy bounties; and glory be to Thee, O my Beloved, that Thou hast manifested the Day-Star of Thy loving-kindness and Thy tender mercies. I yield Thee such thanks as can direct the steps of the wayward towards the splendours of the morning light of Thy guidance, and enable those who yearn towards Thee to attain the seat of the revelation of the effulgence of Thy beauty. I yield Thee such thanks as can cause the sick to draw nigh unto the waters of Thy healing, and can help those who are far from Thee to approach the living fountain of Thy presence. I yield Thee such thanks as can divest the bodies of Thy servants of the garments of mortality and abasement, and attire them in the robes of Thine eternity and Thy glory, and lead the poor unto the shores of Thy holiness and all sufficient riches. I yield Thee such thanks as can enable the Heavenly Dove to warble forth, upon the branches of the Lote-Tree of immortality, her song: *"Verily, Thou art God. No God is there besides Thee. From eternity Thou hast been exalted above the praise of aught else but Thee, and been high above the description of any one except Thyself."* I yield Thee such thanks as can cause the Nightingale of Glory to pour forth its melody in the highest heaven: *"Alí* (the Báb)*, in truth, is Thy servant, Whom Thou hast singled out from among Thy Messengers and Thy chosen Ones, and made Him to be the Manifestation of Thyself in all that pertaineth unto Thee, and that concerneth the revelation of Thine attributes and the evidences of Thy names."* I yield Thee such thanks as can stir up all things to extol Thee, and to glorify Thine Essence, and can unloose the tongues of all beings to magnify the sovereignty of Thy beauty. I yield Thee such thanks as can fill the heavens and the earth with the signs of Thy transcendent Essence, and assist all created things to enter the Tabernacle of Thy nearness and Thy presence. I yield Thee such thanks as can make every created thing to be a book that shall speak of Thee, and a scroll that shall unfold Thy praise. I yield Thee such thanks as can establish the Manifestations of Thy sovereignty upon the throne of Thy governance, and set up the Exponents of Thy glory upon the seat of Thy Divinity. I yield Thee such thanks as can make the corrupt tree to bring forth good fruit through the holy breaths of Thy favours, and revive the bodies of all beings with the gentle winds of Thy transcendent grace. I yield Thee such thanks as can cause the signs of Thine exalted singleness to be sent down out of the heaven of Thy hly unity. I yield Thee such thanks as can teach all things the realities of Thy knowledge and the essence of Thy wisdom, and will not withhold the wretched creatures from the doors of Thy mercy and Thy bountiful favour. I yield Thee such thanks as can enable all who are in heaven and on earth to dispense with all created things, through the treasuries of Thine all-sufficing riches, and can aid all created things to reach unto the summit of Thine almighty favours. I yield Thee such thanks as can assist the hearts of Thine ardent lovers to soar into the atmosphere of nearness to Thee, and of longing for Thee, and kindle the Light of Lights within the land of 'Iráq. I yield Thee such thank as can detach them that are nigh unto Thee from all created things, and draw them to the throne of Thy names and Thine attributes. I yield Thee such thanks as can cause Thee to forgive all sins and trespasses, and to fulfil the needs of the peoples of all religions, and to waft the fragrances of pardon over the entire creation. I yield Thee such thanks as can enable them that recognize Thy unity to scale the heights of Thy love, and cause such as are devoted to Thee to ascend unto the Paradise of Thy presence. I yield Thee such thanks as can satisfy the wants of all such as seek Thee, and realize the aims of them that have recognized Thee. I yield Thee such thanks as can blot out from the hearts of men all suggestions of limitations, and inscribe the signs of Thy unity. I yield Thee such thanks as that with which Thou didst from eternity glorify Thine own Self, and didst exalt it above all peers, rivals, and comparisons, O Thou in Whose hands are the heavens of grace and of bouny, and the kingdoms of glory and of majesty!

Lauded be Thy name, O Lord my God, and my Master! Thou bearest witness, and seest, and knowest the things that have befallen Thy loved ones in Thy days, and the continual trials, and the successive tribulations, and the incessant afflictions, which have been sent down upon Thine elect. Such hath been their plight that the earth became too strait for them, and they were encompassed by the evidences of Thy wrath and the signs of Thy fear in every land, and the doors of Thy mercy and Thy loving-kindness were shut against them, and the garden of their hearts was deprived of the overflowing showers of Thy grace and Thy bountiful favours. Wilt Thou withhold, O my God, from such as love Thee the wonders of Thine ascendancy and triumph? Wilt Thou shatter, O my Beloved, the hopes which they who are devoted to Thee have fixed on Thy manifold bounties and gifts? Wilt Thou keep back, O my Master, those that have recognized Thee from the shores of Thy sanctified knowledge, or wilt Thou cease to rain down upon the hearts of such as desire Thee the showers of Thy transcendent grace? No, no, and to this Thy glory beareth me witness! I testify this very moment that Thy mercy hath surpassed all created things, and Thy loving-kindness encompassed all that are in heaven and all that are on earth. From everlasting the doors of Thy generosity were open to the faces of Thy servants, and the gentle winds of Thy grace were wafted over the hearts of Thy creatures, and the overflowing rains of Thy bounty were showered upon Thy people and the dwellers of Thy realm.

I know full well Thou hast delayed to manifest Thy triumph in the kingdom of creation by reason of Thy knowledge which embraceth both the mysteries of Thy decree, and the hidden things ordained behind the veils of Thine irrevocable purpose, that thereby those who have entered beneath the shadow of Thy transcendent mercy may be separated from those who have dealt disdainfully with Thee, and turned back from Thy presence at the time when Thou didst manifest Thy most exalted Beauty.

Exalted, immeasurably exalted an Thou, therefore, O my Beloved! For-as-much as Thou hast divided, in Thy realm, Thy loved ones from Thine enemies, and hast perfected Thy most weighty testimony and Thy most infallible Proof unto all who are in heaven and on earth, have mercy, then, upon those who were brought low in Thy land, by reason of what hath befallen them in Thy path. Exalt them, then, O my God, through the power of Thy might and the potency of Thy will, and raise them to proclaim Thy Cause through Thine omnipotent sovereignty and purpose.

I swear by Thy glory! My sole purpose in showing forth Thine ascendancy hath been to glorify Thy Cause, and to magnify Thy word. I am persuaded that if Thou wert to delay to send down Thy victory and to demonstrate Thy power, the signs of Thy sovereignty would assuredly perish in Thy land, and the tokens of Thy rule would be blotted out throughout Thy dominion.

My breast is straitened, O my God, and sorrows and vexations have compassed me round, for I hear among Thy servants every praise except Thy wondrous praise, and behold amidst Thy people the evidences of all things save the evidences of what Thou hast prescribed unto them by Thy behest, and destined for them through Thy sovereign will, and ordained unto them by Thine overruling decree. They have strayed so far from Thee that should any of Thy loved ones deliver unto them the wondrous tokens of Thy unity, and the gem-like utterances that attest Thy transcendent oneness, they would thrust their fingers into their ears, and would cavil at him and mock him. All this hast Thou set down through Thine all- encompassing sovereignty, and apprehended through Thine omnipotent supremacy.

Glorified, immeasurably glorified art Thou, O my Master! Look, then, upon the hearts which, in their love for Thee, have been transfixed by the darts of Thine enemies, and the heads which were borne on spears for the sake of the exaltation of Thy Cause and the glorification of Thy name. Have pity, then, upon those hearts which have been consumed by the fire of Thy love, and been touched by such tribulations as are known only unto Thee.

All laud and honour to Thee, O my God! Thou well knowest the things which, for a score of years, have happened in Thy days, and have continued to happen until this hour. No man can reckon, nor can any tongue tell, what hath befallen Thy chosen ones during all this time. They could obtain no shelter, nor find any refuge in which they could abide in safety. Turn, then, O my God, their fear into the evidences of Thy peace and Thy security, and their abasement into the sovereignty of Thy glory, and their poverty into Thine all-sufficient riches, and their distress into the wonders of Thy perfect tranquillity. Vouchsafe unto them the fragrances of Thy might and Thy mercy, and send down upon them, out of Thy marvellous loving-kindness, what will enable them to dispense with all except Thee. and will detach them from aught save thyself, that the sovereignty of Thy oneness may be revealed and the supremacy of Thy grace and Thy bounty demonstrated.

Wilt Thou not, O my God, look upon the tears which Thy loved ones have shed? Wilt Thou not pity, O my Beloved, the eyes which have been dimmed by reason of their separation from Thee, and because of the cessation of the signs of Thy victory? Wilt Thou not behold, O my Master, the hearts wherein have beaten the wings of the dove of longing and love for Thee? By Thy glory! Things have come to such a pass that hope hath well nigh been banished from the hearts of Thy chosen ones, and the breaths of despair and ready to seize them, by reason of what hath befallen them in Thy days.

Behold me, then, O my God, how I have fled from myself unto Thee, and have abandoned my own being that I may attain unto the splendours of the light of Thy Being, and have forsaken all that keepeth me back from Thee, and maketh me forgetful of Thee, in order that I may inhale the fragrances of Thy presence and Thy remembrance. Behold how I have stepped upon the dust of the city of Thy forgiveness and Thy bounty, and dwelt within the precincts of Thy transcendent mercy, and have besought Thee, through the sovereignty of Him Who is Thy Remembrance and Who hath appeared in the robe of Thy most pure and most august Beauty, to send down, in the course of this year, upon Thy loved ones what will enable them to dispense with any one except Thee, and will set them free to recognize the evidences of Thy sovereign will and all-conquering purpose, in such wise that they will seek only what Thou didst wish for them through Thy bidding, and will desire naught except what Thou didst desire for them through Thy will. Sanctify, then, their eyes, O my God, that they may behold the light of Thy Beauty, and purge their ears, that they may listen to the melodies of the Dove of Thy transcendent oneness. Flood, then, their hearts with the wonders of Thy love, and preserve their tongues from mentioning any one save Thee, and guard their faces from trueing to aught else except Thyself. Potent art Thou to do what pleaseth Thee. Thou, verily, are the Almighty, the Help in Peril, the Self Subsisting.

Protect, moreover, O my Beloved, through Thy love for them and through the love they bear to Thee, this servant, who hath sacrificed his all for Thee, and expended whatsoever Thou hast given him in the path of Thy love and Thy good pleasure, and preserve him from all that Thou abhorrest, and from whatsoever may hinder him from entering into the Tabernacle of Thy holy sovereignty, and from attaining the seat of Thy transcendent oneness. Number him, then, O my God, with such as have allowed nothing whatever to deter them from beholding Thy beauty, or from meditating on the wondrous evidences of Thine everlasting handiwork, that he may have fellowship with none except Thee, and turn to naught save Thyself, and discover in whatever hath been created by Thee in the kingdoms of earth and heaven nothing but Thy wondrous Beauty and the revelation of the splendours of Thy face, and be so immersed beneath the billowing oceans of Thine overruling providence and the surging seas of Thy holy unity, that he will forget evey mention except the mention of Thy transcendent oneness, and banish from his soul the traces of all evil suggestions, O Thou in Whose hands are the kingdoms of all names and attributes!

Lauded be Thy name, O Thou Who art the Goal of my desire! I swear by Thy glory! How great is my wish to attain unto a detachment so complete that were there to appear before me those countenances which are hid within the chambers of chastity, and the beauty of which Thou didst veil from the eyes of the entire creation, and whose faces Thou didst sanctify from the sight of all beings, and were they to unveil themselves in all the glory of the splendours of Thine incomparable beauty, I would refuse to look upon them. and would behold them solely for the purpose of discerning the mysteries of Thy handiwork, which have perplexed the minds of such as have drawn nigh unto Thee, and awed the souls of all them that have recognized Thee. I would, by Thy power and Thy might, soar to such heights that nothing whatsoever would have the power to keep me back from the manifold evidences of Thy transcendent dominion, nor would any earthly scheme shut me out from the manifestations of Thy Divine holiness.

Glorified, immeasurably glorified art Thou, O my God, and my Beloved, and my Master, and my Desire! Shatter not the hopes of this lowly one to attain the shores of Thy glory, and deprive not this wretched creature of the immensities of Thy riches, and cast not away this suppliant from the doors of Thy grace, and Thy bounty, and Thy gifts. Have mercy, then, upon this poor and desolate soul who hath sought no friend but Thee, and no companion except Thee, and no comforter save Thee, and no beloved apart from Thee, nor cherished any desire but Thyself.

Cast, then, upon me, O my God, the glances of Thy mercy, and forgive me my trespasses and the trespasses of them that are dear to Thee, and which come in between us and the revelation of Thy triumph and Thy grace. Cancel Thou, moreover, our sins which have shut off our faces from the splendours of the Day-Star of Thy favours. Powerful art Thou to do Thy pleasure. Thou ordainest what Thou wiliest, and art not asked of what Thou wishest through the power of Thy sovereignty, nor canst Thou be frustrated in whatsoever Thou prescribes" through Thine irrevocable decree. No God is there save Thee, the Almighty, the Most Powerful, the Ever-living, the Most Compassionate.[45]

2.2.4 Prayer Revealed by Bahá'u'lláh

Unto Thee be praise, O Lord my God! I entreat Thee, by Thy signs that have encompassed the entire creation, and by the light of Thy countenance that hath illuminated all that are in heaven and on earth, and by Thy mercy that hath surpassed all created things, and by Thy grace that hath suffused the whole universe, to rend asunder the veils that shut me out from Thee, that I may hasten unto the Fountain-Head of Thy mighty inspiration, and to the Day-Spring of Thy Revelation and bountiful favours, and may be immersed beneath the ocean of Thy nearness and pleasure.

Suffer me not, O my Lord, to be deprived of the knowledge of Thee in Thy days, and divest me not of the robe of Thy guidance. Give me to drink of the river that is life indeed, whose waters have streamed forth from the Paradise (Riḍván) in which the throne of Thy Name, the All-Merciful, was established, that mine eyes may be opened, and my face be illumined, and my heart be assured, and my soul be enlightened, and my steps be made firm.

Thou art He Who from everlasting was, through the potency of His might, supreme over all things, and, through the operation of His will, was able to ordain all things. Nothing whatsoever, whether in Thy heaven or on Thy earth, can frustrate Thy purpose. Have mercy, then, upon me, O my Lord, through Thy gracious providence and generosity, and incline mine ear to the sweet melodies of the birds that warble their praise of Thee, amidst the branches of the tree of Thy oneness.

Thou art the Great Giver, the Ever-Forgiving, the Most Compassionate.[46]

---

45. Bahá'u'lláh, *Prayers and Meditations*, no. CLXXXIV, pp. 324-339.
46. Ibid, no. II, pp. 4-5.

2.2.5 Excerpts from the Tablet of Bahá'u'lláh Addressed to Násiri'd-Dín Sháh

O King! I was but a man like others, asleep upon My couch, when lo, the breezes of the All-Glorious were wafted over Me, and taught Me the knowledge of all that hath been. This thing is not from Me, but from One Who is Almighty and All-Knowing. And He bade Me lift up My voice between earth and heaven, and for this there befell Me what hath caused the tears of every man of understanding to flow. The learning current amongst men I studied not; their schools I entered not. Ask of the city wherein I dwelt, that thou mayest be well assured that I am not of them who speak falsely. This is but a leaf which the winds of the will of thy Lord, the Almighty, the All-Praised, have stirred. Can it be still when the tempestuous winds are blowing? Nay, by Him Who is the Lord of all Names and Attributes! They move it as they list. The evanescent is as nothing before Him Who is the Ever-Abiding. His all-compelling summons hath reached Me, and caused Me to speak His praise amidst all people. I was indeed as one dead when His behest was uttered. The hand of the will of thy Lord, the Compassionate, the Merciful, transformed Me. Can any one speak forth of his own accord that for which all men, both high and low, will protest against him? Nay, by Him Who taught the Pen the eternal mysteries, save him whom the grace of the Almighty, the All-Powerful, hath strengthened. The Pen of the Most High addresseth Me saying: Fear not. Relate unto His Majesty the Sháh that which befell thee. His heart, verily, is between the fingers of thy Lord, the God of Mercy, that haply the sun of justice and bounty may shine forth above the horizon of his heart. Thus hath the decree been irrevocably fixed by Him Who is the All-Wise.

Look upon this Youth, O King, with the eyes of justice; judge thou, then, with truth concerning what hath befallen Him. Of a verity, God hath made thee His shadow amongst men, and the sign of His power unto all that dwell on earth. Judge thou between Us and them that have wronged Us without proof and without an enlightening Book. They that surround thee love thee for their own sakes, whereas this Youth loveth thee for thine own sake, and hath had no desire except to draw thee nigh unto the seat of grace, and to turn thee toward the right-hand of justice. Thy Lord beareth witness unto that which I declare.

O King ! Wert thou to incline thine ear unto the shrill of the Pen of Glory and the cooing of the Dove of Eternity which, on the branches of the Lote-Tree beyond which there is no passing, uttereth praises to God, the Maker of all names and Creator of earth and heaven, thou wouldst attain unto a station from which thou wouldst behold in the world of being naught save the effulgence of the Adored One, and wouldst regard thy sovereignty as the most contemptible of thy possessions, abandoning it to whosoever might desire it, and setting thy face toward the Horizon aglow with the light of His countenance. Neither wouldst thou ever be willing to bear the burden of dominion save for the purpose of helping thy Lord, the Exalted, the Most High. Then would the Concourse on high bless thee O how excellent is this most sublime station, couldst thou ascend thereunto through the power of a sovereignty recognized as derived from the Name of God! [47]

2.2.6 *The Day of Star of Truth*, A Tablet from 'Abdu'l-Bahá

O daughter of the Kingdom! Thy letter hath come and its contents make clear the fact that thou hast directed all thy thoughts toward acquiring light from the realms of mystery. So long as the thoughts of an individual are scattered he will achieve no results, but if his thinking be concentrated on a single point wonderful will be the fruits thereof.

One cannot obtain the full force of the sunlight when it is cast on a flat mirror, but once the sun shineth upon a concave mirror, or on a lens that is convex, all its heat will be concentrated on a single point, and that one point will burn the hottest. Thus is it necessary to focus one's thinking on a single point so that it will become an effective force.

Thou didst wish to celebrate the Day of Riḍván with a feast, and to have those present on that day engage in reciting Tablets with delight and joy, and thou didst request me to send thee a letter to be read on that day. My letter is this:

O ye beloved, and ye handmaids of the Merciful! This is the day when the Day-Star of Truth rose over the horizon of life, and its glory spread, and its brightness shone out with such power that it clove the dense and high-piled clouds and mounted the skies of the world in all its splendour. Hence do ye witness a new stirring throughout all created things.

See how, in this day, the scope of sciences and arts hath widened out, and what wondrous technical advances have been made, and to what a high degree the mind's powers have increased, and what stupendous inventions have appeared.

---

47. Bahá'u'lláh, *The Proclamation of Bahá'u'lláh*, pp. 57-9.

This age, is indeed as a hundred other ages: should ye gather the yield of a hundred ages, and set that against the accumulated product of our times, the yield of this one era will prove greater than that of a hundred gone before. Take ye, for an example, the sum total of all the books that were ever written in ages past, and compare that with the books and treatises that our era hath produced: these books, written in our day alone, far and away exceed the total number of volumes that have been written down the ages. See how powerful is the influence exerted by the Day-Star of the world upon the inner essence of all created things!

But alas, a thousand times alas! The eyes see it not, the ears are deaf, and the hearts and minds are oblivious of this supreme bestowal Strive ye then, with all your hears and souls, to awaken those who slumber, to cause the blind to see, and the dead to rise.[48]

2.2.7   Excerpts From a Tablet, Revealed by `Abdu'l-Bahá

Praise be to Him through Whose splendours the earth and the heavens are aglow, through Whose fragrant breathings the gardens of holiness that adorn the hearts of the chosen are trembling for joy, to Him Who hath shed His light and brightened the face of the firmament. Verily there appeared luminous and sparkling stars, glittering, shining out, and casting forth their rays upon the supreme horizon. They derived their grace and brilliance from the bounties of the Abhá Realm, then, stars of guidance, they poured down their lights upon this earth. Praise be to Him Who hath fashioned this new era, this age of majesty, even as an unfolding pageant where the realities of all things can be exposed to view. Now are clouds of bounty raining down and the gifts of the loving Lord are clearly manifest; for both the seen and the unseen worlds have been illumined and the Promised One hath come to earth and the beauty of the Adored One hath shone forth. Salutations, blessings, and welcome to that Universal Reality, that Perfect Word, that Manifest Book, that Splendour which hath dawned in the highest heaven, that Guide of all nations, that Light of the world—the billowing ocean of Whose abounding grace hath flooded all creation, in such wise that the waves thereof have cast upon the sands of this visible world their shining pearls. Now hath the Truth appeared, and falsehood fled away; now hath the day dawned and jubilation taken over, wherefore men's souls are sanctified, their spirits purged, their

---

48. 'Abdu'-Bahá, *Selections From the Writings of 'Abdu'l-Bahá*, pp. 110-112.

hearts rejoiced their minds purified, their secret thoughts made wholesome, their consciences washed clean, their inmost selves made holy: for the Day of Resurrection hath come to pass, and the bestowals of thy Lord, the Forgiving, have encompassed all things. Salutations and praise be unto those luminous, resplendent stars that are shedding down their rays from the highest heaven, those celestial bodies of the girdling zodiac of the Abhá Realm. May glory rest upon them.[49]

• • •

For thy part, rejoice at this best of all glad tidings, and rise up to exalt the Word of God and to spread abroad His sweet savours in all that vast and mighty land. Know thou of a certainty that thy Lord will come to shine aid with a company of the Concourse on high and hosts of the Abhá Kingdom. These will mount the attack, and will furiously assail the forces of the ignorant, the blind. Ere long wilt thou behold the flush of daybreak spreading from out the Most Exalted Realm, and the morn encompassing all regions. It will put the dark to flight and the gloom of night will fade and pass, and the bright brow of the Faith shine forth, and the Day-Star rise and overspread the world. On that day will the faithful rejoice, and the steadfast be blissful; then will the slanderers take themselves off, and the waverers be blotted out, even as deepest shadows fall away at the first light of the breaking dawn.

Greetings be unto thee, and praise.[50]

2.2.8 Riḍván Festival

Twenty-seven days after that mournful Tablet had been so unexpectedly revealed by Bahá'u'lláh, and the fateful communication, presaging His departure to Constantinople had been delivered into His hands, on a Wednesday afternoon (April 22, 1863), thirty-one days after Naw-Rúz, on the third of Dhi'l-Qa'dih, AH 1279, He set forth on the first stage of His four months' journey to the capital of Ottoman Empire. That historic day, forever after designated as the first day of the Riḍván Festival, the culmination of innumerable farewell visits which friends and acquaintances of every class and denomination, had been paying him, was one the like of which the inhabitants of Baghdád had rarely beheld. A concourse of people of both sexes and of every age, comprising friends and strangers, Arabs, Kurds and Persians, nota-

---

49. 'Abdu'l-Bahá, *Selections From the Writings of 'Abdu'l-Bahá*, pp. 38-9.

50. Ibid, p. 43

bles and clerics, officials and merchants, as well as many of the lower classes, the poor, the orphaned, the outcast, some surprised, others heartbroken, many tearful and apprehensive, a few impelled by curiosity or secret satisfaction, thronged the approaches of His house, eager to catch a final glimpse of One Who, for a decade, had, through precept and example, exercised so potent an influence on so large a number of the heterogeneous inhabitants of their city.

Leaving for the last time, amidst weeping and lamentation, His *"Most Holy Habitation"* out of which had *"gone forth the breath of the All-Glorious,"* and from which had poured forth, in *"ceaseless strains,"* the *"melody of the All-Merciful,"* and dispensing on His way with a lavish hand a last alms to the poor He had so faithfully befriended, and uttering words of comfort to the disconsolate who besought Him on every side, He, at length, reached the banks of the river, and was ferried across, accompanied by His sons and amanuensis, to the Najíbíyyih Garden, situated on the opposite shore. *"O My companions,"* He thus addressed that faithful band that surrounded Him before He embarked, *"I entrust to your keeping this city of Baghdád, in the state ye now behold it, when from the eyes of friends and strangers alike, crowding its housetops, its streets and markets, tears like the rain of spring are flowing down, and I depart. With you it now rests to watch lest your deeds and conduct dim the flame of love that gloweth within the breasts of its inhabitants."*

The muezzin had just raised the afternoon call to prayer when Bahá'u'lláh entered the Najíbíyyih Garden, where He tarried twelve days before His final departure from the city. There His friends and companions, arriving in successive waves, attained His presence and bade Him, with feelings of profound sorrow, their last farewell.[51]

2.2.9 Declaration of Bahá'u'lláh

The arrival of Bahá'u'lláh in the Najíbíyyih Garden, subsequently designated by His followers the Garden of Riḍván, signalizes the commencement of what has come to be recognized as the holiest and most significant of all Bahá'í festivals, the festival commemorating the Declaration of His Mission to His companions. So momentous a Declaration may well be regarded both as the logical consummation of that revolutionizing process which was initiated by Himself upon His return from Sulaymáníyyih, and as a prelude to the final proclamation of that same Mission to the world and its rulers from Adrianople.

Through that solemn act the *"delay"*, of no less than a decade, divinely inter-

---

51. Shoghi Effendi, God Passes By, pp. 148-9.

posed between the birth of Bahá'u'lláh's Revelation in the Síyáh-<u>Ch</u>ál and its announcement to the Báb's disciples, was at long last terminated. The *"set time of concealment,"* during which as He Himself has borne witness, the *"signs and tokens of a divinely-appointed Revelation"* were being showered upon Him, was fulfilled. The *"myriad veils of light,"* within which His glory had been wrapped, were, at that historic hour, partially lifted, vouchsafing to mankind *"an infinitesimal glimmer"* of the effulgence of His *"peerless, His most sacred and exalted Countenance"* The *"thousand two hundred and ninety days,"* fixed by Daniel in the last chapter of His Book, as the duration of the "abomination that maketh desolate" had now elapsed. The *"hundred lunar years,"* destined to immediately precede that blissful consummation (1335 days), announced by Daniel in that same chapter, had commenced. The nineteen years, constituting the first *"Váḥid",* preordained in the Persian Bayán by the pen of the Báb, had been completed. The Lord of the Kingdom, Jesus Christ returned in the glory of the Father, was about to ascend His throne, and assume the sceptre of the world-embracing, indestructible sovereignty. The community of the Most Great Name, the *"companions of the Crimson Coloured Ark,"* lauded in glowing terms in the Qayyúmu'l-Asmá', had visibly emerged. The Báb's own prophecy regarding the *"Riḍván,"* the scene of the unveiling of Bahá'u'lláh's transcendent glory, had been literally fulfilled.[52]

Of the exact circumstances attending that epoch-making Declaration we, alas, are but scantily informed. The words Bahá'u'lláh actually uttered on that occasion, the manner of His Declaration, the reaction it produced, its impact on Mírzá Yaḥ yá, the identity of those who were privileged to hear Him, are shrouded in an obscurity which future historians will find it difficult to penetrate. The fragmentary description left to posterity by His chronicler Nabíl is one of the very few authentic records we possess of the memorable days He spent in that garden. *"Every day,"* Nabíl has related, *"ere the hour of dawn, the gardeners would pick the roses which lined the four avenues of the garden, and would pile them in the centre of the floor of His blessed tent. So great would be the heap that when His companions gathered to drink their morning tea in His presence, they would be unable to see each other across it. All these roses Bahá'u'lláh would, with His own hands, entrust to those whom He dismissed from His presence every morning to be delivered, on His behalf, to His Arab and Persian friends in the city."* "One night," he continues, *"the ninth night of the waxing moon, I happened to be one of those who watched beside His blessed tent. As the hour of midnight approached, I saw Him issue from His tent, pass by the places where some of His*

---

52. Shoghi Effendi, *God Passes By*, p. 151.

companions were sleeping, and begin to pace up and down the moonlit, flower-bordered avenues of the garden. So loud was the singing of the nightingales on every side that only those who were near Him could hear distinctly His voice. He continued to walk until, pausing in the midst of one of these avenues, He observed: 'Consider these nightingales. So great is their love for these roses, that sleepless from dusk till dawn, they warble their melodies and commune with burning passion with the object of their adoration. How then can those who claim to be afire with the rose-like beauty of the Beloved choose to sleep?' For three successive nights I watched and circled round His blessed tent. Every time I passed by the couch whereon He lay, I would find Him wakeful, and every day, from morn till eventide, I would see Him ceaselessly engaged in conversing with the stream of visitors who kept flowing in from Baghdád. Not once could I discover in the words He spoke any trace of dissimulation."

As to the significance of that Declaration let Bahá'u'lláh Himself reveal to us its import. Acclaiming that historic occasion as the *"Most Great Festival,"* the *"King of Festivals,"* the *"Festival of God,"* He has in His *Kitáb-i-Aqdas,* characterized it as the Day whereon *"all created things were immersed in the sea of purification,"* whilst in one of His specific Tablets, He has referred to it as the Day whereon *"the breezes of forgiveness were wafted over the entire creation." "Rejoice, with exceeding gladness, O people of Bahá!"* He, in another Tablet, has written, *"as ye call to remembrance the Day of supreme felicity, the Day whereon the Tongue of the Ancient of Days hath spoken, as He departed from His House proceeding to the Spot from which He shed upon the whole of creation the splendours of His Name, the All-Merciful ... Were We to reveal the hidden secrets of that Day, all that dwell on earth and in the heavens would swoon away and die, except such as will be preserved by God, the Almighty, the All- Knowing, the All- Wise. Such is the inebriating effect of the words of God upon the Revealer of His undoubted proofs that His pen can move no longer."* And again: *"The Divine Springtime is come, O most Exalted Pen, for the Festival of the All-Merciful is fast approaching ... The Day-Star of blissfulness shineth above the horizon of Our Name, the Blissful, inasmuch as the Kingdom of the Name of God hath been adorned with the ornament of the Name of Thy Lord, the Creator of the heavens ...Take heed lest anything deter Thee from extolling the greatness of this Day—the Day whereon the Finger of Majesty and Power hath opened the seal of the Wine of Reunion, and called all who are in the heavens and all who are on earth. ...This is the Day whereon the unseen world crieth out: 'Great is thy blessedness, O earth, for thou has been made the footstool of thy God, and been chosen as the seat of His mighty throne.' ...Say ...He it is who hath laid bare before you the hidden and treasured Gem, were ye to seek it. He it is Who is the One Beloved of all things, whether of the past or of the future."* And yet again: *"Arise, and proclaim unto the entire creation the tidings that He who is the All-Merciful hath directed His steps towards the Riḍván and entered it. Guide, then, the people unto the Garden of Delight which God hath made the throne of His Paradise ... Within this Paradise, and from the heights of its loftiest chambers, the Maids of Heaven have cried out and shouted. 'Rejoice, ye dwellers of the realms above, for the fingers of Him Who is the Ancient of Days are ringing, in the name of the All-Glorious, the Most Great Bell, in the midmost heart of the heavens. The hands of bounty have borne round the cups of everlasting life. Approach, and quaff your fill.'"* And finally: *"Forget the world of creation, O Pen, and turn Thou towards the face of Thy Lord, the Lord of all names. Adorn, then, the world with the ornament of the favours of Thy Lord, the King of everlasting days. For We perceive the fragrance of the Day whereon He Who is the Desire of all nations hath shed upon the kingdoms of the unseen and of the seen the splendours of the light of His most excellent names, and enveloped them with the radiance of the luminaries of His most gracious favours, favours which none can reckon except Him Who is the Omnipotent Protector of the entire creation."*

The departure of Bahá'u'lláh from the Garden of Riḍván, at noon, on the 14th of Ḏhi'l-Qa'dih AH 1279. (3 May, 1863), witnessed scenes of tumultuous enthusiasm no less spectacular, and even more touching, than those which greeted Him when leaving His Most Great House in Baghdád. "The great tumult," wrote an eye witness, "associated in our minds with the Day of Gathering, the Day of Judgment, we beheld on that occasion. Believers and unbelievers alike sobbed and lamented. The chiefs and notables who had congregated were struck with wonder. Emotions were stirred to such depths as no tongue can describe, nor could any observer escape their contagion."

Mounted on His steed, a red roan stallion of the finest breed, the best His lovers could purchase for Him, and leaving behind Him a bowing multitude of fervent admirers, He rode forth on the first stage of a journey that was to carry Him to the city of Constantinople. "Numerous were the heads," Nabíl himself a witness of that memorable scene, recounts, "which, on every side, bowed to the dust at the feet of His horse, and kissed its hoofs, and countless were those who pressed forward to embrace His stirrups." "How great the number of those embodiments of fidelity," testifies a fellow-traveller, "who, casting themselves before that charger, preferred death to separation from their Beloved! Methinks, that blessed steed trod upon the bodies of those pure-hearted souls." *"He (God) it was,"* Bahá'u'lláh Himself declares, *"Who enabled Me to depart out of the city (Baghdád), clothed with such majesty as none, except the denier and the malicious, can fail to acknowledge."* These marks of homage and devotion continued to surround Him until He was installed in Constantinople. Mírzá Yaḥyá, while hurrying on foot, by his own choice, behind Bahá'u'lláh's carriage, on the day of His arrival in that city, was overheard by Nabíl to remark to Siyyid Muḥammad: "Had I not chosen to hide myself, had I revealed my identity, the honour accorded Him (Bahá'u'lláh) on this day would have been mine too.[53]

2.2.10 The Station of Bahá'u'lláh

He Who in such dramatic circumstances was made to sustain the overpowering weight of so glorious a Mission was none other than the One Whom posterity will acclaim, and Whom innumerable followers already recognize, as the Judge, the Lawgiver and Redeemer of all mankind, as the Organizer of the entire planet, as the Unifier of the children of men, as the Inaugurator of the long-awaited millennium, as the Originator of a new *"Universal Cycle,"* as the Establisher of the Most Great Peace, as the Fountain of the Most Great Justice, as the Proclaimer of the coming of age of the entire human race, as the creator of a new World Order, and as the Inspirer and Founder of a world civilization.

To Israel He was neither more nor less than the incarnation of the *"Everlasting Father,"* the *"Lord of Hosts"* come down *"with ten thousands of saints"*; to Christendom Christ returned *"in the glory of the Father,"* to Shí'ih Islám the return of the Imám Ḥusayn; to Sunní Islam the descent of the *"Spirit of God"* (Jesus Christ); to the Zoroastrians the promised S̲h̲áh-Bahrám; to the Hindus the reincarnation of Krishna; to the Buddhists the fifth Buddha.

In the name He bore He combined those of the Imám Husayn, the most illustrious of the successors of the Apostle of God—the brightest *"star"* shining in the *"crown"* mentioned in the Revelation of St John—and the Imám Alí, the Commander of the Faithful, the second of the two *"witnesses"* extolled in that same Book. He was formally designated Bahá'u'lláh, an appellation specifically recorded in the Persian Bayán, signifying at once the glory, the light and the splendour of God, and was styled the *"Lord of Lords,"* the *"Most Great Name,"* the *"Ancient Beauty,"* the *"Pen of the Most High,"* the *"Hidden Name,"* the *"Preserved Treasure,"* *"He Whom God will make mani*fest," the *"Most Great Light,"* the *"All-Highest Horizon,"* the *"Most Great Ocean,"* the *"Supreme Heaven,"* the *"Pre-Existent Root,"* the *"Self-Subsistent,"* the *"Day-Star of the Universe,"* the *"Great Announcement,"* the *"Speaker on Sinai,"* the *"Sifter of Men,"* the *"Wronged One of the World,"* the *"Desire of Nations,"* the *"Lord of the Covenant,"* the *"Tree beyond-which there is no passing"*. He derived His descent, on the one hand from Abraham (The Father of the Faithful) through his wife Katurah, and on the other from Zoroaster, as

---

53. Shoghi Effendi, *God Passes By*, pp. 153-5.

well, as from Yazdigird, the last king of the Sásáníyán dynasty. He was moreover a descendant of Jesse, and belonged, through His father, Mírzá 'Abbás, better known as Mírzá Buzurg—a nobleman closely associated with the ministerial circles of the Court of Fath-'Alí Sháh-to one of the most ancient and renowned families of Mázindarán.

To Him Isaiah, the greatest of the Jewish prophets, had alluded as the *"Glory of the Lord,"* the *"Everlasting Father,"* the *"Prince of Peace,"* and *"Wonderful,"* the *"Counsellor,"* the *"Rod come forth out of the stem of Jesse,"* and the *"Branch grown out of His roots,"* Who *"shall be established upon the throne of David,"* Who *"will come with strong hand,"* Who *"shall judge among the nations,"* Who *"shall smite the earth with the rod of His mouth, and with the breath of His lips slay the wicked,"* and Who *"shall assemble the outcasts of Israel, and gather together the dispersed of Judah from the four corners of the earth."* Of Him David had sung in his Psalms, acclaiming Him as the *"Lord of Hosts"* and the *"King of Glory."* To Him Haggai had referred as the *"Desire of all nations,"* and Zachariah as the *"Branch,"* Who *"shall grow up out of His place,"* and *"shall build the Temple of the Lord."* Ezekiel had extolled Him as the *"Lord,"* Who *"shall be king over all the earth,"* while to His day Joel and Zephaniah had both referred as the *"day of Jehovah,"* the latter describing it as *"a day of wrath, a day of trouble and distress, a day of wasteness and desolation, a day of darkness and gloominess, a day of clouds and thick darkness, a day of the trumpet and alarm against the fenced cities, and against the high towers."* His Day Ezekiel and Daniel had, moreover, both acclaimed as the *"day of the Lord,"* and Malachi described as *"the great and dreadful day of the Lord,"* when *"the Sun of Righteousness,"* will *"arise, with healing in His wings,"* whilst Daniel had pronounced His advent as signalizing the end of the *"abomination that maketh desolate."*

To His Dispensation the sacred books of the followers of Zoroaster had referred as that in which the sun must needs be brought to a standstill for no less than one whole month. To Him Zoroaster must have alluded when, according to tradition, He foretold that a period of three thousand years of conflict and contention must needs precede the advent of the World-Saviour Sháh-Bahrám, Who would triumph over Ahriman and usher in an era of blessedness and peace.

He alone is meant by the prophecy attributed to Gautama Buddha Himself, that *"a Buddha named Maitreye, the Buddha of universal fellowship"* should, in the fullness of time, arise and reveal *"His boundless glory."* To Him the Bhagavad-Gita of the Hindus had referred as the *"Most Great Spirit,"* the *"Tenth Avatar,"* the *"Immaculate Manifestation of Krishna."*

To Him Jesus Christ had referred as the *"Prince of this world,"* as the *"Comforter"* Who will *"reprove the world of sin, and of righteousness, and of judgment,"* as the *"Spirit of Truth"* Who *"will guide you into all truth,"* Who *"shall not speak of Himself, but whatsoever He shall hear, that shall He speak,"* as the *"Lord of the Vineyard,"* and as the *"Son of Man"* Who *"shall come in the glory of His Father" "in the clouds of heaven with power and great glory,"* with *"all the holy angels"* about Him, and *"all nations"* gathered before His throne. To Him the Author of the Apocalypse had alluded as the *"Glory of God,"* as *"Alpha and Omega," "the Beginning and the End," "the First and the Last."* Identifying His Revelation with the *"third woe,"* he, moreover, had extolled His Law as *"a new heaven and a new earth,"* as the *"Tabernacle of God,"* as the *"Holy City,"* as the *"New Jerusalem, coming down from God out of heaven, prepared as a bride adorned for her husband."* To His Day Jesus Christ Himself had referred as *"the regeneration when the Son of Man shall sit in the throne of His glory."* To the hour of His advent St Paul had alluded as the hour of the *"last trump,"* the *"trump of God,"* whilst St Peter had spoken of it as the *"Day of God, wherein the heavens being on fire shall be dissolved, and the elements shall melt with fervent heat."* His Day he, furthermore, had described as *"the times of refreshing," "the times of restitution of all things, which God hath spoken by the mouth of all His holy Prophets since the world began."*

To Him Muḥammad, the Apostle of God, had alluded in His Book as the *"Great Announcement,"* and declared His Day to be the Day whereon *"God"* will *"come down" "overshadowed with clouds,"* the Day whereon *"thy Lord shall come and the angels rank on rank,"* and *"The Spirit shall arise and the angels shall be ranged in order."* His advent He, in that Book, in a súrih said to have been termed by Him *"the heart of the Qur'án,"* had foreshadowed as that of the *"third"* Messenger, sent down to *"strengthen"* the two who preceded Him. To His Day He, in the pages of that same Book, had paid a glowing tribute, glorifying it as the *"Great day,"* the *"Last Day,"* the *"Day of God,"* the *"Day of Judgment,"* the *"Day of Reckoning,"* the *"Day of Mutual Deceit,"* the *"Day of Severing,"* the *"Day of Sighing,"* the *"Day of Meeting,"* the Day *"when the Decree shalt be accomplished,"* the Day whereon the second *"Trumpet blast"* will be sounded, the *"Day when mankind shall stand before the Lord of the world,"* and *"all shall come to Him in humble guise,"* the Day when *"thou shalt see the mountains, which thou thinkest so firm, pass away with the passing of a cloud,"* the Day *"wherein account shall be taken," "the approaching Day, when men's hearts shall rise up, choking them, into their throats,"* the Day when *"all that are in the heavens and all that are on the earth shall be terror-stricken, save him whom God pleaseth to deliver,"* the Day whereon *"every suckling woman shall forsake her sucking babe, and every woman that hath a burden in her womb shall cast her burden,"* the Day *"when the earth shall shine with the light of her Lord, and the Book shall be set, and the Prophets shall be brought up, and the witnesses, and judgment shall be given between them with equity, and none shall be wronged."*

The plenitude of His glory the Apostle of God had, moreover, as attested by Bahá'u'lláh Himself, compared to the *"full moon on its fourteenth night."* His station the Imám 'Alí, the Commander of the Faithful, had, according to the same testimony, identified with *"Him Who conversed with Moses from the Burning Bush on Sinai."* To the transcendent character of His mission the Imám Husayn had, again according to Bahá'u'lláh, borne witness as a *"Revelation whose Revealer will be He Who revealed"* the Apostle of God Himself.

About Him Shaykh Ahmad-i-Ahsá'i, the herald of the Bábí Dispensation, who had foreshadowed the *"strange happenings"* that would transpire *"between the years sixty and sixty-seven,"* and had categorically affirmed the inevitability of His Revelation had, as previously mentioned, written the following: *"The Mystery of this Cause must needs be manifest, and the Secret of this Message must needs be divulged. I can say no more, I can appoint no time. His Cause will be made known after Hín (68)"* (i.e., after a while).

Siyyid Kázim-i-Rashtí, Shaykh Ahmad's disciple and successor, had likewise written: *"The Qá'im must needs be put to death. After He has been slain the world will have attained the age of eighteen."* In his Sharh-i-Qasídiy-i-Lámíyyih he had even alluded to the name *"Bahá."* Furthermore, to his disciples, as his days drew to a close, he had significantly declared: *"Verily, I say, after the Qá'im the Qayyúm will be made manifest. For when the star of the former has set the sun of the beauty of Ḥusayn will rise and illuminate the whole world. Then will be unfolded in all its glory the 'Mystery' and the 'Secret' spoken of by Shaykh Ahmad …To have attained unto the Day of Days is to have attained unto the crowning glory of past generations, and one goodly deed performed in that age is equal to the pious worship of countless centuries."* [54]

2.2.11 The First, Ninth and Twelfth Days of Riḍván

As regards various matters you raised in your letters, the reason we commemorate the 1st, 9th and 12th days of Riḍván as Holidays (Holy Days) is because one is the first day, one is the last day, and third one is the ninth day, which of course is associated with the number 9. All 12 days could not be holidays, therefore these t three were chosen." [55]

---

54. Shoghi Effendi, *God Passes By*, pp. 93-7.

55. Shoghi Effendi, quoted in *Lights of Guidance* (First Edition), no. 624.

House of the Báb Exterior Window
Shiraz, Iran

2.3
Declaration of the Báb
May 23, 1844

O Monk of the Incomparable One! Ring out the Bell, inasmuch as the Day of the Lord hath shone forth and the Beauty of the All-Glorious is established upon His holy and resplendent Throne.[56]

Suggested Readings

---

56. Bahá'u'lláh, quoted by Adib Taherzadeh in *The Revelation of Bahá'u'lláh*, vol. 2, p. 19.

2.3.1 Prayer Revealed by Bahá'u'lláh

Praised be Thou, O Lord my God! Every time I am reminded of Thee and muse on Thy virtues, I am seized with such ecstasies and am so enravished by Thee that I find myself unable to make mention of Thy name and to extol Thee. I am carried back to such heights that I recognize my self to be the same as the remembrance of Thee in Thy realm, and the essence of Thy praise among Thy servants. As long as that self endureth, so long will Thy praise continue to be shed abroad among Thy creatures and Thy remembrance glorified by Thy people.

Every man endued with insight among Thy servants is persuaded that my self liveth eternally and can never perish, inasmuch as remembrance of Thee is eternal and will endure so long as Thine own Self endureth, and Thy praise is everlasting and will last as long as Thine own sovereignty will last. By its means Thou art glorified by such of Thy chosen ones as call upon Thee and by the sincere among Thy servants. Nay, the praise wherewith any one, in the entire creation, praiseth Thee proceedeth from this exalted self and returneth unto it, even as the sun which, while it shineth, sheddeth its splendour upon whatsoever may be exposed to its rays. From this sun is generated, and unto it must return, the light which is shed over all things.

Exalted, immeasurably exalted art Thou above any attempt to measure the greatness of Thy Cause, above any comparison that one may seek to make, above the efforts of the human tongue to utter its import! From everlasting Thou hast existed, alone with no one else beside Thee, and wilt, to everlasting, continue to remain the same, in the sublimity of Thine essence and the inaccessible heights of Thy glory.

And when Thou didst purpose to make Thyself known unto men, Thou didst successively reveal the Manifestations of Thy Cause, and ordained each to be a sign of Thy Revelation among Thy people, and the Day-Spring of Thine invisible Self amidst Thy creatures, until the time when, as decreed by Thee, all Thy previous Revelations culminated in Him Whom Thou hast appointed as the Lord of all who are in the heaven of revelation and the kingdom of creation, Him Whom Thou hast established as the Sovereign Lord of all who are in the heavens and all who are on the earth. He it was Whom Thou hast determined to be the Herald of Thy Most Great Revelation and the Announcer of Thy Most Ancient Splendour. In this Thou hadst no other purpose except to try them who have manifested Thy most excellent titles unto all who are in heaven and on earth. He it was Whom Thou hast commanded to establish His covenant with all created things.

And when Thy promise came to pass and the set time was fulfilled, He Who is the Possessor of all Names and Attributes was made manifest unto men. Thereupon all that were in the heavens and all that were on the earth were terror-stricken save those whom Thou didst keep under Thy protection and preserve within the shelter of Thy power and gracious providence. There befell Him, at the hands of such of Thy creatures as have transgressed against Thee, that which the tongue of no one of Thy servants can recount.

Look down, then, upon Him, O my God, with the eye of Thy tender mercy, and send down upon Him and upon those that love Him all the good Thou didst ordain in the heaven of Thy will and the Tablet of Thy decree. Aid them, then, with Thy succour, for Thou art, verily, the Almighty, the Most Exalted, the All-Glorious, the All-Compelling.[57]

2.3.2 An Evidence of the Truth of His Manifestation

And among the evidences of the truth of His manifestation were the ascendancy, the transcendent power, and supremacy which He, the Revealer of being and Manifestation of the Adored, hath, unaided and alone, revealed throughout the world. No sooner had the eternal Beauty revealed Himself in <u>Sh</u>íráz, in the year sixty [AH 1260], and rent asunder the veil of concealment, than the signs of the ascendancy, the might, the sovereignty, and power, emanating from the Essence of Essences and Sea of Seas, were manifest in every land. So much so, that from every city there appeared the signs, the evidences, the tokens, the testimonies of that divine Luminary. How many were those pure and kindly hearts which faithfully reflected the light of that eternal Sun, and how manifold the emanations of knowledge from that Ocean of divine wisdom which encompassed all beings! In every city, all the divines and dignitaries rose to hinder and repress them, and girded up the loins of malice, of envy, and tyranny for their suppression. How great the number of those holy souls, those essences of justice, who, accused of tyranny, were put to death! And how many embodiments of purity, who showed forth naught but true knowledge and stainless deeds, suffered an agonizing death! Notwithstanding all this, each of these holy beings, up to his last moment, breathed the Name of God, and soared in the realm of submission and resignation. Such was the

---

57. Bahá'u'lláh, *Prayers and Meditations*, no. LXXVIII, pp. 127-129.

potency and transmuting influence which He exercised over them, that they ceased to cherish any desire but His will, and wedded their soul to His remembrance.[58]

2.3.3 Excerpts from the Writings of the Báb

And from the moment when the Tree of the Bayán appeared until it disappeareth is the Resurrection of the Apostle of God, as is divinely foretold in the Qur'án; the beginning of which was when two hours and eleven minutes had passed on the eve of the fifth of Jamádíyu'l-Avval, AH 1260[59] which is the year 1270[60] of the Declaration of the Mission of Muḥammad. This was the beginning of the Day of Resurrection of the Qur'án, and until the disappearance of the Tree of divine Reality is the Resurrection of the Qur'án.[61]

• • •

O people of the Bayán! If ye believe in Him Whom God shall make manifest, to your own behoof do ye believe. He hath been and ever will remain independent of all men. For instance, were ye to place unnumbered mirrors before the sun, they would all reflect the sun and produce impressions thereof, whereas the sun is in itself wholly independent of the existence of the mirrors and of the suns which they reproduce. Such are the bounds of the contingent beings in their relation to the manifestation of the Eternal Being ... [62]

• • •

I swear by the holy Essence of God, were all in the Bayán to unite in helping Him Whom God shall make manifest in the days of His Revelation, not a single soul, nay, not a created thing would remain on earth that would not gain admittance into Paradise. Take good heed of yourselves, for the sum total of the religion of God is but to help Him, rather than to observe, in the time of His appearance, such deeds as are prescribed in the Bayán. [63]

---

58. Bahá'u'lláh, *The Kitáb-i-Íqán*, pp. 234-5.

59. 22 May 1844.

60. Muḥammad is supposed to have publicly declared His mission about AD 613. Hence, AH 1260 (the start date of the Muslim calendar is based on the date of the Hijrah or Muḥammad's Emirgration in AD 622) would be 1270 years after His public announcement. - H. M. Balyuzi, *Muḥammad and the Course of Islám*, p. 24.

61. The Báb, *Selections From the Writings of the Báb*, p. 107.

62. Ibid., p. 93

63. Ibid., p 85.

• • •

Since all men have issued forth from the shadow of the signs of His Divinity and Lordship, they always tend to take a path, lofty and high. And because they are bereft of a discerning eye to recognize their Beloved, they fall short of their duty to manifest meekness and humility towards Him. Nevertheless, from the beginning of their lives till the end thereof, in conformity with the laws established in the previous religion, they worship God, piously adore Him, bow themselves before His divine Reality and show submissiveness toward His exalted Essence. At the hour of His manifestation, however, they all turn their gaze toward their own selves and are thus shut out from Him, inasmuch as they fancifully regard Him as one like unto themselves. Far from the glory of God is such a comparison. Indeed that august Being resembleth the physical sun, His verses are like its rays, and all believers, should they truly believe in Him, are as mirrors wherein the sun is reflected. Their light is thus a mere reflection. [64]

• • •

I swear by the most holy Essence of God—exalted and glorified be He—that in the Day of the appearance of Him Whom God shall make manifest a thousand perusals of the Bayán cannot equal the perusal of a single verse to be revealed by Him Whom God shall make manifest.[65]

• • •

O Thou Remnant of God! I have sacrificed myself wholly for Thee; I have accepted curses for Thy sake, and have yearned for naught but martyrdom in the path of Thy love. Sufficient witness unto me is God, the Exalted, the Protector, the Ancient of Days.[66]

2.3.4 Declaration of the Báb

The opening scene of the initial act of this great drama was laid in the upper chamber of the modest residence of the son of a mercer of Shíráz, in an obscure corner of that city. The time was the hour before sunset, on the 22nd day of May, 1844. The participants were the Báb, a twenty-five year old siyyid, of pure and holy lineage, and the young Mullá Ḥusayn, the first to believe in Him. Their meeting immediately before that interview seemed to be purely fortuitous. The interview itself was protracted till the hour of dawn. The Host remained closeted alone with His guest, nor was the sleeping city remotely

---

64. The Báb, Selections From the Writings of the Báb, 92.

65. Ibid., p. 104.

66. Ibid., p. 59.

House of the Báb, Declaration Chamber
Shíráz, Iran

aware of the import of the conversation they held with each other. No record has passed to posterity of that unique night save the fragmentary but highly illuminating account that fell from the lips of Mullá Ḥusayn.

"I sat spellbound by His utterance, oblivious of time and of those who awaited me," he himself has testified, after describing the nature of the questions he had put to his Host and the conclusive replies he had received from Him, replies which had established beyond the shadow of a doubt the validity of His claim to be the promised Qá'im. "Suddenly the call of the Mu'adhdhin, summoning the faithful to their morning prayer, awakened me from the state of ecstasy into which I seemed to have fallen. All the delights, all the ineffable glories, which the Almighty has recounted in His Book as the priceless possessions of the people of Paradise —these I seemed to be experiencing that night. Me thinks I was in a place of which it could be truly said: *Therein no toil shall reach us, and therein no weariness shall touch us;' 'no vain discourse shall they hear therein, nor any falsehood, but only the cry, "Peace! Peace!"' 'their cry therein shall be "Glory to Thee, O God!" and their salutation therein, "Peace!"* and the close of their cry, *"Praise be to God, Lord of all creatures!"'* Sleep had departed from me that night. I was enthralled by the music of that voice which rose and fell as He chanted; now swelling forth as He revealed verses of the *Qayyúmu'l-Asmá'* again acquiring ethereal, subtle harmonies as He uttered the prayers He was revealing. At the end of each invocation, He would repeat this verse: *Far from the glory of thy Lord, the All-Glorious, be that which His creatures affirm of Him! And peace be upon His Messengers! And praise be to God, the Lord of all being!'* "

"This Revelation," Mullá Ḥusayn has further testified, "so suddenly and impetuously thrust upon me, came as a thunderbolt which, for a time, seemed to have benumbed my faculties. I was blinded by its dazzling splendour and overwhelmed by its crushing force. Excitement, joy, awe, and wonder stirred the depths of my soul. Predominant among these emotions was a sense of gladness and strength which seemed to have transfigured me. How feeble and impotent, how dejected and timid, I had felt previously! Then I could neither write nor walk, so tremulous were my hands and feet. Now, however, the knowledge of His Revelation had galvanized my being. I felt possessed of such courage and power that were the world, all its peoples and it potentates, to rise against me, I would, alone and undaunted, withstand their onslaught. The universe seemed but a handful of dust in my grasp. I seemed to be the voice of Gabriel personified, calling unto all mankind: 'Awake, for, lo! the morning Light has broken. Arise, for His Cause is made manifest. The portal of His grace is open wide; enter therein, O peoples of the world! For He Who is your promised One is come!'"

A more significant light, however, is shed on this episode, marking the Declaration of the Mission of the Báb, by the perusal of that *"first, greatest and mightiest"* of all books in the Bábí Dispensation, the celebrated commentary on the Súrih of Joseph, the first chapter of which, we are assured, proceeded, in its entirety, in the course of that night of nights from the pen of its divine Revealer. The description of this episode by Mullá Husayn, as well as the opening pages of that Book attest the magnitude and force of that weighty Declaration. A claim to be no less than the mouthpiece of God Himself, promised by the Prophets of bygone ages; the assertion that He was, at the same time, the Herald of One immeasurably greater than Himself; the summons which He trumpeted forth to the kings and princes of the earth; the dire warnings directed to the Chief Magistrate of the realm, Muḥammad Sháh; the counsel imparted to Hájí Mírzá Áqásí to fear God, and the peremptory command to abdicate his authority as grand vizir of the Sháh and submit to the One Who is the *"Inheritor of the earth and all that is therein"*; the challenge issued to the rulers of the world proclaiming the self-sufficiency of His Cause, denouncing the vanity of their ephemeral power, and calling upon them to *"lay aside, one and all, their dominion,"* and deliver His Message to *"lands in both the East and the West"*—these constitute the dominant features of that initial contact that marked the birth, and fixed the date, of the inception of the most glorious era in the spiritual life of mankind.[67]

2.3.5 Nabíl's Narrative on the Declaration of the Báb

On that very day, a few hours before sunset, whilst walking outside the gate of the city, his eyes fell suddenly upon a Youth of radiant countenance, who wore a green turban and who, advancing towards him, greeted him with a smile of loving welcome. He embraced Mullá Ḥusayn with tender affection as though he had been his intimate and lifelong friend. Mullá Ḥusayn thought Him at first to be a disciple of Siyyid Kázim who, on being informed of his approach to Shíráz, had come out to welcome him.

Mírzá Aḥmad-i-Qazvíní, the martyr, who on several occasions had heard Mullá Ḥusayn recount to the early believers the story of his moving and historic interview with the Báb, related to me the following: "I have heard Mullá Ḥusayn repeatedly and graphically describe the circumstances of that remarkable interview: 'The Youth who met me outside the gate of Shíráz overwhelmed me with expressions of affection and loving-kindness. He extended to me a warm invitation to visit His home, and there refresh myself after the fatigues of my journey. I prayed to be excused, pleading that my two companions had already arranged for my stay in that city, and were now awaiting my return. "Commit them to the care of God," was His reply; "He will surely protect and watch over them." Having spoken these words, He bade me follow Him. I was profoundly impressed by the gentle yet compelling manner in which that strange Youth spoke to me. As I followed Him, His gait, the charm of His voice, the dignity of His bearing, served to enhance my first impressions of this unexpected meeting.

"'We soon found ourselves standing at the gate of a house of modest appearance. He knocked at the door, which was soon opened by an Ethiopian servant. "Enter therein in peace, secure," were His words as He crossed the threshold and motioned me to follow Him. His invitation, uttered with power and majesty, penetrated my soul. I thought it a good augury to be addressed in such words, standing as I did on the threshold of the first house I was entering in Shíráz, a city the very atmosphere of which had produced already an indescribable impression upon me. Might not my visit to this house, I thought to myself, enable me to draw nearer to the Object of my quest? Might it not hasten the termination of a period of intense longing, of strenuous search, of increasing anxiety, which such a quest involves? As I entered the house and followed my Host to His chamber, a feeling of unutterable joy invaded my being. Immediately we were seated, He ordered a ewer of water to be brought, and bade me wash away from my hands and feet the stains of travel. I pleaded permission to retire from His presence and perform my ablutions in an adjoining room. He refused to grant my request, and proceeded to pour the water over my hands. He then gave me to drink of a refreshing beverage, after which He asked for the samovar and Himself prepared the tea which He offered me.

"'Overwhelmed with His acts of extreme kindness, I arose to depart. "The time for evening prayer is approaching," I ventured to observe. "I have promised my friends to join them at that hour in the Masjid-i-Ílkhání." With extreme courtesy and calm He replied: "You must surely have made the hour of your return conditional upon the will and pleasure of God. It seems that His will has decreed otherwise. You need have no fear of having broken your pledge." His dignity and self-assurance silenced me. I renewed my ablutions and prepared for prayer. He, too, stood beside me and prayed. Whilst praying, I unburdened my soul, which was much oppressed, both by the mystery of this interview and the strain and stress of my search. I breathed this prayer: "I have striven with all my soul, O my God, and until now have failed to find Thy promised Messenger. I testify that Thy word faileth not, and that Thy promise is sure."

"That night, that memorable night, was the eve preceding the fifth day of Jamádíyu'l-Avval, in the year AH 1260.[68] It was about an hour after sunset when my youthful Host began to converse with me. "Whom, after Siyyid Kázim," He asked me, "do you regard as his successor and your leader?" "At the hour of his death," I replied, "our departed teacher insistently exhorted us to forsake our homes, to scatter far and wide, in the quest of the promised Beloved. I have, accordingly journeyed to Persia, have arisen to accomplish his will, and am still engaged in my quest." "Has your teacher," He further enquired, "given you any detailed indications as to the distinguishing features of the promised One?" "Yes," I replied, "He is of pure lineage, is of illustrious descent, and of the seed of Fátimih. As to His age, He is more than twenty and less than thirty. He is endowed with innate knowledge. He is of medium height, abstains from smoking, and is free from bodily deficiency." He paused for a while and then with vibrant voice declared: "Behold, all these signs are manifest in Me!" He then considered each of the above-mentioned signs separately, and conclusively demonstrated that each and all were applicable to His person. I was greatly surprised, and politely observed: "He whose advent we await is a Man of unsurpassed holiness, and the Cause He is to reveal, a Cause of tremendous power. Many and diverse are the requirements which He who claims to be its visible embodiment must needs fulfil. How often has Siyyid Kázim referred to the vastness of the knowledge of the promised One! How often did he say: 'My own knowledge is but a drop compared with that with which He has been endowed. All my attainments are but a speck of dust in the face of the immensity of His knowledge. Nay, immeasurable is the difference!'" "No sooner had those words dropped from my lips than I found myself seized with fear and remorse, such as I could neither conceal nor explain. I bitterly reproved myself, and resolved at that very moment to alter my attitude and to soften my tone. I vowed to God that should my Host again refer to the subject, I would, with the utmost humility, answer and say: "If you be willing to substantiate your claim, you will most assuredly deliver me from the anxiety and suspense which so heavily oppress my soul. I shall truly be indebted to you for such deliver-

---

68. Corresponding with the evening of 22 May 1844 A.D.

ance." When I first started upon my quest, I determined to regard the two following standards as those whereby I could ascertain the truth of whosoever might claim to be the promised Qá'im. The first was a treatise which I had myself composed, bearing upon the abstruse and hidden teachings propounded by Shaykh Aḥmad and Siyyid Káẓim. Whoever seemed to me capable of unravelling the mysterious allusions made in that treatise, to him I would next submit my second request, and would ask him to reveal, without the least hesitation or reflection, a commentary on the Súrih of Joseph, in a style and language entirely different from the prevailing standards of the time. I had previously requested Siyyid Káẓim, in private, to write a commentary on that same Súrih, which he refused, saying: "This is, verily, beyond me. He, that great One, who comes after me will, unasked, reveal it for you. That commentary will constitute one of the weightiest testimonies of His truth, and one of the clearest evidences of the loftiness of His position."

"I was revolving these things in my mind, when my distinguished Host again remarked: "Observe attentively. Might not the Person intended by Siyyid Káẓim be none other than I?" I thereupon felt impelled to present to Him a copy of the treatise which I had with me. "Will you," I asked Him, "read this book of mine and look at its pages with indulgent eyes? I pray you to overlook my weaknesses and failings." He graciously complied with my wish. He opened the book, glanced at certain passages, closed it, and began to address me. Within a few minutes He had, with characteristic vigour and charm, unravelled all its mysteries and resolved all its problems. Having to my entire satisfaction accomplished, within so short a time, the task I had expected Him to perform, He further expounded to me certain truths which could be found neither in the reported sayings of the imáms of the Faith nor in the writings of Shaykh Aḥmad and Siyyid Káẓim. These truths, which I had never heard before, seemed to be endowed with refreshing vividness and power. "Had you not been My guest," He afterwards observed, "your position would indeed have been a grievous one. The all-encompassing grace of God has saved you. It is for God to test His servants, and not for His servants to judge Him in accordance with their deficient standards. Were I to fail to resolve your perplexities, could the Reality that shines within Me be regarded as powerless, or My knowledge be accused as faulty? Nay, by the righteousness of God! it behoves, in this day, the peoples and nations of both the East and the West to hasten to this threshold, and here seek to obtain the reviving grace of the Merciful. Whoso hesitates will indeed be in grievous loss. Do not the peoples of the earth testify that the

71

fundamental purpose of their creation is the knowledge and adoration of God? It behoves them to arise, as earnestly and spontaneously as you have arisen, and to seek with determination and constancy their promised Beloved." He then proceeded to say: "Now is the time to reveal the commentary of the Súrih of Joseph." He took up His pen and with incredible rapidity revealed the entire Súrih of Mulk, the first chapter of His commentary on the Súrih of Joseph. The overpowering effect of the manner in which He wrote was heightened by the gentle intonation of His voice which accompanied His writing. Not for one moment did He interrupt the flow of the verses which streamed from His pen. Not once did He pause till the Súrih of Mulk was finished. I sat enraptured by the magic of His voice and the sweeping force of His revelation. At last I reluctantly rose from my seat and begged leave to depart. He smilingly bade me be seated, and said: "If you leave in such a state, whoever sees you will assuredly say: 'This poor youth has lost his mind.' " At that moment the clock registered two hours and eleven minutes after sunset. That night, the eve of the fifth day of Jamádíyu'l-Avval, in the year AH 1260, corresponded with the eve preceding the sixty-fifth day after Naw-Rúz, which was also the eve of the sixth day of Khurdád, of the year Nahang. "This night," He declared, "this very hour will, in the days to come, be celebrated as one of the greatest and most significant of all festivals. Render thanks to God for having graciously assisted you to attain your heart's desire, and for having quaffed from the sealed wine of His utterance. 'Well is it with them that attain "thereunto."'

"At the third hour after sunset, my Host ordered the dinner to be served. That same Ethiopian servant appeared again and spread before us the choicest food. That holy repast refreshed alike my body and soul. In the presence of my Host, at that hour, I felt as though I were feeding upon the fruits of Paradise. I could not but marvel at the manners and the devoted attentions of that Ethiopian servant whose very life seemed to have been transformed by the regenerating influence of his Master. I then, for the first time, recognised the significance of this well-known traditional utterance ascribed to Muḥammad: "I have prepared for the godly and righteous among My servants what eye hath seen not, ear heard not, nor human heart conceived." Had my youthful Host no other claim to greatness, this were sufficient—that He received me with that quality of hospitality and loving-kindness which I was convinced no other human being could possibly reveal.

"'I sat spellbound by His utterance, oblivious of time and of those who awaited me. Suddenly the call of the Mu'adhdhin, summoning the faithful to their morning prayer, awakened me from the state of ecstasy into which I seemed to have fallen. All the delights, all the ineffable glories, which the Almighty has recounted in His Book as the priceless possessions of the people of Paradise—these I seemed to be experiencing that night. Me-thinks I was in a place of which it could be truly said: "Therein no toil shall reach us, and therein no weariness shall touch us"; "No vain discourse shall they hear therein, nor any falsehood, but only the cry, 'Peace! Peace!' "; "Their cry therein shall be, 'Glory be to Thee, O God!' and their salutation therein, 'Peace!' And the close of their cry, 'Praise be to God, Lord of all creatures!'"

Sleep had departed from me that night. I was enthralled by the music of that voice which rose and fell as He chanted; now swelling forth as He revealed verses of the *Qayyúmu'l-Asmá*, again acquiring ethereal, subtle harmonies as He uttered the prayers He was revealing. At the end of each invocation, He would repeat this verse: "Far from the glory of thy Lord, the All-Glorious, be that which His creatures affirm of Him! And peace be upon His Messengers! And praise be to God, the Lord of all beings!"

"'He then addressed me in these words: "O thou who art the first to believe in Me! Verily I say, I am the Báb, the Gate of God, and thou are the Bábu'l-Báb, the gate of that Gate. Eighteen souls must, in the beginning, spontaneously and of their own accord, accept Me and recognise the truth of My Revelation. Unwarned and uninvited, each of these must seek independently to find Me. And when their number is complete, one of them must needs be chosen to accompany Me on My pilgrimage to Mecca and Medina. There I shall deliver the Message of God to the Sharíf of Mecca. I then shall return to Kúfih, where again, in the Masjid of that holy city, I shall manifest His Cause. It is incumbent upon you not to divulge, either to your companions or to any other soul, that which you have seen and heard. Be engaged in the Masjid-i-Ílkhání in prayer and in teaching. I, too, will there join you in congregational prayer. Beware lest your attitude towards Me betray the secret of your faith. You should continue in this occupation and maintain this attitude until our departure for Ḥijáz. Ere we depart, we shall appoint unto each of the eighteen souls his special mission, and shall send them forth to accomplish their task. We shall instruct them to teach the Word of God and to quicken the souls of men." Having spoken these words to me, He dismissed me from His presence. Accompanying me to the door of the house, He committed me to the care of God.[69]

---

69. Nabíl-i-A'ẓam, *The Dawnbreakers*, pp. 52-65.

2.3.6 Station of the Báb

Dearly-beloved friends! That the Báb, the inaugurator of the Bábí Dispensation, is fully entitled to rank as one of the self-sufficient Manifestations of God, that He has been invested with sovereign power and authority, and exercises all the rights and prerogatives of independent Prophethood, is yet another fundamental verity which the Message of Bahá'u'lláh insistently proclaims and which its followers must uncompromisingly uphold. That He is not to be regarded merely as an inspired Precursor of the Bahá'í Revelation, that in His person, as He Himself bears witness in the Persian *Bayán*, the object of all the Prophets gone before Him has been fulfilled, is a truth which I feel it my duty to demonstrate and emphasize. We would assuredly be failing in our duty to the Faith we profess and would be violating one of its basic and sacred principles if in our words or by our conduct we hesitate to recognize the implications of this root principle of Bahá'í belief, or refuse to uphold unreservedly its integrity and demonstrate its truth. Indeed the chief motive actuating me to undertake the task of editing and translating Nabíl's immortal Narrative has been to enable every follower of the Faith in the West to better understand and more readily grasp the tremendous implications of His exalted station and to more ardently admire and love Him.

There can be no doubt that the claim of the twofold station ordained for the Báb by the Almighty, a claim which He Himself has so boldly advanced, which Bahá'u'lláh has repeatedly affirmed, and to which the *Will and Testament of 'Abdu'l-Bahá* has finally given the sanction of its testimony, constitutes the most distinctive feature of the Bahá'í Dispensation. It is a further evidence of its uniqueness, a tremendous accession to the strength, to the mysterious power and authority with which this holy cycle has been invested. Indeed the greatness of the Báb consists primarily, not in His being the divinely-appointed Forerunner of so transcendent a Revelation, but rather in His having been invested with the powers inherent in the inaugurator of a separate religious Dispensation, and in His wielding, to a degree unrivalled by the Messengers gone before Him, the sceptre of independent Prophethood.

The short duration of His Dispensation, the restricted range within which His laws and ordinances have been made to operate, supply no criterion whatever wherewith to judge its Divine origin and to evaluate the potency of its message. *"That so brief a span,"* Bahá'u'lláh Himself explains, *"should have separated this most mighty and wondrous Revelation from Mine own previous Manifestation, is a secret that no man can unravel and a mystery such as no mind can fathom. Its duration had been fore-ordained, and no man shall ever discover its reason unless and until he be informed of the contents of My Hidden Book."* *"Behold,"* Bahá'u'lláh further explains in the *Kitáb-i-Bádi,* one of His works refuting the arguments of the people of the Bayán, *"behold, how immediately upon the completion of the ninth year of this wondrous, this most holy and merciful Dispensation, the requisite number of pure, of wholly consecrated and sanctified souls had been most secretly consummated."*

The marvellous happenings that have heralded the advent of the Founder of the Bábí Dispensation, the dramatic circumstances of His own eventful life, the miraculous tragedy of His martyrdom, the magic of His influence exerted on the most eminent and powerful among His countrymen, to all of which every chapter of Nabíl's stirring narrative testifies, should in themselves be regarded as sufficient evidence of the validity of His claim to so exalted a station among the Prophets.

However graphic the record which the eminent chronicler of His life has transmitted to posterity, so luminous a narrative must pale before the glowing tribute paid to the Báb by the pen of Bahá'u'lláh. This tribute the Báb Himself has, by the clear assertion of His claim, abundantly supported, while the written testimonies of 'Abdu'l-Bahá have powerfully reinforced its character and elucidated its meaning.

Where else if not in the *Kitáb-i-Íqán* can the student of the Bábí Dispensation seek to find those affirmations that unmistakably attest the power and spirit which no man, except he be a Manifestation of God, can manifest? *"Could such a thing,"* exclaims Bahá'u'lláh, *"be made manifest except through the power of a Divine Revelation and the potency of God's invincible Will? By the righteousness of God! Were any one to entertain so great a Revelation in his heart the thought of such a declaration would alone confound him! Were the hearts of all men to be crowded into his heart, he would still hesitate to venture upon so awful an enterprise."* *"No eye,"* He in another passage affirms, *"hath beheld so great an outpouring of bounty, nor hath any ear heard of such a Revelation of loving-kindness ...The Prophets 'endowed with constancy,' whose loftiness and glory shine as the sun, were each honoured with a Book which all have seen, and the verses of which have been duly ascertained. Whereas the verses which have rained from this Cloud of divine mercy have been so abundant that none hath yet been able to estimate their number... How can they belittle this Revelation? Hath any age witnessed such momentous happenings?"*

Commenting on the character and influence of those heroes and martyrs whom the spirit of the Báb had so magically transformed Bahá'u'lláh reveals the following: *"If these companions be not the true strivers after God, who else could be called by this name? ...If these companions, with all their marvellous testimonies and wondrous works, be false, who then is worthy to claim for himself the truth? ...Has the world since the days of Adam witnessed such tumult, such violent commotion? ...Methinks, patience was revealed only by virtue of their fortitude, and faithfulness itself was begotten only by their deeds."*

Wishing to stress the sublimity of the Báb's exalted station as compared with that of the Prophets of the past, Bahá'u'lláh in that same epistle asserts: *"No understanding can grasp the nature of His Revelation, nor can any knowledge comprehend the full measure of His Faith."* He then quotes, in confirmation of His argument, these prophetic words: *"Knowledge is twenty and seven letters. All that the Prophets have revealed are two letters thereof. No man thus far hath known more than these two letters. But when the Qá'im shall arise, He will cause the remaining twenty and five letters to be made manifest."* *"Behold,"* He adds, *"how great and lofty is His station! His rank excelleth that of all the Prophets and His Revelation transcendeth the comprehension and understanding of all their chosen ones."* *"Of His Revelation,"* He further adds, *"the prophets of God, His saints and chosen ones, have either not been informed, or in pursuance of God's inscrutable decree, they have not disclosed."*

Of all the tributes which Bahá'u'lláh's unerring pen has chosen to pay to the memory of the Báb, His *"Best-Beloved,"* the most memorable and touching is this brief, yet eloquent passage which so greatly enhances the value of the concluding passages of that same epistle. *"Amidst them all,"* He writes, referring to the afflictive trials and dangers besetting him in the city of Baghdád, *"We stand life in hand wholly resigned to His Will, that perchance through God's loving kindness and grace, this revealed and manifest Letter* (Bahá'u'lláh) *may lay down His life as a sacrifice in the path of the Primal Point, the most exalted Word* (the Báb). *By Him, at Whose bidding the Spirit hath spoken, but for this yearning of Our soul, We would not, for one moment, have tarried any longer in this city."*

Dearly-beloved friends! So resounding a praise, so bold an assertion issued by the pen of Bahá'u'lláh in so weighty a work, are fully re-echoed in the language in which the Source of the Bábí Revelation has chosen to clothe the claims He Himself has advanced. *"I am the Mystic Fane,"* the Báb thus proclaims His station in the Qayyúmu'l-Asmá', *"which the Hand of Omnipotence hath reared. I am the lamp which the Finger of God hath lit within its niche and caused to shine with deathless splendour. I am the Flame of that supernal Light that glowed upon Sinai in the gladsome Spot, and lay concealed in the midst of the Burning Bush."* *"O Qurratu'l-'Ayn!"* He, addressing Himself in the same commentary, exclaims, *"I recognize in Thee none other except the 'Great Announcement'—the Announcement voiced by the Concourse on high. By this name, I bear witness, they that circle the Throne of Glory have ever known*

Thee." "With each and every Prophet, Whom We have sent down in the past," He further adds, "We have established a separate Covenant concerning the 'Remembrance of God' and His Day. Manifest, in the realm of glory and through the power of truth, are the 'Remembrance of God' and His Day before the eyes of the angels that circle His mercy-seat." "Should it be Our wish," He again affirms, "it is in Our power to compel, through the agency of but one letter of Our Revelation, the world and all that is therein to recognize, in less than the twinkling of an eye, the truth of Our Cause."

"I am the Primal Point," the Báb thus addresses Muhammad Sháh from the prison-fortress of Máh-Kú, "from which have been generated all created things ...I am the Countenance of God Whose splendour can never be obscured, the light of God whose radiance can never fade ...All the keys of heaven God hath chosen to place on My right hand, and all the keys of hell on My left ...I am one of the sustaining pillars of the Primal Word of God. Whosoever hath recognized Me, hath known all that is true and right, and hath attained all that is good and seemly ...The substance wherewith God hath created Me is not the clay out of which others have been formed. He hath conferred upon Me that which the worldly-wise can never comprehend, nor the faithful discover." "Should a tiny ant," the Báb, wishing to stress the limitless potentialities latent in His Dispensation, characteristically affirms, "desire in this day to be possessed of such power as to be able to unravel the abstrusest and most bewildering passages of the Qur'án, its wish will no doubt be fulfilled, inasmuch as the mystery of eternal might vibrates within the innermost being of all created things." "If so helpless a creature," is 'Abdu'l-Bahá's comment on so startling an affirmation, "can be endowed with so subtle a capacity, how much more efficacious must be the power released through the liberal effusions of the grace of Bahá'u'lláh!"

To these authoritative assertions and solemn declarations made by Bahá'u'lláh and the Báb must be added 'Abdu'l-Bahá's own incontrovertible testimony. He, the appointed interpreter of the utterances of both Bahá'u'lláh and the Báb, corroborates, not by implication but in clear and categorical language, both in His Tablets and in His Testament, the truth of the statements to which I have already referred.

In a Tablet addressed to a Bahá'í in Mázindarán, in which He unfolds the meaning of a misinterpreted statement attributed to Him regarding the rise of the Sun of Truth in this century, He sets forth, briefly but conclusively, what should remain for all time our true conception of the relationship between the two Manifestations associated with the Bahá'í Dispensation. "In making such a statement," He explains, "I had in mind no one else except the Báb and Bahá'u'lláh, the character of whose Revelations it had been my purpose to elucidate. The Revelation of the Báb may be likened to the sun, its station corresponding to the first sign of the Zodiac—the sign

Aries—which the sun enters at the Vernal Equinox. The station of Bahá'u'lláh's Revelation, on the other hand, is represented by the sign Leo, the sun's mid-summer and highest station. By this is meant that this holy Dispensation is illumined with the light of the Sun of Truth shining from its most exalted station, and in the plenitude of its resplendency, its heat and glory."

"*The Báb, the Exalted One,*" 'Abdu'l-Bahá more specifically affirms in another Tablet, "*is the Morn of Truth, the splendour of Whose light shineth throughout all regions. He is also the Harbinger of the Most Great Light, the Abhá Luminary. The Blessed Beauty is the One promised by the sacred books of the past, the revelation of the Source of light that shone upon Mount Sinai, Whose fire glowed in the midst of the Burning Bush. We are, one and all, servants of their threshold, and stand each as a lowly keeper at their door.*"

"*Every proof and prophecy,*" is His still more emphatic warning, "*every manner of evidence, whether based on reason or on the text of the Scriptures and traditions, are to be regarded as centred in the persons of Bahá'u'lláh and the Báb. In them is to be found their complete fulfilment.*"

And finally, in His *Will and Testament,* the repository of His last wishes and parting instructions, He in the following passage, specifically designed to set forth the guiding principles of Bahá'í belief, sets the seal of His testimony on the Báb's dual and exalted station: "*The foundation of the belief of the people of Bahá (may my life be offered up for them) is this: His holiness the exalted One* (the Báb) *is the Manifestation of the unity and oneness of God and the Forerunner of the Ancient Beauty* (Bahá'u'lláh). *His holiness, the Abhá Beauty* (Bahá'u'lláh) *(may my life be offered up as a sacrifice for His steadfast friends) is the supreme Manifestation of God and the Dayspring of His most divine Essence.*" "*All others,*" He significantly adds, "*are servants unto Him and do His bidding.*"[70]

2.3.7 The Báb's Address to the Letters of the Living

O My beloved friends![71] You are the bearers of the name of God in this Day. You have been chosen as the repositories of His mystery. It behoves each one of you to manifest the attributes of God, and to exemplify by your deeds and words the signs of His righteousness, His power and glory. The very members of your body must bear witness to the loftiness of your purpose, the integrity of your life, the reality of your faith, and the exalted character of your

---

70. Shoghi Effendi, *The World Order of Bahá'u'lláh*, pp. 123-8.
71. Words addressed by the Báb to the remaining Letters of the Living after the departure of Mullá 'Alí.

devotion. For verily I say, this is the Day spoken of by God in His Book:[72] 'On that day will We set a seal upon their mouths; yet shall their hands speak unto Us, and their feet shall bear witness to that which they shall have done.' Ponder the words of Jesus addressed to His disciples, as He sent them forth to propagate the Cause of God. In words such as these, He bade them arise and fulfil their mission: 'Ye are even as the fire which in the darkness of the night has been kindled upon the mountain-top. Let your light shine before the eyes of men. Such must be the purity of your character and the degree of your renunciation, that the people of the earth may through you recognise and be drawn closer to the heavenly Father who is the Source of purity and grace. For none has seen the Father who is in heaven. You who are His spiritual children must by your deeds exemplify His virtues, and witness to His glory. You are the salt of the earth, but if the salt have lost its savour, wherewith shall it be salted? Such must be the degree of your detachment, that into whatever city you enter to proclaim and teach the Cause of God, you should in no wise expect either meat or reward from its people. Nay, when you depart out of that city, you should shake the dust from your feet. As you have entered it pure and undefiled, so must you depart from that city. For verily I say, the heavenly Father is ever with you and keeps watch over you. If you be faithful to Him, He will assuredly deliver into your hands all the treasures of the earth, and will exalt you above all the rulers and kings of the world.' O My Letters! Verily I say, immensely exalted is this Day above the days of the Apostles of old. Nay, immeasurable is the difference! You are the witnesses of the Dawn of the promised Day of God. You are the partakers of the mystic chalice of His Revelation. Gird up the loins of endeavour, and be mindful of the words of God as revealed in His Book:[73] 'Lo, the Lord thy God is come, and with Him is the company of His angels arrayed before Him!' Purge your hearts of worldly desires, and let angelic virtues be your adorning. Strive that by your deeds you may bear witness to the truth of these words of God, and beware lest, by 'turning back,' He may 'change you for another people,' who 'shall not be your like,' and who shall take from you the Kingdom of God. The days when idle worship was deemed sufficient are ended. The time is come when naught but the purest motive, supported by deeds of stainless purity, can ascend to the throne of the Most High and be acceptable unto Him. 'The good word riseth up unto Him, and

---

72. *The Qur'án.*
73. Ibid.

the righteous deed will cause it to be exalted before Him.' You are the lowly, of whom God has thus spoken in His Book:[74] 'And We desire to show favour to those who were brought low in the land, and to make them spiritual leaders among men, and to make them Our heirs.' You have been called to this station; you will attain to it, only if you arise to trample beneath your feet every earthly desire, and endeavour to become those 'honoured servants of His who speak not till He hath spoken, and who do His bidding,'[The Báb] You are the first Letters that have been generated from the Primal Point, the first Springs that have welled out from the Source of this Revelation. Beseech the Lord your God to grant that no earthly entanglements, no worldly affections, no ephemeral pursuits, may tarnish the purity, or embitter the sweetness, of that grace which flows through you. I am preparing you for the advent of a mighty Day. Exert your utmost endeavour that, in the world to come, I, who am now instructing you, may, before the mercy-seat of God, rejoice in your deeds and glory in your achievements. The secret of the Day that is to come is now concealed. It can neither be divulged nor estimated. The newly born babe of that Day excels the wisest and the most venerable men of this time, and the lowliest and most unlearned of that period shall surpass in understanding the most erudite and accomplished divines of this age. Scatter throughout the length and breadth of this land, and, with steadfast feet and sanctified hearts, prepare the way for His coming. Heed not your weaknesses and frailty; fix your gaze upon the invincible power of the Lord, your God, the Almighty. Has He not, in past days, caused Abraham, in spite of His seeming helplessness, to triumph over the forces of Nimrod? Has He not enabled Moses, whose staff was His only companion, to vanquish Pharaoh and his hosts? Has He not established the ascendancy of Jesus, poor and lowly as He was in the eyes of men, over the combined forces of the Jewish people? Has He not subjected the barbarous and militant tribes of Arabia to the holy and transforming discipline of Muḥammad, His Prophet? Arise in His name, put your trust wholly in Him, and be assured of ultimate victory.[75]

---

74. The Qur'án.
75. The Báb, quoted in The Dawnbreakers, pp. 92-4.

Mansion of Bahji

2.4
Ascension of Bahá'u'lláh
May 29, 1892

The Sun of Truth, that Most Great Light, hath set upon the horizon of the world to rise with deathless splendour over the Realm of the Limitless.[76]

Suggested Readings

2.4.1   Prayer Revealed by Bahá'u'lláh
2.4.2   *Let not Your Hearts Be Perturbed*, Tablet Revealed by Bahá'u'lláh
2.4.3   *Kitáb-i-Ahd* (Book of the Covenant), Revealed by Bahá'u'lláh
2.4.4   *Let not Fear Fall Upon You*, from the Writings of 'Abdu'l-Bahá
2.4.5   *He Came and Went As He Wished*, A Talk Given by 'Abdul-Bahá
2.4.6   *What An Educator This Glorious Being Was*, Talk by 'Abdu'l-Bahá
2.4.7   *Bahá'u'lláh and His Sufferings*, from Nabíl's Narrative
2.4.8   *Ascension of Bahá'u'lláh*, from the Writings of Shoghi Effendi
2.4.9   *Ascension of Bahá'u'lláh*, An Account by Nabíl
2.4.10   *The Tablet of Visitation*

---

76. 'Abdu'l-Bahá, *Selections From the Writings of 'Abdu'l-Bahá*, p.18.

2.4.1   Prayer Revealed by Bahá'u'lláh

O Thou Who art the Ruler of earth and heaven and the Author of all names! Thou hearest the voice of my lamentation which from the fortress-town of Àkká ascendeth towards Thee, and beholdest how my captive friends have fallen into the hands of the workers of iniquity.

We render Thee thanks, O our Lord, for all the troubles which have touched us in Thy path. Oh, that the span of my earthly life could be so extended as to embrace the lives of the former and the latter generations, or could even be so lengthened that no man on the face of the earth could measure it, and be afflicted every day and every moment with a fresh tribulation for love of Thee and for Thy pleasure's sake!

Thou well knowest, however, O my God, that my wish is wholly dissolved in Thy wish, and that Thou hast irrevocably decreed that my soul should ascend unto the loftiest mansions of Thy Kingdom, and pass into the presence of my all-glorious Companion.

Hasten, by Thy grace and bounty, my passing, O my Lord, and pour forth upon all them that are dear to Thee what will preserve them from fear and trembling after me. Powerful art Thou to do whatsoever may please Thee. No God is there except Thee, the All-Glorious, the All-Wise.

Thou seest, O my Lord, how Thy servants have left their homes in their longing to meet Thee, and how they have been hindered by the ungodly from looking upon thy face, and from circumambulating the sanctuary of Thy grandeur. Pour out thy steadfastness and send down Thy calm upon them, O my Lord! Thou art, in truth, the Ever-Forgiving, the Most Compassionate.[77]

2.4.2   *Let Not Your Hearts Be Perturbed*, Tablet Revealed by Bahá'u'lláh

Let not your hearts be perturbed, O people, when the glory of My Presence is withdrawn, and the ocean of My utterance is stilled. In My presence amongst you there is a wisdom, and in My absence there is yet another, inscrutable to all but God, the Incomparable, the All-Knowing. Verily, We behold you from Our realm of glory, and shall aid whosoever will arise for the triumph of Our Cause with the hosts of the Concourse on high and a company of Our favoured angels.

O peoples of the earth! God, the Eternal Truth, is My witness that streams

---

77. Bahá'u'lláh, *Prayers and Meditations*, no. XV, pp. 17-18.

of fresh and soft-flowing waters have gushed from the rocks, through the sweetness of the words uttered by your Lord, the Unconstrained; and still ye slumber. Cast away that which ye possess, and, on the wings of detachment, soar beyond all created things. Thus biddeth you the Lord of creation, the movement of Whose Pen hath revolutionized the soul of mankind.

Know ye from what heights your Lord, the All-Glorious, is calling? Think ye that ye have recognized the Pen where with your Lord, the Lord of all names, commandeth you? Nay, by My life! Did ye but know it, ye would renounce the world, and would hasten with your whole hearts to the presence of the Well-Beloved. Your spirits would be so transported by His Word as to throw into commotion the Greater World—how much more this small and petty one! Thus have the showers of My bounty been poured down from the heaven of My loving-kindness, as a token of My grace; that ye may be of the thankful.

...Beware lest the desires of the flesh and of a corrupt inclination provoke divisions among you. Be ye as the fingers of one hand, the members of one body. Thus counselleth you the Pen of Revelation, if ye be of them that believe.

Consider the mercy of God and His gifts. He enjoineth upon you that which shall profit you, though He Himself can well dispense with all creatures. Your evil doings can never harm Us, neither can your good works profit Us. We summon you wholly for the sake of God. To this every man of understanding and insight will testify. [78]

2.4.3 *Kitáb-i-'Ahd* (Book of the Covenant)

Although the Realm of Glory hath none of the vanities of the world, yet within the treasury of trust and resignation We have bequeathed to Our heirs an excellent and priceless heritage. Earthly treasures We have not bequeathed, nor have We added such cares as they entail. By God! In earthly riches fear is hidden and peril is concealed. Consider ye and call to mind that which the All-Merciful hath revealed in the Qur'án: *'Woe betide every slanderer and defamer, him that layeth up riches and counteth them.'* Fleeting are the riches of the world; all that perisheth and changeth is not, and hath never been, worthy of attention, except to a recognized measure.

The aim of this Wronged One in sustaining woes and tribulations, in revealing the Holy Verses and in demonstrating proofs hath been naught but to quench

---

78. Bahá'u'lláh, *The Kitáb-i-Aqdas*, pp. 39-40.

House of Abbud

the flame of hate and enmity, that the horizon of the hearts of men may be illumined with the light of concord and attain real peace and tranquillity. From the dawning-place of the divine Tablet the day-star of this utterance shineth resplendent, and it behoveth everyone to fix his gaze upon it: We exhort you, O peoples of the world, to observe that which will elevate your station. Hold fast to the fear of God and firmly adhere to what is right. Verily I say, the tongue is for mentioning what is good, defile it not with unseemly talk. God hath forgiven what is past. Henceforward everyone should utter that which is meet and seemly, and should refrain from slander, abuse and whatever causeth sadness in men. Lofty is the station of man! Not long ago this exalted Word streamed forth from the treasury of Our Pen of Glory: Great and blessed is this Day— the Day in which all that lay latent in man hath been and will be made manifest. Lofty is the station of man, were he to hold fast to righteousness and truth and to remain firm and steadfast in the Cause. In the eyes of the All-Merciful a true man appeareth even as a firmament; its sun and moon are his sight and hearing, and his shining and resplendent character its stars. His is the loftiest station, and his influence educateth the world of being.

Every receptive soul who hath in this Day inhaled the fragrance of His garment and hash, with a pure heart, set his face towards the all-glorious Horizon is reckoned among the people of Bahá in the Crimson Book. Grasp ye, in My Name, the chalice of My loving-kindness, drink then your fill in My glorious and wondrous remembrance.

O ye that dwell on earth! The religion of God is for love and unity; make it not the cause of enmity or dissension. In the eyes of men of insight and the beholders of the Most Sublime Vision, whatsoever are the effective means for safeguarding and promoting the happiness and welfare of the children of men hath already been revealed by the Pen of Glory. But the foolish ones of the earth, being nurtured in evil passions and desires, have remained heedless of the consummate wisdom of Him Who is, in truth, the All-Wise, while their words and deeds are prompted by idle fancies and vain-imaginings.

O ye the loved ones and the trustees of God! Kings are the manifestations of the power, and the daysprings of the might and riches, of God. Pray ye on their behalf. He hath invested them with the rulership of the earth and hath singled out the hearts of men as His Own domain.

Conflict and contention are categorically forbidden in His Book. This is a decree of God in this Most Great Revelation. It is divinely preserved from annulment and is invested by Him with the splendour of His confirmation.

Verily He is the All-Knowing, the All-Wise.

It is incumbent upon everyone to aid these dayprings of authority and sources of command who are adorned with the ornament of equity and justice. Blessed are the rulers and the learned among the people of Bahá. They are My trustees among My servants and the manifestations of My commandments amidst My people. Upon them rest My glory, My blessings and My grace which have pervaded the world of being. In this connection the utterances revealed in the *Kitáb-i-Aqda*s are such that from the horizon of their words the light of divine grace shineth luminous and resplendent.

O ye My Branches! A mighty force, a consummate power lieth concealed in the world of being. Fix your gaze upon it and upon its unifying influence, and not upon the differences which appear from it.

The Will of the divine Testator is this: It is incumbent upon the Aghsán, the Afnán[79] and My Kindred to turn, one and all, their faces towards the Most Mighty Branch. Consider that which We have revealed in Our Most Holy Book: 'When the ocean of My presence hath ebbed and the Book of My Revelation is ended, turn your faces toward Him Whom God hath purposed, Who hath branched from this Ancient Root.' The object of this sacred verse is none other except the Most Mighty Branch ['Abdu'l-Bahá]. Thus have We graciously revealed unto you our potent Will, and I am verily the Gracious, the All-Powerful. Verily God hath ordained the station of the Greater Branch [Muḥammad 'Alí] to be beneath that of the Most Great Branch ['Abdu'l-Bahá]. He is in truth the Ordainer, the All-Wise. We have chosen 'the Greater' after 'the Most Great', as decreed by Him Who is the All-Knowing, the All-Informed.

It is enjoined upon everyone to manifest love towards the Aghsán, but God hath not granted them any right to the property of others.

O ye My Aghṣán, My Afnán and My Kindred! We exhort you to fear God, to perform praiseworthy deeds and to do that which is meet and seemly and serveth to exalt your station. Verily I say, fear of God is the greatest commander that can render the Cause of God victorious, and the hosts which best befit this commander have ever been and are an upright character and pure and goodly deeds.

---

79. The Afnán (twigs) are designated by Bahá'u'lláh to be the Báb's kinsmen descended from His three maternal uncles and His wife's two brothers. The Aghṣan (branches) are the sons and male descendants of Bahá'u'lláh. - Adib Taherzadeh, *The Revelation of Bahá'u'lláh*, vol. I, footnote p. 134.

Say: O servants! Let not the means of order be made the cause of confusion and the instrument of union an occasion for discord. We fain would hope that the people of Bahá may be guided by the blessed words: 'Say: all things are of God.' This exalted utterance is like unto water for quenching the fire of hate and enmity which smouldereth within the hearts and breasts of men. By this single utterance contending peoples and kindreds will attain the light of true unity. Verily He speaketh the truth and leadeth the way. He is the All-Powerful, the Exalted, the Gracious.

It is incumbent upon everyone to show courtesy to, and have regard for the Aghṣán, that thereby the Cause of God may be glorified and His Word exalted. This injunction hath time and again been mentioned and recorded in the Holy Writ. Well is it with him who is enabled to achieve that which the Ordainer, the Ancient of Days hath prescribed for him. Ye are bidden moreover to respect the members of the Holy Household, the Afnán and the kindred. We further admonish you to serve all nations and to strive for the betterment of the world.

That which is conducive to the regeneration of the world and the salvation of the peoples and kindreds of the earth hath been sent down from the heaven of the utterance of Him Who is the Desire of the world. Give ye a hearing ear to the counsels of the Pen of Glory. Better is this for you than all that is on the earth. Unto this beareth witness My glorious and wondrous Book.[80]

2.4.4 *Let Not Fear Fall Upon You*, from the Writings of 'Abdu'l-Bahá

The world's great Light, once resplendent upon all mankind, hath set, to shine everlastingly from the Abhá Horizen, His Kingdom of fadeless glory, shedding splendour upon His loved ones from on high and breathing into their hearts and souls the breath of eternal life.

Ponder in your hearts that which He hath foretold, in His Tablet of the Divine Vision that hath been spread throughout the world. Therein He saith: 'Thereupon she wailed and exclaimed: "May the world and all that is therein be a ransom for Thy woes. O Sovereign of heaven and earth! Wherefore hast Thou left Thyself in the hands of the dwellers of this prison-city of 'Akká? Hasten Thou to other dominions, to Thy retreats above, whereon the eyes of the people of names have never fallen." We smiled and spake not. Reflect upon

---

80. Bahá'u'lláh, *Tablets of Bahá'u'lláh*, pp. 219-23.

these most exalted words, and comprehend the purpose of this hidden and sacred mystery.'

O ye beloved of the Lord! Beware, beware lest ye hesitate and waver. Let not fear fall upon you, neither be troubled nor dismayed. Take ye good heed lest this calamitous day slacken the flames of your ardour, and quench your tender hopes. Today is the day for steadfastness and constancy. Blessed are they that stand firm and immovable as the rock and brave the storm and stress of this tempestuous hour. They, verily, shall be the recipients of God's grace; they, verily, shall receive His divine assistance, and shall be truly victorious. They shall shine amidst mankind with a radiance which the dwellers of the Pavilion of Glory laud and magnify. To them is proclaimed this celestial call, revealed in His Most Holy Book: 'Let not your hearts be perturbed, O people, when the glory of My Presence is withdrawn, and the ocean of My utterance is stilled. In My presence amongst you there is a wisdom, and in My absence there is yet another, inscrutable to all but God, the Incomparable, the All-Knowing. Verily, We behold you from Our realm of glory, and shall aid whosoever will arise for the triumph of Our Cause with the hosts of the Concourse on high and a company of Our favoured angels.'

The Sun of Truth, that Most Great Light, hath set upon the horizon of the world to rise with deathless splendour over the Realm of the Limitless. In His Most Holy Book He calleth the firm and steadfast of His friends: 'Be not dismayed, O peoples of the world, when the day-star of My beauty is set, and the heaven of My tabernacle is concealed from your eyes. Arise to further My Cause, and to exalt My Word amongst men.' [81]

2.4.5 *He Came and Went as He Wished*, A Talk Given by 'Abdu'l-Bahá.

I will speak to you today of Bahá'u'lláh. In the third year after the Báb had declared his Mission, Bahá'u'lláh, being accused by fanatical Mullás of believing in the new doctrine, was arrested and thrown into prison. The next day, however, several ministers of the Government and other influential men caused him to be set free. Later on he was again arrested, and the priests condemned him to death! The Governor hesitated to have this sentence carried out for fear of a revolution. The priests met together in the Mosque, before which was the place of execution. All the people of the town gathered in crowds outside the

---

81. 'Abdu'l-Bahá, *Selections From the Writings of 'Abdu'l-Bahá*, pp. 17-18.

Mosque. The carpenters brought their saws and hammers, the butchers came with their knives, the bricklayers and builders shouldered their spades, all these men, incited by the frenzied Mullás, were eager to share in the honour of killing Him. Inside the Mosque were assembled the doctors of religion. Bahá'u'lláh stood before them, and answered all their questions with great wisdom. The chief sage in particular, was completely silenced by Bahá'u'lláh, who refuted all his arguments.

A discussion arose between two of these priests as to the meaning of some words in the writings of the Báb; accusing Him of inaccuracy, they challenged Bahá'u'lláh to defend Him if he were able. These priests were entirely humiliated, for Bahá'u'lláh proved before the whole assembly that the Báb was absolutely right, and that the accusation was made in ignorance.

The defeated ones now put Him to the torture of the bastinado, and more infuriated than before brought Him out before the walls of the Mosque unto the place of execution, where the misguided people were awaiting His coming.

Still the Governor feared to comply with the demand of the priests for His execution. Realizing the danger in which the dignified prisoner was placed, some men were sent to rescue Him. In this they succeeded by breaking through the wall of the Mosque and leading Bahá'u'lláh through the opening into a place of safety, but not of freedom; for the Governor shifted the responsibility from off his own shoulders by sending him to Ṭihrán. Here He was imprisoned in an underground dungeon, where the light of day was never seen. A heavy chain was placed about His neck by which He was chained to five other Bábís; these fetters were locked together by strong, very heavy bolts and screws. His clothes were torn to pieces, also His fez. In this terrible condition He was kept for four months.

During this time none of His friends were able to get access to Him.

A prison official made an attempt to poison Him, but beyond causing Him great suffering, this poison had no effect.

After a time Governor liberated Him and exiled Him and His family to Baghdád, where He remained for eleven years. During this time He underwent severe persecutions, being surrounded by the watchful hatred of His enemies.

He bore all evils and torments with the greatest courage and fortitude. Often when He arose in the morning, He knew not whether He would live until the sun should set. Meanwhile, each day, the priests came and questioned Him on religion and metaphysics.

At length the Turkish Governor exiled Him to Constantinople, whence He was sent to Adrianople; here He stayed for five years. Eventually, He was sent to the far off prison fortress of St. Jean d'Acre. Here He was imprisoned in the military portion of the fortress and kept under the strictest surveillance. Words would fail me to tell you of the many trials He had to suffer, and all the misery He endured in that prison. Notwithstanding, it was from this prison that Bahá'u'lláh wrote to all the Monarchs of Europe, and these letters with one exception were sent through the post.

The Epistle to Náṣiri'd-Dín Sháh was confided to a Persian Bahá'í, Mírzá Bádí Khurásání, who undertook to deliver it into the Sháh's own hands. This brave man waited in the neighbourhood of Ṭihrán for the passing of the Sháh, who had the intention to journey by that way to his summer Palace. The courageous messenger followed the Sháh to his Palace, and waited on the road near the entrance for several days. Always in the same place was he seen waiting on the road, until the people began to wonder why he should be there. At last the Sháh heard of him, and commanded his servants that the man should be brought before him.

'Oh! servants of the Sháh, I bring a letter, which I must deliver into his own hands,' Bádí said, and then Bádí said to the Sháh, 'I bring you a letter from Bahá'u'lláh.'

He was immediately seized and questioned by those who wished to elicit information which would help them in the further persecutions of Bahá'u'lláh. Bádí would not answer a word; then they tortured him, still he held his peace! After three days they killed him, having failed to force him to speak! These cruel men photographed him whilst he was under torture.

The Sháh gave the letter from Bahá'u'lláh to the priests that they might explain it to him. After some days these priests told the Sháh that the letter was from a political enemy. The Sháh grew angry and said, 'This is no explanation, I pay you to read and answer my letters, therefore obey!'

The spirit and meaning of the Tablet to Náṣiri'd-Dín Sháh was, in short, this: 'Now that the time has come, when the Cause of the Glory of God has appeared, I ask that I may be allowed to come to Ṭihrán and answer any questions the priests may put to Me.'

'I exhort to detach yourself from the worldly magnificence of your Empire. Remember all those great kings who have lived before you—their glories have passed away!'

The letter was written in a most beautiful manner, and continued warning the King and telling him of the future triumph of the Kingdom of Bahá'u'lláh, both in the Eastern and in the Western World.

The Sháh paid no attention to the warning of this letter and continued to live in the same fashion until the end.

Although Bahá'u'lláh was in prison the great Power of the Holy Spirit was with Him!

None other in prison could have been like unto Him. In spite of all the hardships He suffered, He never complained.

In the dignity of His Majesty, He always refused to see the Governor, or the influential people of the town.

Although the surveillance was unremittingly strict He came and went as He wished! He died in a house situated about three kilometres from St. Jean D'Acre.[82]

2.4.6 *What An Educator!*, A Talk by 'Abdu'l-Bahá

To sum up, both his antagonists and His partisans, as well as all those who were received in the sacred spot, acknowledged and bore witness to the greatness of Bahá'u'lláh, though they did not believe in him, still they acknowledged His grandeur, and as soon as they entered the sacred spot, the presence of Bahá'u'lláh produced such an effect on most of them that they could not utter a word.[83]

For fifty years Bahá'u'lláh faced His enemies like a mountain all wished to annihilate Him and sought His destruction. A thousand times they planned to crucify and destroy Him, and during the fifty years He was in constant danger.[84]

Finally we must be just, and acknowledge what an educator this Glorious Being was, what marvellous signs were manifested by Him, and what power and might have been realised in the world through Him.[85]

2.4.7 *Bahá'u'lláh and His Sufferings*, from Nabíl's Narrative

The eighth Naw-Rúz after the Declaration of the Báb, which fell on the twenty-seventh day of the month of Jamádíyu'l-Avval, in the year AH 1268.,[86] found Bahá'u'lláh still in 'Iráq, engaged in spreading the teachings, and making firm the foundations, of the New Revelation. Displaying an enthusiasm and

---

82. 'Abdu'l-Bahá, *Paris Talks*, pp. 75-9.

83. 'Abdu'l-Bahá, *Some Answered Questions*, p. 34.

84. Ibid., p. 35.

85. Ibid., p. 35.

86. 1852 AD.

ability that recalled His activities in the early days of the Movement in Núr and Mázindarán, He continued to devote Himself to the task of reviving the energies, of organising the forces, and of directing the efforts, of the Báb's scattered companions. He was the sole light amidst the darkness that encompassed the bewildered disciples who had witnessed, on the one hand, the cruel martyrdom of their beloved Leader and, on the other, the tragic fate of their companions. He alone was able to inspire them with the needful courage and fortitude to endure the many afflictions that had been heaped upon them; He alone was capable of preparing them for the burden of the task they were destined to bear, and of inuring them to brave the storm and perils they were soon to face. [87]

• • •

Bahá'u'lláh proceeded to Lavásán, and was staying in the village of Afchih, the property of the Grand Vazír, when the news of the attempt on the life of Náṣiri'd-Dín Sháh reached Him. Ja'far-Qulí Khán was still acting as His host on behalf of the Amír-Niẓám. That criminal act was committed towards the end of the month of Shavvál, in the year AH 1268 by two obscure and irresponsible young men, one named Ṣádiq-i-Tabrízí, and the other Fatḥu'lláh-i-Qumí, both of whom earned their livelihood in Ṭihrán. At a time when the imperial army, headed by the Sháh himself, had encamped in Shimírán, these two ignorant youths in a frenzy of despair, arose to avenge the blood of their slaughtered brethren.

The folly that characterised their act was betrayed by the fact that in making such an attempt on the life of their sovereign, instead of employing effective weapons which would ensure the success of their venture, these youths charged their pistols with shot which no reasonable person would ever think of using for such a purpose. Had their action been instigated by a man of judgment and common sense, he would certainly never have allowed them to carry out their intention with such ridiculously ineffective instruments.

That act, though committed by wild and feeble-minded fanatics, and in spite of its being from the very first emphatically condemned by no less responsible a person than Bahá'u'lláh, was the signal for the outbreak of a series of persecutions and massacres of such barbarous ferocity as could be compared only to the atrocities of Mázindarán and Zanján. The storm to which that act gave rise plunged the whole of Ṭihrán into consternation and distress. It in-

---

87. Nabíl-i-A'ẓam, *The Dawn Breakers*, p. 595.

volved the life of the leading companions who had survived the calamities to which their Faith had been so cruelly and repeatedly subjected. The storm was still raging when Bahá'u'lláh, with some of His ablest lieutenants, was plunged into a filthy, dark, and fever-stricken dungeon, whilst chains of such weight as only notorious criminals were condemned to carry, were placed upon His neck. For no less than four months He bore the burden, and such was the intensity of His suffering that the marks of that cruelty remained imprinted upon His body all the days of His life.

So grave a menace to their sovereign and to the institutions of his realm stirred the indignation of the entire body of the ecclesiastical order of Persia. To them so bold a deed called for immediate and condign punishment. Measures of unprecedented severity, they clamoured, should be undertaken to stem the tide that was engulfing both the government and the Faith of Islám. Despite the restraint which the followers of the Báb had exercised ever since the inception of the Faith in every part of the land; despite the repeated charges of the chief disciples to their brethren enjoining them to refrain from acts of violence, to obey their government loyally, and to disclaim any intention of a holy war, their enemies persevered in their deliberate efforts to misrepresent the nature and purpose of that Faith to the authorities. Now that an act of such momentous consequences had been committed, what accusations would not these same enemies be prompted to attribute to the Cause with which those guilty of the crime had been associated!

The moment seemed to have come when they could at last awaken the rulers of the country to the necessity of extirpating as speedily as possible a heresy which seemed to threaten the very foundations of the State.

Ja'far-Qulí Khán, who was in Shimírán when the attempt on the Sháh's life was made, immediately wrote a letter to Bahá'u'lláh and acquainted Him with what had happened. "The Sháh's mother," he wrote, "is inflamed with anger. She is denouncing you openly before the court and people as the 'would-be murderer' of her son. She is also trying to involve Mírzá Áqá Khán in this affair, and accuses him of being your accomplice." He urged Bahá'u'lláh to remain for a time concealed in that neighbourhood until the passion of the populace had subsided. He despatched to Afchih an old and experienced messenger whom he ordered to be at the disposal of his Guest and to hold himself in readiness to accompany Him to whatever place of safety He might desire.

Bahá'u'lláh refused to avail Himself of the opportunity Ja'far-Qulí Khán offered Him. Ignoring the messenger and rejecting his offer, He rode out, the next morning, with calm confidence, from Lavásán, where He was sojourning, to the headquarters of the imperial army, which was then stationed in Níyávarán, in the Shimírán district. Arriving at the village of Zarkandih, the seat of the Russian legation, which lay at a distance of one maydán from Níyávarán, He was met by Mírzá Majíd, His brother-in-law, who acted as secretary to the Russian minister, and was invited by him to stay at his home, which adjoined that of his superior. The attendants of Ḥájí 'Alí Khán the Hájibu'd-Dawlih, recognised Him and went straightway to inform their master, who in turn brought the matter to the attention of the Sháh.

The news of the arrival of Bahá'u'lláh greatly surprised the officers of the imperial army. Náṣiri'd-Dín Sháh himself was amazed at the bold and unexpected step which a man who was accused of being the chief instigator of the attempt upon his life had taken. He immediately sent one of his trusted officers to the legation, demanding that the Accused be delivered into his hands. The Russian minister refused, and requested Bahá'u'lláh to proceed to the home of Mírzá Áqá Khán, the Grand Vazír, a place he thought to be the most appropriate under the circumstances. His request was granted, whereupon the minister formally communicated to the Grand Vazír his desire that the utmost care should be exercised to ensure the safety and protection of the Trust his government was delivering into his keeping, warning him that he would hold him responsible should he fail to disregard his wishes.

Mírzá Áqá Khán, though he undertook to give the fullest assurances that were required, and received Bahá'u'lláh with every mark of respect into his home, was, however, too apprehensive for the safety of his own position to accord his Guest the treatment he was expected to extend.

As Bahá'u'lláh was leaving the village of Zarkandih, the minister's daughter, who felt greatly distressed at the dangers which beset His life, was so overcome with emotion that she was unable to restrain her tears. "Of what use," she was heard expostulating with her father, "is the authority with which you have been invested, if you are powerless to extend your protection to a guest whom you have received in your house?" The minister, who had a great affection for his daughter, was moved by the sight of her tears, and sought to comfort her by his assurances that he would do all in his power to avert the danger that threatened the life of Bahá'u'lláh.

That day the army of Náṣiri'd-Dín Sháh was thrown into a state of violent tumult. The peremptory orders of the sovereign, following so closely upon the attempt on his life, gave rise to the wildest rumours and excited the fiercest passions in the hearts of the people of the neighbourhood. The agitation spread to Ṭihrán and fanned into flaming fury the smouldering embers of hatred which the enemies of the Cause still nourished in their hearts. Confusion, unprecedented in its range, reigned in the capital. A word of denunciation, a sign, or a whisper was sufficient to subject the innocent to a persecution which no pen dare try to describe. Security of life and property had completely vanished. The highest ecclesiastical authorities in the capital joined hands with the most influential members of the government to deal what they hoped would be the fatal blow to a foe who, for eight years, had so gravely shaken the peace of the land, and whom no cunning or violence had yet been able to silence.

Bahá'u'lláh, now that the Báb was no more, appeared in their eyes to be the arch-foe whom they deemed it their first duty to seize and imprison. To them He was the reincarnation of the Spirit the Báb had so powerfully manifested, the Spirit through which He had been able to accomplish so complete a transformation in the lives and habits of His countrymen. The precautions the Russian minister had taken, and the warning he had uttered, failed to stay the hand that had been outstretched with such determination against that precious Life.

From Shimírán to Ṭihrán, Bahá'u'lláh was several times stripped of His garments, and was overwhelmed with abuse and ridicule. On foot and exposed to the fierce rays of the midsummer Sun, He was compelled to cover, barefooted and bareheaded the whole distance from Shimírán to the dungeon already referred to. All along the route, He was pelted and vilified by the crowds whom His enemies had succeeded in convincing that He was the sworn enemy of their sovereign and the wrecker of his realm. Words fail me to portray the horror of the treatment which was meted out to Him as He was being taken to the Síyáh-Chál of Ṭihrán. As he was approaching that dungeon, an old and decrepit woman was seen to emerge from the midst of the crowd, with a stone in her hand, eager to cast it at the face of Bahá'u'lláh. Her eyes glowed with a determination and fanaticism of which few women of her age were capable. Her whole frame shook with rage as she stepped forward and raised her hand to hurl her missile at Him. "By the Siyyidu'sh-Shuhadá,[88] I adjure you," she pleaded, as she ran to overtake those into whose hands Bahá'u'lláh had been delivered, "give me a chance to fling my stone in his face!" "Suffer not this woman to be disappointed," were Bahá'u'lláh's words to His guards, as He saw her hastening behind Him. "Deny her not what she regards as a meritorious act in the sight

---

88. The Imám Husayn

of God."

The Síyáh-<u>Ch</u>ál, into which Bahá'u'lláh, was thrown, originally a reservoir of water for one of the public baths of Ṭihrán, was a subterranean dungeon in which criminals of the worst type were wont to be confined. The darkness, the filth, and the character of the prisoners, combined to make of that pestilential dungeon the most abominable place to which human beings could be condemned. His feet were placed in stocks, and around His neck was fastened the Qará-Guhar chains, infamous throughout Persia for their galling weight. For three days and three nights, no manner of food or drink was given to Bahá'u'lláh. Rest and sleep were both impossible to Him. The place was infested with vermin, and the stench of that gloomy abode was enough to crush the very spirits of those who were condemned to suffer its horrors.

Such were the conditions under which He was held down that even one of the executioners who were watching over Him was moved with pity. Several times this man attempted to induce Him to take some tea which he had managed to introduce into the dungeon under the cover of his garments. Bahá'u'lláh, however, would refuse to drink it. His family often endeavoured to persuade the guards to allow them to carry the food they had prepared for Him into His prison. Though at first no amount of pleading would induce the guards to relax the severity of their discipline, yet gradually they yielded to His friends' importunity. No one could be sure, however, whether that food would eventually reach Him, or whether He would consent to eat it whilst a number of His fellow-prisoners were starving before His eyes. Surely greater misery than had befallen these innocent victims of the wrath of their sovereign, could hardly be imagined.[89]

● ● ●

I have heard the Most Great Branch ['Abdu'l-Bahá], who in those days was a child of only eight years of age, recount one of His experiences as He ventured to leave the house in which He was then residing. "We had sought shelter," He told us, "in the house of My uncle, Mírzá Ismá'íl. Ṭihrán was in the throes of wildest excitement. I ventured at times to sally forth from that house and to cross the street on My way to the market. I would hardly cross the threshold and step into the street, when boys of My age, who were running about, would crowd around Me crying, 'Bábí! Bábí!' Knowing well the state of excitement into which all the inhabitants of the capital, both young and old, had fallen, I

---

89. Nabíl-i-A'ẓam, *The Dawn Breakers,* pp. 599-609.

would deliberately ignore their clamour and quietly steal away to My home. One day I happened to be walking alone through the market on My way to My uncle's house. As I was looking behind Me, I found a band of little ruffians running fast to overtake Me. They were pelting Me with stones and shouting menacingly, 'Bábí! Bábí!' To intimidate them seemed to be the only way I could avert the danger with which I was threatened. I turned back and rushed towards them with such determination that they fled away in distress and vanished. I could hear their distant cry, 'The little Bábí is fast pursuing us! He will surely overtake and slay us all!' As I was directing My steps towards home, I heard a man shouting at the top of his voice: 'Well done, you brave and fearless child! No one of your age would ever have been able, unaided, to withstand their attack.' From that day onward, I was never again molested by any of the boys of the streets, nor did I hear any offensive word fall from their lips." [90]

● ● ●

I now proceed to relate what befell the remaining companions of the Báb, those who had been privileged to share the horrors of the confinement with Bahá'u'lláh. From His own lips I have often heard the following account: "All those who were struck down by the storm that raged during that memorable year in Ṭihrán were Our fellow-prisoners in the Síyáh-Chál, where We were confined We were all huddled together in one cell, our feet in stocks, and around our necks fastened the most galling of chains. The air we breathed was laden with the foulest impurities, while the floor on which we sat was covered with filth and infested with vermin. No ray of light was allowed to penetrate that pestilential dungeon or to warm its icy-coldness. We were placed in two rows, each facing the other. We had taught them to repeat certain verses which, every night, they chanted with extreme fervour. 'God is sufficient unto me; He verily is the All-sufficing!' one row would intone, while the other would reply: 'In Him let the trusting trust.' The chorus of these gladsome voices would continue to peal out until the early hours of the morning. Their reverberation would fill the dungeon, and, piercing its massive walls, would reach the ears of Náṣiri'd-Dín Sháh, whose palace was not far distant from the place where we were imprisoned. 'What means this sound?' he was reported to have exclaimed. 'It is the anthem the Bábís are intoning in their prison,' they replied. The Sháh made no further remarks, nor did he attempt to restrain the enthusiasm his prisoners, despite the horrors of their confinement, continued to display.

---

90. Nabíl-i-A'ẓam, *The Dawn Breakers,* p. 616.

"One day, there was brought to Our prison, a tray of roasted meat, which they informed Us the Sháh had ordered to be distributed among the prisoners. 'The Sháh,' We were told, 'faithful to a vow he made, has chosen this day to offer to you all this lamb in fulfilment of his pledge.' A deep silence fell upon Our companions, who expected Us to make answer on their behalf. 'We return this gift to you,' We replied; 'we can well dispense with this offer.' The answer We made would have greatly irritated the guards had they not been eager to devour the food we had refused to touch. Despite the hunger with which Our companions were afflicted, only one among them, a certain Mírzá Ḥusayn-i-Mutavallíy-i-Qumí, showed any desire to eat of the food the sovereign had chosen to spread before us. With a fortitude that was truly heroic, Our fellow-prisoners submitted, without a murmur, to endure the piteous plight to which they were reduced. Praise of God, instead of complaint of the treatment meted out to them by the Sháh, fell unceasingly from their lips—praise with which they sought to beguile the hardships of a cruel captivity.

"Every day Our gaolers, entering Our cell, would call the name of one of Our companions, bidding him arise and follow them to the foot of the gallows. With what eagerness would the owner of that name respond to that solemn call! Relieved of his chains, he would spring to his feet and, in a state of uncontrollable delight, would approach and embrace Us. We would seek to comfort him with the assurance of an everlasting life in the world beyond, and, filling his heart with hope and joy, would send him forth to win the crown of glory. He would embrace, in turn, the rest of his fellow-prisoners and then proceed to die as dauntlessly as he had lived. Soon after the martyrdom of each of these companions, We would be informed by the executioner, who had grown to be friendly to Us, of the circumstances of the death of his victim, and of the joy with which he had endured his sufferings to the very end.

"We were awakened one night, ere break of day, by Mírzá 'Abdu'l-Vahháb-i-Shírazí, who was bound with Us to the same chains. He had left Kázimayn and followed Us to Ṭihrán, where he was arrested and thrown into prison. He asked Us whether We were awake, and proceeded to relate to Us his dream. 'I have this night,' he said, 'been soaring into a space of infinite vastness and beauty. I seemed to be uplifted on wings that carried me wherever I desired to go. A feeling of rapturous delight filled my soul. I flew in the midst of that immensity with a swiftness and ease that I cannot describe.' 'To-day,' We replied, 'it will be your turn to sacrifice yourself for this Cause. May you remain firm and steadfast to the end. You will then find yourself soaring in that same limitless space of which you dreamed, traversing with the same ease and swiftness the realm of immortal sovereignty, and gazing with that same rapture upon the Infinite Horizon.'

"That morning saw the gaoler again enter Our cell and call out the name of 'Abdu'l-Vahháb. Throwing off his chains, he sprang to his feet, embraced each of his fellow-prisoners, and, taking Us into his arms, pressed Us lovingly to his heart. That moment We discovered that he had no shoes to wear. We gave him Our own, and, speaking a last word of encouragement and cheer, sent him forth to the scene of his martyrdom. Later on, his executioner came to Us, praising in glowing language the spirit which that youth had shown. How thankful We were to God for this testimony which the executioner himself had given!"

All this suffering and the cruel revenge the authorities had taken on those who attempted the life of their sovereign failed to appease the anger of the Sháh's mother. Day and night she persisted in her vindictive clamour, demanding the execution of Bahá'u'lláh, whom she still regarded as the real author of the crime. "Deliver him to the executioner!" she insistently cried to the authorities. "What greater humiliation than this, that I, who am the mother of the Sháh, should be powerless to inflict upon that criminal the punishment so dastardly an act deserves!" Her cry for vengeance, which an impotent rage served to intensify, was doomed to remain unanswered. Despite her machinations, Bahá'u'lláh was saved from the fate she had so importunately striven to precipitate. The Prisoner was eventually released from His confinement, and was able to unfold and establish, beyond the confines of the kingdom of her son, a sovereignty the possibility of which she could never have even dreamed of. The blood shed in the course of that fateful year in Ṭihrán by that heroic band with whom Bahá'u'lláh had been imprisoned, was the ransom paid for His deliverance from the hand of a foe that sought to prevent Him from achieving the purpose for which God had destined Him. Ever since the time He espoused the Cause of the Báb, He had never neglected one single occasion to champion the Faith He had embraced. He had exposed Himself to the perils which the followers of the Faith had to face in its early days. He was the first of the Báb's disciples to set the example of renunciation and service to the Cause. Yet His life, beset as it was by the risks and dangers that a career such as His was sure to encounter, was spared by that same Providence who had chosen Him for a task which He, in His wisdom, deemed it as yet too soon to proclaim publicly.

The terror that convulsed Ṭihrán was but one of the many risks and dangers to which Bahá'u'lláh's life was exposed. Men, women and children in the capital trembled at the ruthlessness with which the enemy pursued their victims. A youth named 'Abbás, a former servant of Hájí Sulaymán Khán and fully informed, owing to the wide circle of friends whom his master cultivated, of the names, the number, and the dwelling places of the Báb's disciples, was employed by the enemy as an instrument ready to hand for the prosecution of its designs. He had identified himself with the Faith of his master, and regarded himself as one of its zealous supporters. At the outset of the turmoil he was arrested and compelled to betray all those whom he knew to be associated with the Faith. They sought by every manner of reward to induce him to reveal those who were his master's fellow-disciples, and warned him that, should he refuse to disclose their names, he would be subjected to inhuman tortures. He pledged his word that he would act according to their wishes and would inform the assistants of Hájí 'Alí Khán, the Hájibu'd-Dawlih, the Farrásh-Báshí, of their names and abodes. He was taken through the streets of Ṭihrán and directed to point out everyone he recognised as being a follower of the Báb. A number of people whom he had never met and known were in this manner delivered in the hands of Hájí 'Alí Khán's assistants—people who had never had any connection with the Báb and His Cause. These were able to recover their freedom only after having paid a heavy bribe to those who had captured them. Such was the greed of the Hájibu'd-Dawlih's attendants that they specially requested 'Abbás to salute as a sign of betrayal every person who he thought would be willing and able to pay large sums for his deliverance. They would even force him to betray such persons, threatening that his refusal would be fraught with grave danger to his own life. They would frequently promise to give him a share of the money they determined to extort from their victims.

This 'Abbás was taken to the Síyáh-Chál and introduced to Bahá'u'lláh, whom he had met previously on several occasions in the company of his master, in the hope that he would betray Him. They promised that the mother of the Sháh would amply reward him for such a betrayal. Every time he was taken into Bahá'u'lláh's presence, 'Abbás, after standing a few moments before Him and gazing upon His face, would leave the place, emphatically denying ever having seen Him. Having failed in their efforts, they resorted to poison, in the hope of obtaining the favour of the mother of their sovereign. They were able to intercept the food that their Prisoner was permitted to receive from His home, and mixed it with the poison they hoped would be fatal to Him. This measure, though impairing the health of Bahá'u'lláh for years, failed to achieve its purpose.

The enemy was finally induced to cease regarding Him as the prime mover of that attempt, and decided to transfer the responsibility for this act to 'Azím, whom they now accused of being the real author of the crime. By this means they endeavoured to obtain the favour of the mother of the Sháh, a favour they greatly coveted. Hájí 'Alí Khan was only too happy to second their efforts. As he himself had taken no share in imprisoning Bahá'u'lláh, he seized upon the occasion which offered itself to denounce 'Azím, whom he had already succeeded in arresting, as the chief and responsible instigator.

The Russian minister, who, through one of his agents, was watching the developments of the situation and keeping in close touch with the condition of Bahá'u'lláh, addressed, through his interpreter, a strongly worded message to the Grand Vazír, in which he protested against his action, suggesting that a messenger should proceed, in the company of one of the government's trusted representatives and of Hájíbu-d-Dawlih, to the Síyáh-Chál and there ask the newly recognised leader to declare publicly his opinion regarding Bahá'u'lláh's position. "Whatever that leader may declare," he wrote, "whether in praise or denunciation, I think ought to be immediately recorded and should serve as a basis for the final judgment which should be pronounced in this affair."

The Grand Vazír promised the interpreter that he would follow the minister's advice, and even appointed a time for the messenger to join the government representative and Hájibu'd-Dawlih and proceed with them to the Síyáh-Chál.

When 'Azím was questioned as to whether he regarded Bahá'u'lláh as the responsible leader of the group that had made the attempt on the Sháh's life, he answered: "The Leader of this community was none other than the Siyyid-i-Báb, who was slain in Tabríz, and whose martyrdom induced me to arise and avenge His death. I alone conceived this plan and endeavoured to execute it. The youth who threw the Sháh from his horse was none other than Sádiq-i-Tabrízí, a servitor in a confectioner's shop in Tihrán who had been for two years in my service. He was fired with a desire even more burning than my own to avenge the martyrdom of his Leader. He acted too hastily, however, and failed to make certain the success of his attempt."

The words of his declaration were taken down by both the minister's interpreter and the Grand Vazír's representative, who submitted their records to Mírzá Áqá Khán. The documents which were placed in his hands were chiefly responsible for Bahá'u'lláh's release from His imprisonment.[91]

91. Nabíl-i-A'zam, *The Dawn Breakers,* pp. 646-50.

• • •

The confession of 'Aẓím freed Bahá'u'lláh from the danger to which His life had been exposed. The circumstances of the death of him who had declared himself the chief instigator of that crime served to abate the wrath with which an enraged populace clamoured for the immediate punishment of so daring an attempt. The cries of rage and vengeance, the appeals for immediate retribution, which had hitherto been focussed on Bahá'u'lláh were now diverted from Him. The ferocity of those claimant denunciations was, by degrees, much allayed. The conviction grew firmer in the minds of the responsible authorities in Ṭihrán that Bahá'u'lláh, hitherto regarded as the arch-foe of Náṣiri'd-Dín Sháh, was by no means involved in any conspiracy against the sovereign's life. Mírzá Áqá Khán was therefore encouraged to send his trusted representative, a man named Ḥájí 'Alí, to the Síyáh-Chál, and to present the order for His release to the Prisoner.

Upon his arrival, the sight which the emissary beheld filled him with grief and surprise. The spectacle which met his eyes was one he could scarcely believe. He wept as he saw Bahá'u'lláh chained to a floor that was infested with vermin, His neck weighed down by galling chains, His face laden with sorrow, ungroomed and dishevelled, breathing the pestilential atmosphere of the most terrible of dungeons. "Accursed be Mírzá Áqá Khán!" he burst, forth, as his eyes recognised Bahá'u'lláh in the gloom that surrounded Him. "God knows I had never imagined that you could have been subjected to so humiliating a captivity. I should never have thought that the Grand Vazír could have dared commit so heinous an act."

He removed the mantle from his shoulders and presented it to Bahá'u'lláh, entreating Him to wear it when in the presence of the minister and his counsellors. Bahá'u'lláh refused his request, and, wearing the dress of a prisoner, proceeded straightway to the seat of the imperial government.

The first word the Grand Vazír was moved to address to his Captive was the following: "Had you chosen to take my advice, and had you dissociated yourself from the faith of the Siyyid-i-Báb, you would never have suffered the pains and indignities that have been heaped upon you." "Had you, in your turn," Bahá'u'lláh replied, "followed my counsels, the affairs of the government would not have reached so critical a stage."

He was immediately reminded of the conversation he had had with Him on the occasion of the Báb's martyrdom. The words, "the flame that has been kindled will blaze forth more fiercely than ever," flashed through the mind of

Mírzá Áqá Khán. "The warning you uttered," he remarked, "has, alas, been fulfilled. What is it that you advise me now to do?" "Command the governors of the realm," was the instant reply, "to cease shedding the blood of the innocent, to cease plundering their property, to cease dishonouring their women and injuring their children. Let them cease the persecution of the Faith of the Báb; let them abandon the idle hope of wiping out its followers."

That same day orders were given, through a circular addressed to all the governors of the realm, bidding them desist from their acts of cruelty and shame. "What you have done is enough," Mírzá Áqá Khán wrote them. "Cease arresting and punishing the people. Disturb no longer the peace and tranquillity of your countrymen." The Sháh's government had been deliberating as to the most effective measures that should be taken to rid the country, once and for all, of the curse with which it had been afflicted. No sooner had Bahá'u'lláh recovered His freedom than the decision of the government was handed to Him, informing Him that within a month of the issuing of this order, He, with His family, was expected to leave Ṭihrán for a place beyond the confines of Persia.

The Russian minister, as soon as he learned of the action which the government contemplated taking, volunteered to take Bahá'u'lláh under his protection, and invited Him to go to Russia. He refused the offer and chose instead to leave for 'Iraq. Nine months after His return from Karbilá, on the first day of the month of Rabi'u'th-Tháni, in the year AH 1269,[92] Bahá'u'lláh accompanied by the members of His family, among whom were the Most Great Branch and Áqáy-i-Kalím, and escorted by a member of the imperial body-guard and an official representing the Russian legation, set out from Ṭihrán on His journey to Baghdád.[93]

2.4.8 *Ascension of Bahá'u'lláh*, from the Writings of Shoghi Effendi

Well nigh half a century had passed since the inception of the Faith. Cradled in adversity, deprived in its infancy of its Herald and Leader, it had been raised from the dust, in which a hostile despot had thrown it, by its second and greatest Luminary Who, despite successive banishments, had, in less than half a century, succeeded in rehabilitating its fortunes, in proclaiming its Message, in enacting its laws and ordinances, in formulating its principles and in ordaining its institu-

92. 12 January 1853 AD.

93. Nabíl-i-A'ẓam, *The Dawn Breakers,* pp. 646-50.

tions, and it had just begun to enjoy the sunshine of a prosperity never previously experienced, when suddenly it was robbed of its Author by the Hand of Destiny, its followers were plunged into sorrow and consternation, its repudiators found their declining hopes revive, and its adversaries, political as well as ecclesiastical, began to take heart again.

Already nine months before His ascension Bahá'u'lláh, as attested by 'Abdu'l-Bahá, had voiced His desire to depart from this world. From that time onward it became increasingly evident, from the tone of His remarks to those who attained His presence, that the close of His earthly life was approaching though He refrained from mentioning it openly to any one. On the night preceding the eleventh of Shavvál AH 1309, (8 May 1892) He contracted a slight fever, which, though it mounted the following day, soon after subsided. He continued to grant interviews to certain of the friends and pilgrims, but it soon became evident that He was not well. His fever returned in a more acute form than before, His general condition grew steadily worse, complications ensued which at last culminated in His ascension, at the hour of dawn, on the 2nd of Dhi'l-Qa'dih 1309 A.H. (29 May 1892), eight hours after sunset, in the 75th year of His age. His spirit, at long last released from the toils of a life crowded with tribulations, had winged its flight to His *"other dominions,"* dominions *"whereon the eyes of the people of names have never fallen,"* and to which the *"Luminous Maid," "clad in white,"* had bidden Him hasten, as described by Himself in the *Lawḥ-i-Ru'yá* (Tablet of the Vision), revealed nineteen years previously, on the anniversary of the birth of His Forerunner.

Six days before He passed away He summoned to His presence, as He lay in bed leaning against one of His sons, the entire company of believers, including several pilgrims, who had assembled in the Mansion, for what proved to be their last audience with Him, *"I am well pleased with you all,"* He gently and affectionately addressed the weeping crowd that gathered about Him. *"Ye have rendered many services, and been very assiduous in your labours. Ye have come here every morning and every evening. May God assist you to remain united. May He aid you to exalt the Cause of the Lord of being."* To the women, including members of His own family, gathered at His bedside, He addressed similar words of encouragement, definitely assuring them that in a document entrusted by Him to the Most Great Branch He had commended them all to His care.

The news of His ascension was instantly communicated to Sulṭán 'Abdu'l-Ḥamíd in a telegram which began with the words "the Sun of Bahá has set" and in which the monarch was advised of the intention of interring the sacred remains within the precincts of the Mansion, an arrangement to which he readily assented. Bahá'u'lláh was accordingly laid to rest in the northernmost room of the house which served as a dwelling-place for His son-in-law, the most northerly of the three houses lying to the west of, and adjacent to, the Mansion. His interment took place shortly after sunset, on the very day of His ascension.

The inconsolable Nabíl, who had had the privilege of a private audience with Bahá'u'lláh during the days of His illness; whom 'Abdu'l-Bahá had chosen to select those passages which constitute the text of the Tablet of Visitation now recited in the Most Holy Tomb; and who, in his uncontrollable grief, drowned himself in the sea shortly after the passing of his Beloved, thus describes the agony of those days: "Methinks, the spiritual commotion set up in the world of dust had caused all the worlds of God to tremble ... My inner and outer tongue are powerless to portray the condition we were in ... In the midst of the prevailing confusion a multitude of the inhabitants of 'Akká and of the neighbouring villages, that had thronged the fields surrounding the Mansion, could be seen weeping, beating upon their heads, and crying aloud their grief."

For a full week a vast numbers of mourners, rich and poor alike, tarried to grieve with the bereaved family, partaking day and night of the food that was lavishly dispensed by its members. Notables, among whom were numbered Shí'ahs, Sunnís, Christians, Jews and Druzes, as well as poets, 'ulumás and government officials, all joined in lamenting the loss, and in magnifying the virtues and the greatness of Bahá'u'lláh, many of them paying to Him their written tributes, in verse and in prose, in both Arabic and Turkish. From cities as far afield as Damascus, Aleppo, Beirut and Cairo similar tributes were received. These glowing testimonials were, without exception, submitted to 'Abdu'l-Bahá, Who now represented the Cause of the departed Leader, and Whose praises were often mingled in these eulogies with the homage paid to His Father.

And yet these effusive manifestations of sorrow and expressions of praise and of admiration, which the ascension of Bahá'u'lláh had spontaneously evoked among the unbelievers in the Holy Land and the adjoining countries, were but a drop when compared with the ocean of grief and the innumerable evidences of unbounded devotion which, at the hour of the setting of the Sun of Truth, poured forth from the hearts of the countless thousands who had espoused His Cause, and were determined to carry aloft its banner in Persia, India, Russia, 'Iráq, Turkey, Palestine, Egypt and Syria.[94]

94. Shoghi Effendi, *God Passes By*, pp. 221-3.

2.4.9 *Ascension of Bahá'u'lláh*, An Account by Nabíl

As attested by the Most Great Branch, nine months before this most griev-ous event—His ascension—Bahá'u'lláh had voiced His desire to depart from this world. During these nine months, from the tone of His exhortations and remarks to those friends who attained His presence it became increasingly ap-parent that the end of His earthly life was approaching. He seemed to be arranging the affairs with a sense of urgency. But He never spoke openly about the approaching end of His life.

On the eve of Sunday, the eleventh of the month of Shavvál AH 1309 (8 May 1892), fifty days after Naw-Rúz, He contracted a fever, though He did not mention it to anyone. The following morning a number of the friends attained His presence. Late in the afternoon the fever was intensified. In the evening only one of the companions who had an urgent demand was admitted to His pres-ence. On Monday (the second day of His illness) only one of the friends was admitted. On Tuesday this helpless servant was given the honour of an audi-ence with His blessed Person. At noon He summoned me to His presence alone and spoke to me for about half an hour, sometimes seated and some-times pacing up and down. He vouchsafed unto me His infinite bounties and His exalted utterances reached the acme of perfection.

I wish I had known that this was going to be my last audience with Him, so that I could have clung to the hem of His holy vesture and begged Him to accept me as a sacrifice in His path, to relieve me from the vanity of this world and admit me into the realm of everlasting joy. Alas! Alas! what had been pre-ordained did come to pass.

In the afternoon of that day Ḥájí Niyaz {a well-known believer] arrived from Egypt and, along with some others, was permitted to attain the presence of Bahá'u'lláh. Till sunset a number of the friends were admitted into His presence in groups. The following day the door of union with Him was closed to the face of the believers, no one was able to attain His presence, and an atmosphere of gloom and sorrow descended upon the hearts of His forlorn lovers. This situation remained unchanged for a few days, until Monday (the ninth day) which proved to be the day of grief for the friends. On that day the Most Great Branch left the presence of Bahá'u'lláh and went to the Pilgrim House. He conveyed Bahá'u'lláh's greetings to all, and said that the Ancient Beauty had stated: *'All the friends must remain patient and steadfast, and arise for the promotion of the Cause of God. They should not become perturbed, because I shall always be with them, and will remember and care for them.'* On hearing these piercing words the hearts of the believers were crying out with grief, for the tone of 'Abdu'l-Bahá's remarks indicated that the end of the earthly life of the One who was the Lord of all creation was fast approaching. The friends were thrown into such turmoil and dismay that they were about to expire.

This being so, the bounties of the Incomparable Beloved were vouchsafed unto all, and the following day, Tuesday (the tenth day), was turned into a joyful day. The day-star of delight and blissfulness shone forth and the Most Great Branch conveyed at the hour of dawn the joyful news of the well-being of His blessed Person. Happy and smiling, He arrived at the Pilgrim House, and like unto a musk-laden breeze which had wafted from the abode of the Beloved, or as the holy Spirit of the Mercy of the Lord, He awoke the friends one by one, bade them arise, drink their morning tea with the utmost joy, and offer thanksgiving to God, for, Praise be to His Most Exalted and Glorious Being, perfect health had returned to His blessed Person, and the signs of the most great favours were manifested in His countenance. Truly, on that day the joy and happiness of the friends, those who circled around the throne of the Beauty of their Lord, were such that all the inhabitants of 'Akká and indeed the people of Syria were influenced and affected by their condition. All the people both low and high were congratulating each other as in a day of festival.

The reason for this was that on the same day that Bahá'u'lláh contracted the fever, the government rounded up about one thousand farmers and poor people, clad them in military uniforms and held them against their will as conscripts. They were receiving military training to be dispatched to far-off lands in a few days' time. The tents of these oppressed people were near the grounds of the Mansion of Bahjí, and the cries of their weeping and lamenting and those of their families could be heard by day and by night. However, in the morning of the 'day of joy', a royal telegram was unexpectedly received ordering the release of the conscripts. This news was rapturously received by the people who were filled with delight. The Most Great Branch on that day distributed food among the conscripts, the poor, the inmates of prison and the orphans. Consequently the people of 'Akká and outside were heartily offering thanks to Bahá'u'lláh for His loving favours and gifts. No one among the inhabitants of Syria could remember having seen a day as blissful as that day.

That same day the Most Great Branch went to 'Akká, visited every Bahá'í household and conveyed to every single believer, man and woman alike, loving greetings from the Blessed Beauty. On Sunday (the fifteenth day) afternoon, all the friends who were present at the Mansion, together with pilgrims and resident Bahá'ís, were summoned to Bahá'u'lláh's presence. The entire body of the friends, weeping and grief-stricken, attained His presence as He lay in bed leaning against the Most Great Branch (may my life be a sacrifice for Him). The Tongue of Grandeur gently and affectionately addressed them all saying: *'I am well pleased with you all, you have rendered many services, and been very assiduous in your labours. You have come here every morning and evening. May God assist you to remain united. May He aid you to exalt the Cause of the Lord of being.'. This was the last audience with Him. The birds of the hearts of His lovers were addressed from on high: 'Verily the door of union is closed to all who are in heaven and on earth...'*

On the eve of Saturday (twenty-first day after contracting fever), the 2nd of Dhi'l-Qa'dih AH 1309 (29 May 1892) ... 13th of the month of 'Azamat 49, Bahá'í Era ... seventy days after Naw-Rúz, while there was no sign of fever, the will of the King of Eternity to leave the prison of 'Akká and to ascend to His *'other dominions whereon the eyes of the people of names have never fallen'*, mentioned in the *Tablet of Ru'yá* revealed ... nineteen years previously, was at long last realized. Methinks, the spiritual commotion set up in the world of dust had caused all the worlds of God to tremble. Eight hours after sunset on that darksome night when the heavens wept over the earth, what had been revealed in the *Kitáb-i-Aqdas* was finally realized. My inner and outer tongue are powerless to portray the condition we were in... In the midst of the prevailing confusion, a multitude of the inhabitants of 'Akká and of the neighbouring villages, that had thronged the fields surrounding the Mansion, could be seen weeping, beating upon their heads, and crying aloud their grief ...

For a full week after that great calamity, a great number of mourners, the rich, the poor, the orphans and the oppressed partook of the food that was generously dispensed by the bereaved family ... From the second day of the ascension of the Ever-Living, the Self-Subsistent Lord to His Most Holy and exalted Dominions on high, men of learning and poets, both Muslim and Christian, began to send telegrams of condolence to the presence of the Most Great Branch. They sent poems eloquently extolling the virtues and lamenting the loss of the Beloved ... [95]

2.4.10 Tablet of Visitation

The praise which hath dawned from Thy most august Self, and the glory which hath shone forth from Thy most effulgent Beauty, rest upon Thee, O

---

95. Nabíl-i-A'ẓam, quoted by Adib Taherzadeh in *The Revelation of Bahá'u'lláh,* vol. 4, pp. 414-7.

Thou Who art the Manifestation of Grandeur, and the King of Eternity, and the Lord of all who are in heaven and on earth! I testify that through Thee the sovereignty of God and His dominion, and the majesty of God and His grandeur, were revealed, and the Day-Stars of ancient splendour have shed their radiance in the heaven of Thine irrevocable decree, and the Beauty of the Unseen hath shone forth above the horizon of creation. I testify, moreover, that with but a movement of Thy Pen Thine injunction 'Be Thou' hath enforced, and God's hidden Secret hath been divulged, and all created things have been called into being, and all the Revelations have been sent down.

I bear witness, moreover, that through Thy beauty the beauty of the Adored One hath been unveiled, and through Thy face the face of the Desired One hath shone forth, and that through a word from Thee Thou hast decided between all created things, causing them who are devoted to Thee to ascend unto the summit of glory, and the infidels to fall into the lowest abyss.

I bear witness that he who hath known Thee hath known God, and he who hath attained unto Thy presence hath attained unto the presence of God. Great, therefore, is the blessedness of him who hath believed in Thee, and in Thy signs, and hath humbled himself before Thy sovereignty, and hath been honoured with meeting Thee, and hath attained the good pleasure of Thy will, and circled around Thee, and stood before Thy throne. Woe betide him that hath transgressed against Thee, and hath denied Thee, and repudiated Thy signs, and gainsaid Thy sovereignty, and risen up against Thee, and waxed proud before Thy face, and hath disputed Thy testimonies, and fled from Thy rule and Thy dominion, and been numbered with the infidels whose names have been inscribed by the fingers of Thy behest upon Thy holy Tablets.

Waft, then, unto me, O my God and my Beloved, from the right hand of Thy mercy and Thy loving-kindness, the holy breaths of Thy favours, that they may draw me away from myself and from the world unto the courts of Thy nearness and Thy presence. Potent art Thou to do what pleaseth Thee. Thou, truly, hast been supreme over all things.

The remembrance of God and His praise, and the Glory of God and His splendour, rest upon Thee, O Thou who art His Beauty! I bear witness that the eye of creation hath never gazed upon one wronged like Thee. Thou wast immersed all the days of Thy life beneath an ocean of tribulations. At one time Thou wast in chains and fetters; at another Thou west threatened by the sword of Thine enemies. Yet, despite all this, Thou didst enjoin upon all men to observe what had been prescribed unto Thee by Him Who is the All- Knowing, the All-Wise.

May my spirit be a sacrifice to the wrongs Thou didst suffer, and my soul be a ransom for the adversities Thou didst sustain. I beseech God, by Thee and by them whose faces have been illumined with the splendours of the light of Thy countenance, and who, for love of Thee, have observed all whereunto they were bidden, to remove the veils that have come in between Thee and Thy creatures, and to supply me with the good of this world and the world to come. Thou art, in truth, the Almighty, the Most Exalted, the All-Glorious, the Ever-Forgiving, the Most Compassionate.

Bless Thou, O Lord my God, the Divine Lote-Tree and its leaves, and its boughs, and its branches, and its stems, and its offshoots, as long as Thy most excellent titles will endure and Thy most august attributes will last. Protect it, then, from the mischief of the aggressor and the hosts of tyranny. Thou art, in truth, the Almighty, the Most Powerful. Bless Thou, also, O Lord my God, Thy servants and Thy handmaidens who have attained unto Thee. Thou, truly, art the All-Bountiful, Whose grace is infinite. No God is there save Thee, the Ever-Forgiving, the Most Generous.[96]

96. Bahá'u'lláh, *Prayers and Meditations*, no. CLXXX, pp. 310-3.

Prison of Bahá'u'lláh in 'Akká

2.5
Martyrdom of the Báb
July 9, 1850

> ... His life must be one of those events in the last hundred years which is really worth study.[97]

Suggested Readings

---

97. Sir Francis Younghusband, quoted in *The Bahá'í World*, vol. XIII, p. 816.

2.5.1 Prayer Revealed by Bahá'u'lláh

Thou seest Thy dear One, O my God, lying at the mercy of Thine enemies, and hearest the voice of His lamentation from the midst of such of Thy creatures as have dealt wickedly in Thy sight. He it is, O my Lord, through Whose name Thou didst beautify Thy Tablets, and for Whose greater glory Thou didst send down the Bayán, and at Whose separation from Thee Thou didst weep continually. Look Thou, then, upon His loneliness, O my God, and behold Him fallen into the hands of them that have disbelieved in Thy signs, have turned their backs upon Thee, and have forgotten the wonders of Thy mercy. He it is, O my God, about Whom Thou hast said: "But for Thee the Scriptures would have remained unrevealed, and the Prophets unsent." And no sooner had He, by Thy behest, been manifested and spoken forth Thy praise, than the wicked doers among Thy creatures compassed Him round, with the swords of hate drawn against Him, O Thou the Lord of all names! Thou well knowest what befell Him at the hands of such as have rent asunder the veil of Thy grandeur, and cast behind their backs Thy Covenant and Thy Testament, of Thou Who art the Maker of the heavens! He is the One for Whose sake Thou (the Báb) hast yielded Thy life, and hast consented to be touched by the manifold ills of the world that He may manifest Himself, and summoned all mankind in His name. As soon as He came down, however, from the heaven of majesty and power, Thy servants stretched out against Him the hands of cruelty and sedition, and caused Him to be afflicted with such troubles that the scrolls of the world are insufficient to contain a full recital of them.

Thou seest, therefore, O Thou Beloved of the world, Him Who is dear to Thee in the clutches of such as have denied Thee, and beholdest Thy heart's desire under the swords of the ungodly. Methinks He, from His most exalted station, saith unto me: "Would that my soul, O Prisoner, could be a ransom for Thy captivity, and my being, O wronged One, be sacrificed for the adversities Thou didst suffer! Thou art He through Whose captivity the standards of Thine almighty power were hoisted, and the day-star of Thy revelation shone forth above the horizon of tribulation, in such wise that all created things bowed down before the greatness of Thy majesty.

"The more they strove to hinder Thee from remembering Thy God and from extolling His virtues, the more passionately didst Thou glorify Him and the more loudly didst Thou call upon Him. And every time the veils of the perverse came in between Thee and Thy servants, Thou didst shed the splendours of the light of Thy countenance out of the heaven of Thy grace. Thou art, in very truth, the Self-Subsisting as testified by the tongue of God, the All-Glorious, the one alone Beloved; and Thou art the Desire of the world as attested by what hath flowed down from the Pen of Him Who hath announced unto Thy servants Thy hidden Name, and adorned the entire creation with the ornament of Thy love, the Most Precious, the Most Exalted.

"The eyes of the world were gladdened at the sight of Thy luminous countenance, and yet the peoples have united to put out Thy light, O Thou in Whose hands are the reins of the worlds! All the atoms of the earth have celebrated Thy praise, and all created things have been set ablaze with the drops sprinkled by the ocean of Thy love, and yet the people still seek to quench Thy fire. Nay—and to this Thine own Self beareth me witness—they are all weakness, and Thou, verily, art the All-Powerful; and they are but paupers and Thou, in truth, art the All-Possessing; and they are impotent and Thou art, truly, the Almighty. Naught can ever frustrate Thy purpose, neither can the dissensions of the world harm Thee. Through the breaths of Thine utterance the heaven of understanding hath been adorned, and by the effusions of Thy pen every moldering bone hath been quickened. Grieve not at what hath befallen Thee, neither do Thou lay hold on them for the things they have committed in Thy days. Do Thou be forbearing toward them. Thou art the Ever-Forgiving, the Most Compassionate." [98]

2.5.2 The Day Star of the Bayán

Give ear, O My servant, unto that which is being sent down unto thee from the Throne of thy Lord, the Inaccessible, the Most Great. There is none other God but Him. He hath called into being His creatures, that they may know Him, Who is the Compassionate, the All-Merciful. Unto the cities of all nations He hath sent His Messengers Whom He hath commissioned to announce unto men tidings of the Paradise of His good pleasure, and to draw them nigh unto the Haven of abiding security, the Seat of eternal holiness and transcendent glory.

Some were guided by the Light of God, gained admittance into the court of His presence, and quaffed, from the hand of resignation, the waters of everlasting life, and were accounted of them that have truly recognized and believed in Him. Others rebelled against Him, and rejected the signs of God, the Most Powerful, the Almighty, the All-Wise.

---

98. Bahá'u'lláh, *Prayers and Meditations*, no. XXXII, pp. 144-9.

Shrine of the Báb

Ages rolled away, until they attained their consummation in this, the Lord of days, the Day whereon the Day Star of the Bayán manifested itself above the horizon of mercy, the Day in which the Beauty of the All-Glorious shone forth in the exalted person of 'Alí-Muḥammad, the Báb. No sooner did He reveal Himself, than all the people rose up against Him. By some He was denounced as one that hath uttered slanders against God, the Almighty, the Ancient of Days. Others regarded Him as a man smitten with madness, an allegation which I, Myself, have heard from the lips of one of the divines. Still others disputed His claim to be the Mouthpiece of God, and stigmatized Him as one who had stolen and used as his the words of the Almighty, who had perverted their meaning, and mingled them with his own. The Eye of Grandeur weepeth sore for the things which their mouths have uttered, while they continue to rejoice upon their seats.

"God," said He, "is My witness, O people! I am come to you with a Revelation from the Lord, your God, the Lord of your fathers of old. Look not, O people, at the things ye possess. Look rather at the things God hath sent down unto you. This, surely, will be better for you than the whole of creation, could ye but perceive it. Repeat the gaze, O people, and consider the testimony of God and His proof which are in your possession, and compare them unto the Revelation sent down unto you in this Day, that the truth, the infallible truth, may be indubitably manifested unto you. Follow not, O people, the steps of the Evil One; follow ye the Faith of the All-Merciful, and be ye of them that truly believe. What would it profit man, if he were to fail to recognize the Revelation of God? Nothing whatever. To this Mine own Self, the Omnipotent, the Omniscient, the All-Wise, will testify."

The more He exhorted them, the fiercer grew their enmity, till, at the last, they put Him to death with shameful cruelty. The curse of God be upon the oppressors!

A few believed in Him; few of Our servants are the thankful. These He admonished, in all His Tablets— nay, in every passage of His wondrous writings—not to give themselves up in the Day of the promised Revelation to anything whatever, be it in the heaven or in the earth. "O people!" said He, "I have revealed Myself for His Manifestation, and have caused My Book, the Bayán, to descend upon you for no other purpose except to establish the truth of His Cause. Fear ye God, and contend not with Him as the people of the Qur'án have contended with Me. At whatever time ye hear of Him, hasten ye towards Him, and cleave ye to whatsoever He may reveal unto you. Naught else besides Him can ever profit you, no, not though ye produce from first to last the testimonies of all those who were before you."

And when after the lapse of a few years the heaven of Divine decree was cleft asunder, and the Beauty of the Báb appeared in the clouds of the names of God, arrayed in a new raiment, these same people maliciously rose up against Him, Whose light embraceth all created things. They broke His Covenant, rejected His truth, contended with Him, cavilled at His signs, treated His testimony as falsehood, and joined the company of the infidels. Eventually, they determined to take away His life. Such is the state of them who are in a far-gone error!

And when they realized their powerlessness to achieve their purpose, they arose to plot against Him. Witness how every moment they devise a fresh device to harm Him, that they may injure and dishonour the cause of God. Say: Woe be to you! By God! Your schemings cover you with shame. Your Lord, the God of mercy, can well dispense with all creatures. Nothing whatever can either increase or diminish the things He doth possess. If ye believe, to your own behoof will ye believe; and if ye believe not, ye yourselves will suffer. At no time can the hand of the infidel profane the hem of His Robe.

O My servant that believest" in God! By the righteousness of the Almighty! Were I to recount to thee the tale of the things that have befallen Me, the souls and minds of men would be incapable of sustaining its weight. God Himself beareth Me witness. Watch over thyself, and follow not the footsteps of these people. Meditate diligently upon the Cause of thy Lord. Strive to know Him through His own Self and not through others. For no one else besides Him can ever profit thee. To this all created things will testify, could thou but perceive it.

Emerge from behind the veil, by the leave of thy Lord, the All-Glorious, the Most Powerful, and seize, before the eyes of those who are in the heavens and those who are on the earth, the Chalice of Immortality, in the name of thy Lord, the Inaccessible, the Most High, and quaff thy fill, and be not of them that tarry. I swear by God! The moment thou touchest" the Cup with thy lips, the Concourse on high will acclaim thee saying, "Drink with healthy relish, O man that hast truly believed in God!" and the inhabitants of the Cities of Immortality will cry out, "Joy be to thee, O thou that hast drained the Cup of His love!" and the Tongue of Grandeur will hail thee, "Great is the blessedness that awaiteth thee, O My servant, for thou has attained unto that which none hath attained, except such as have detached themselves from all that is in the heavens and all that is on the earth, and who are the emblems of true detachment." [99]

2.5.3 Prayer Revealed by the Báb

How can I praise Thee, O Lord, for the evidences of Thy mighty splendour and for Thy wondrous sweet savours which Thou hast imparted to Me in this fortress, in such measure that nothing in the heavens or on the earth can compare with them? Thou hast watched over Me in the heart of this mountain where I am compassed by mountains on all sides. One hangeth above Me, others stand on My right and My left and yet another riseth in front of Me. Glory be unto Thee, no God is there but Thee. How often have I seen rocks from the mountain hurtling down upon Me, and Thou didst protect Me therefrom and preserved Me within the stronghold of Thy divine Unity.

Glorified and exalted art Thou, and praise be unto Thee for whatsoever Thou lovest and desirest, and thanks be unto Thee for that which Thou hast decreed and preordained. From time immemorial Thy tender mercy hath been sent down and the process of Thy creation hath been and ever is ceaseless. Thy handiwork is unlike the work of anyone besides Thee, and Thy goodly gifts are unparalleled by the gifts of anyone other than Thyself.

Praise be unto Thee, O My Beloved, and magnified be Thy Name. Ever since the hour I set foot upon this fortress till the moment I shall have departed therefrom, I behold Thee established upon Thy seat of glory and majesty, sending down upon Me the manifold tokens of Thy bountiful favour and grace. Thou beholdest that My dwelling place is but the heart of the mountains, and Thou discernest naught in My Person except the evidences of abasement and loneliness.

Lauded be Thy Name; I render Thee thanks for every instance of Thine inscrutable Decree and offer My praise for every token of Thy tribulations. Having suffered Me to be cast into the prison, Thou didst turn it into a garden of Paradise for Me and caused it to become a chamber of the court of everlasting fellowship.

How numerous the verses Thou didst send down unto Me, and the prayers Thou didst hear Me offer unto Thee. How diverse the revelations which Thou didst call into being through Me and the experiences Thou didst witness in Met

Magnified be Thy Name. Manifold trials have been powerless to deter Me from yielding thanks unto Thee and My shortcomings have failed to keep Me back from extolling Thy virtues. The infidels had purposed to turn My abode

---

99. Bahá'u'lláh, *Gleanings from the Writings of Bahá'u'lláh*, no. LXXVI, pp. 144-9.

into one of disgrace and humiliation. But Thou hast glorified Me through My remembrance of Thee, hast exalted Me through My praise of Thee, hast graciously aided Me through the revelations of Thy oneness, and hast conferred upon Me a great honour through the effulgent splendours of Thine ancient eternity. To the fire Thou dost command, 'Be thou a soothing balm unto My Servant', and to the prison, 'Be thou a seat of tender compassion to My Servant, as a token from My presence'. Yea, I swear by Thy glory; to Me the prison hath proved to be naught but the most delightful garden of Paradise and hath served as the noblest spot in the realm above.

Praised and glorified art Thou. How often did adversities descend upon Me and Thou didst temper them and avert them through Thy gracious favour; and how many times were commotions stirred up against Me at the hand of the people, while Thou didst cause them to subside through Thy tender mercy. How numerous the occasions when the Nimrods kindled fires wherewith to burn Me, but Thou didst make them balm for Me; and how manifold the instances when the infidels decreed My humiliation and Thou didst turn them into marks of honour for Me... .

Verily Thou art the highest aspiration of every earnest seeker and the Goal of the desire of them that yearn after Thee. Thou art He Who is ready to answer the call of such as recognize Thy divine unity, and He before Whom the faint-hearted stand in awe. Thou art the Helper of the needy, the Deliverer of the captives, the Abaser of the oppressors, the Destroyer of the wrong-doers, the God of all men, the Lord of all created things. Thine are the kingdoms of Creation and Revelation, O Thou Who art the Lord of all the worlds.

O All-Sufficient One! Thou dost suffice Me in every hardship that may descend upon Me and in every affliction that may wax great before Me. Thou art My sole Companion in My loneliness, the Delight of My heart in My solitude and My Best Beloved in My prison and in My Abode. No God is there but Thee!

Whomsoever Thou dost suffice shall not be put to grief; whomsoever Thou dost protect shall never perish; whomsoever Thou dost help shall never be abased; and he unto whom Thou turnest Thy gaze shall never be far removed from Thee.

Write down for us then whatsoever is of Thee, and forgive us for what we are. Verily Thou art the Lord of power and glory, the Lord of all the worlds. Far be the glory of Thy Lord, the Lord of all greatness, from what they impute to Him, and peace be upon his Apostles, and praise be unto God, the Lord of all the worlds.[100]

2.5.4 *The Execution of the Báb*, Described by Shoghi Effendi

Immediately before and soon after this humiliating treatment meted out to the Báb, two highly significant incidents occurred, incidents that cast an illuminating light on the mysterious circumstances surrounding the opening phase of His martyrdom. The farrásh-bashí had abruptly interrupted the last conversation which the Báb was confidentially having in one of the rooms of the barracks with His amanuensis Siyyid Ḥusayn, and was drawing the latter aside, and severely rebuking him, when he was thus addressed by his Prisoner: *"Not until I have said to him all those things that I wish to say can any earthly power silence Me. Though all the world be armed against Me, yet shall it be powerless to deter Me from fulfilling, to the last word, My intention."* To the Christian Sám Khán—the colonel of the Armenian regiment ordered to carry out the execution—who, seized with fear lest his act should provoke the wrath of God, had begged to be released from the duty imposed upon him, the Báb gave the following assurance: *"Follow your instructions, and if your intention be sincere, the Almighty is surely able to relieve you of your perplexity."*

Sám Khán accordingly set out to discharge his duty. A spike was driven into a pillar which separated two rooms of the barracks facing the square. Two ropes were fastened to it from which the Báb and one of his disciples, the youthful and devout Mirza Muḥammad-'Alí-Zunúzí, surnamed Anís, who had previously flung himself at the feet of his Master and implored that under no circumstances he be sent away from Him, were separately suspended. The firing squad ranged itself in three files, each of two hundred and fifty men. Each file in turn opened fire until the whole detachment had discharged its bullets. So dense was the smoke from the seven hundred and fifty rifles that the sky was darkened. As soon as the smoke had cleared away the astounded multitude of about ten thousand souls, who had crowded onto the roof of the barracks, as well as the tops of the adjoining houses, beheld a scene which their eyes could scarcely believe.

The Báb had vanished from their sight! Only his companion remained, alive and unscathed, standing beside the wall on which they had been suspended. The ropes by which they had been hung alone were severed. "The Siyyid-i-Báb has gone from our sight!" cried out the bewildered spectators. A frenzied search

---

100. The Báb, *Selections from the Writings of the Báb*, pp. 183-6.

immediately ensued. He was found, unhurt and unruffled, in the very room He had occupied the night before, engaged in completing His interrupted conversation with His amanuensis. *"I have finished My conversation with Siyyid Ḥusayn"* were the words with which the Prisoner, so providentially preserved, greeted the appearance of the farrá<u>sh</u>-ba<u>sh</u>í, *"Now you may proceed to fulfil your intention."* Recalling the bold assertion his Prisoner had previously made, and shaken by so stunning a revelation, the farrá<u>sh</u>-ba<u>sh</u>í quitted instantly the scene, and resigned his post.

Sám <u>Kh</u>án, likewise, remembering, with feelings of awe and wonder, the reassuring words addressed to him by the Bab, ordered his men to leave the barracks immediately, and swore, as he left the courtyard, never again, even at the cost of his life, to repeat that act Áqá Ján-i-<u>Kh</u>amsih, colonel of the body-guard, volunteered to replace him. On the same wall and in the same manner the Báb and His companion were again suspended, while the new regiment formed in line and opened fire upon them. This time, however, their breasts were riddled with bullets, and their bodies completely dissected, with the exception of their faces which were but little marred. *"O wayward generation!"* were the last words of the Báb to the gazing multitude as the regiment prepared to fire its volley, *"Had you believed in Me every one of you would have followed the example of this youth, who stood in rank above most of you and would have willingly sacrificed himself in My path The day will come when you will have recognized Me; that day I shall have ceased to be with you."*

Nor was this all. The very moment the shots were fired a gale of exceptional violence arose and swept over the city. From noon till night a whirlwind of dust obscured the light of the sun, and blinded the eyes of the people. In <u>Sh</u>iráz an "earthquake," foreshadowed in no less weighty a Book than the *Revelation of St. John*, occurred in AH 1268 which threw the whole city into turmoil and wrought havoc amongst its people, a havoc that was greatly aggravated by the outbreak of cholera, by famine and other afflictions. In that same year no less than two hundred and fifty of the firing squad, that had replaced Sám <u>Kh</u>án's regiment, met their death, together with their officers, in a terrible earthquake, while the remaining five hundred suffered, three years later, as a punishment for their mutiny, the same fate as that which their hands had inflicted upon the Báb. To insure that none of them had survived, they were riddled with a second volley, after which their bodies, pierced with spears and lances, were exposed to the gaze of the people of Tabríz. The prime instigator of the Báb's death, the implacable Amir-Niẓám, together with his brother, his chief accomplice,

124

met their death within two years of that savage act.

On the evening of the very day of the Báb's execution, which fell on the ninth of July 1850 (28th of Sha'bán AH 1266), during the thirty-first year of His age and the seventh of His ministry, the mangled bodies were transferred from the courtyard of the barracks to the edge of the moat outside the gate of the city. Four companies, each consisting of ten sentinels, were ordered to keep watch in turn over them. On the following morning the Russian Consul in Tabríz visited the spot, and ordered the artist who had accompanied him to make a drawing of the remains as they lay beside the moat. In the middle of the following night a follower of the Báb, Ḥájí Sulaymán Khán, succeeded, through the instrumentality of a certain Ḥájí Allah-Yár, in removing the bodies to the silk factory owned by one of the believers of Mílán, and laid them, the next day, in a specially made wooden casket, which he later transferred to a place of safety. Meanwhile the Mullás were boastfully proclaiming from the pulpits that, whereas the holy body of the Immaculate Imám would be preserved from beasts of prey and from all creeping things, this man's body had been devoured by wild animals. No sooner had the news of the transfer of the remains of the Báb and of His fellow sufferer been communicated to Bahá'u'lláh than He ordered that same Sulaymán Khán to bring them to Ṭihrán, where they were taken to the Imám-Zádih-Ḥasan, from whence they were removed to different places, until the time when in pursuance of 'Abdu'l-Bahá's instructions, they were transferred to the Holy Land, and were permanently and ceremoniously laid to rest by Him in a specially erected mausoleum on the slopes of Mt. Carmel.

Thus ended a life which posterity will recognize as standing at the confluence of two universal prophetic cycles, the Adamic Cycle stretching back as far as the first dawnings of the world's recorded religious history and the Bahá'í Cycle destined to propel itself across the unborn reaches of time for a period of no less than five thousand centuries. The apotheosis in which such a life attained its consummation marks, as already observed, the culmination of the most heroic phase of the Heroic Age of the Bahá'í Dispensation. It can, moreover, be regarded in no other light except as the most dramatic, the most tragic event transpiring within the entire range of the first Bahá'í century. Indeed it can be rightly acclaimed as unparalleled in the annals of the lives of all the Founders of the world's existing -religious systems.

So momentous an event could hardly fail to arouse widespread and keen interest even beyond the confines of the land in which it had occurred. "C'est un des plus magnifiques exemples de courage qu'il ait ete donne a l'humanité de contempler," is the testimony recorded by a Christian scholar and government official who had lived in Persia and had familiarized himself with the life and teachings of the Báb, 'et c'est aussi une admirable preuve de ['amour que notre heros portait a ses con citoyens. Il s'est sacrifie pour l'humanite: pour elle il a donne son corps et son ame, pour elle il a subi les privations, les affronts, les injures, la torture et le martyre. Il a scelle de son sang le pacte de la fraternise universelle, et comme Jesus il a paye de sa vie l'annonce du regne de la concorde, de l'equite et de ['amour du prochain." "Un fait etrange, unique dans les annales de l'humanite," is a further testimony from the pen of that same scholar commenting on the circumstances attending the Báb's martyrdom. "A veritable miracle," is the pronouncement made by a noted French Orientalist. "A true God-man," is the verdict of a famous British traveller and writer. "The finest product of his country," is the tribute paid Him by a noted French publicist. "That Jesus of the age...a prophet, and more than a prophet," is the judgment passed by a distinguished English divine. "The most important religious movement since the foundation of Christianity," is the possibility that was envisaged for the Faith the Báb had established by that far-famed Oxford scholar, the late Master of Balliol.[101]

2.5.5   *The Execution of the Báb*, Recorded by Nabíl

Deprived of His turban and sash, the twin emblems of His noble lineage, the Báb, together with Siyyid Ḥusayn, His amanuensis, was driven to yet another confinement which He well knew was but a step further on the way leading Him to the goal He had set Himself to attain. That day witnessed a tremendous commotion in the city of Tabríz. The great convulsion associated in the ideas of its inhabitants with the Day of Judgment seemed at last to have come upon them. Never had that city experienced a turmoil so fierce and so mysterious as the one which seized its inhabitants on the day the Báb was led to that place which was to be the scene of His martyrdom. As He approached the courtyard of the barracks, a youth suddenly leaped forward who, in his eagerness to overtake Him, had forced his way through the crowd, utterly ignoring the risks and perils which such an attempt might involve. His face was haggard, his feet were bare, and his hair dishevelled. Breathless with excitement and exhausted with fatigue, he flung imself at the feet of the Báb and, seizing the hem of His

---

101. Shoghi Effendi, *God Passes By*, pp. 507-22.

garment, passionately implored Him: "Send me not from Thee, O Master. Wherever Thou goest, suffer me to follow Thee." "Muḥammad-'Alí," answered the Báb, "arise, and rest assured that you will be with Me. To-morrow you shall witness what God has decreed." Two other companions, unable to contain themselves, rushed forward and assured Him of their unalterable loyalty. These, together with Mírzá Muḥammad-'Alí-i-Zunúzí, were seized and placed in the same cell in which the Báb and Siyyid Ḥusayn were confined.

I have heard Siyyid Ḥusayn bear witness to the following: "That night the face of the Báb was aglow with joy, a joy such as had never shone from His countenance. Indifferent to the storm that raged about Him, He conversed with us with gaiety and cheerfulness. The sorrows that had weighed so heavily upon Him seemed to have completely vanished. Their weight appeared to have dissolved in the consciousness of approaching victory. 'To-morrow,' He said to us, 'will be the day of My martyrdom. Would that one of you might now arise and, with his hands, end My life. I prefer to be slain by the hand of a friend rather than by that of the enemy.' Tears rained from our eyes as we heard Him express that wish. We shrank, however, at the thought of taking away with our own hands so precious a life. We refused, and remained silent. Mírzá Muḥammad-'Alí suddenly sprang to his feet and announced himself ready to obey whatever the Báb might desire. 'This same youth who has risen to comply with My wish,' the Báb declared, as soon as we had intervened and forced him to abandon that thought, 'will together with Me, suffer martyrdom. Him will I choose to share with Me its crown.'"

Early in the morning, Mírzá Ḥasan Khán ordered his farrásh-bashí to conduct the Báb into the presence of the leading mujtahids of the city and to obtain from them the authorisation required for His execution. As the Báb was leaving the barracks, Siyyid Ḥusayn asked Him what he should do. "Confess not your faith," He advised him. "Thereby you will be enabled, when the hour comes, to convey to those who are destined to hear you, the things of which you alone are aware." He was engaged in a confidential conversation with him when the farrásh-bashí suddenly interrupted and, holding Siyyid Ḥusayn by the hand, drew him aside and severely rebuked him. "Not until I have said to him all those things that I wish to say," the Báb warned the farrásh-bashí, "can any earthly power silence Me. Though all the world be armed against Me, yet shall they be powerless to deter Me from fulfilling, to the last word, My intention." The farrásh-bashí was amazed at such a bold assertion. He made, however, no reply, and bade Siyyid Ḥusayn arise and follow him.

When Mírzá Muḥammad-'Alí was ushered into the presence of the mujtahids, he was repeatedly urged, in view of the position which his stepfather, Siyyid 'Alí-i-Zunúzí, occupied, to recant his faith. "Never," he exclaimed, "will I renounce my Master. He is the essence of my faith, and the object of my truest adoration. In Him I have found my paradise, and in the observance of His law I recognise the ark of my salvation." "Hold your peace!" thundered Mullá Muḥammad-i-Mámáqání, before whom that youth was brought. "Such words betray your madness; I can well excuse the words for which you are not responsible." "I am not mad," he retorted. "Such a charge should rather be brought against you who have sentenced to death a man no less holy than the promised Qá'im. He is not a fool who has embraced His Faith and is longing to shed his blood in His path."

The Báb was, in His turn, brought before Mullá Muḥammad-i-Mámáqání. No sooner had he recognised Him than he seized the death-warrant he himself had previously written and, handing it to his attendant, bade him deliver it to the Farrásh-Bashí. "No need," he cried, "to bring the Siyyid-i-Báb into my presence. This death-warrant I penned the very day I met him at the gathering presided over by the Valí-'Ahd. He surely is the same man whom I saw on that occasion, and has not, in the meantime, surrendered any of his claims."

From thence the Báb was conducted to the house of Mírzá Báqir, the son of Mírzá Aḥmad, to whom he had recently succeeded. When they arrived, they found his attendant standing at the gate and holding in his hand the Báb's death-warrant. "No need to enter," he told them. "My master is already satisfied that his father was right in pronouncing the sentence of death. He can do no better than follow his example."

Mullá Murtaḍá-Qulí, following in the footsteps of the other two mujtahids, had previously issued his own written testimony and refused to meet face to face his dreaded opponent. No sooner had the Farrásh-Bashí secured the necessary documents than he delivered his Captive into the hands of Sám Khán, assuring him that he could proceed with his task now that he had obtained the sanction of the civil and ecclesiastical authorities of the realm.

Siyyid Ḥusayn had remained confined in the same room in which he had spent the previous night with the Báb. They were proceeding to place Mírzá Muḥammad-'Alí in that same room, when he burst forth into tears and entreated them to allow him to remain with his Master. He was delivered into the hands of Sám Khán, who was ordered to execute him also, if he persisted in his refusal to deny his Faith.

Sám Khán was, in the meantime, finding himself increasingly affected by the behaviour of his Captive and the treatment that had been meted out to Him. He was seized with great fear lest his action should bring upon him the wrath of God. "I profess the Christian Faith," he explained to the Báb, "and entertain no ill will against you. If your Cause be the Cause of Truth, enable me to free myself from the obligation to shed your blood." "Follow your instructions," the Báb replied, "and if your intention be sincere, the Almighty is surely able to relieve you from your perplexity."

Sám Khán ordered his men to drive a nail into the pillar that lay between the door of the room that Siyyid Ḥusayn occupied and the entrance to the adjoining one, and to make fast two ropes to that nail, from which the Báb and His companion were to be separately suspended. Mírzá Muḥammad-'Alí begged Sám Khán to be placed in such a manner that his own body would shield that of the Báb. He was eventually suspended in such a position that his head reposed on the breast of his Master. As soon as they were fastened, a regiment of soldiers ranged itself in three files, each of two hundred and fifty men, each of which was ordered to open fire in its turn until the whole detachment had discharged the volleys of its bullets. The smoke of the firing of the seven hundred and fifty rifles was such as to turn the light of the noonday sun into darkness. There had crowded onto the roof of the barracks, as well as the tops of the adjoining houses, about ten thousand people, all of whom were witnesses to that sad and moving scene.

As soon as the cloud of smoke had cleared away, an astounded multitude were looking upon a scene which their eyes could scarcely believe. There, standing before them alive and unhurt, was the companion of the Báb, whilst He Himself had vanished uninjured from their sight. Though the cords with which they were suspended had been rent in pieces by the bullets, yet their bodies had miraculously escaped the volleys. Even the tunic which Mírzá Muḥammad-'Alí was wearing had, despite the thickness of the smoke, remained unsullied. "The Siyyid-i-Báb has gone from our sight!" rang out the voices of the bewildered multitude. They set out in a frenzied search for Him, and found Him, eventually, seated in the same room which He had occupied the night before, engaged in completing His interrupted conversation, with Siyyid Ḥusayn. An expression of unruffled calm was upon His face. His body had emerged unscathed from the shower of bullets which the regiment had directed against Him. "I have finished My conversation with Siyyid Ḥusayn," the Báb told the farrásh-bashí. "Now you may proceed to fulfil your intention." The man was too much shaken to resume what he had already attempted. Refusing to accomplish his duty, he, that same moment, left the scene and resigned his post. He related all that he had seen to his neighbour, Mírzá Siyyid Muḥsin, one of the notables of Tabríz, who, as soon as he heard the story, was converted to the Faith.

I was privileged to meet, subsequently, this same Mírzá Siyyid Muḥsin, who conducted me to the scene of the Báb's martyrdom and showed me the wall where He had been suspended. I was taken to the room in which He had been found conversing with Siyyid Ḥusayn, and was shown the very spot where He had been seated. I saw the very nail which His enemies had hammered into the wall and to which the rope which had supported His body had been attached.

Sám Khán was likewise stunned by the force of this tremendous revelation. He ordered his men to leave the barracks immediately, and refused ever again to associate himself and his regiment with any act that involved the least injury to the Báb. He swore, as he left that courtyard, never again to resume the task even though his refusal should entail the loss of his own life.

No sooner had Sám Khán departed than Áqá Ján Khán-i-Khamsih, Colonel of the body-guard, known also by the names of Khamsih and Naṣírí, volunteered to carry out the order for execution. On the same wall and in the same manner, the Báb and His companion were again suspended, while the regiment formed in line to open fire upon them. Contrariwise to the previous occasion, when only the cord with which they were suspended had been shot into pieces, this time their bodies were shattered and were blended into one mass of mingled flesh and bone. "Had you believed in Me, O wayward generation" were the last words of the Báb to the gazing multitude as the regiment was preparing to fire the final volley, "every one of you would have followed the example of this youth, who stood in rank above most of you, and willingly would have sacrificed himself in My path. The day will come when you will have recognised Me; that day I shall have ceased to be with you."

The very moments the shots were fired, a gale of exceptional severity arose and swept over the whole city. A whirlwind of dust of incredible density obscured the light of the sun and blinded the eyes of the people. The entire city remained enveloped in that darkness from noon till night. Even so strange a phenomenon, following immediately in the wake of that still more astounding failure of Sám Khán's regiment to injure the Báb, was unable to move the hearts of the people of Tabríz, and to induce them to pause and reflect upon the significance of such momentous events. They witnessed the effect which so marvellous an occurrence had produced upon Sám Khán; they beheld the consternation of the farrásh- bashí and saw him make his irrevocable decision; they could even examine that tunic which, despite the discharge of so many bullets, had remained whole and stainless; they could read in the face of the Báb, who had emerged unhurt from that storm, the expression of undisturbed serenity as He resumed His conversation with Siyyid Ḥusayn; and yet none of them troubled himself to enquire as to the significance of these unwonted signs and wonders.

The martyrdom of the Báb took place at noon on Sunday, the twenty-eighth of Sha'bán, in the year AH 1266, thirty-one lunar years, seven months, and twenty-seven days from the day of His birth in Shíráz.

On the evening of that same day, the mangled bodies of the Báb and His companion were removed from the courtyard of the barracks to the edge of the moat outside the gate of the city. Four companies, each consisting of ten sentinels, were ordered to keep watch in turn over them. On the morning following the day of martyrdom, the Russian consul in Tabríz, accompanied by an artist, went to that spot and ordered that a sketch be made of the remains as they lay beside the moat.

I have heard Ḥájí'Alí'Askar relate the following: "An official of the Russian consulate, to whom I was related, showed me that same sketch on the very day it was drawn. It was such a faithful portrait of the Báb that I looked upon! No bullet had struck His forehead, His cheeks, or His lips. I gazed upon a smile which seemed to be still lingering upon His countenance. His body, however, had been severely mutilated. I could recognise the arms and head of His companion, who seemed to be holding Him in his embrace. As I gazed horror-struck upon that haunting picture, and saw how those noble traits had been disfigured, my heart sank within me. I turned away my face in anguish and, regaining my house, locked myself within my room. For three days and three nights, I could neither sleep nor eat, so overwhelmed was I with emotion. That short and tumultuous life, with all its sorrows, its turmoils, its banishments, and eventually the awe-inspiring martyrdom with which it had been crowned, seemed again to be re- enacted before my eyes. I tossed upon my bed, writhing inagony and pain."

On the afternoon of the second day after the Báb's martyrdom Ḥájí Sulaymán Khán, son of Yaḥyá Khán, arrived at Bágh-Mishih, a suburb of Tabríz, and was received at the house of the Kalantar, one of his friends and confidants, who was a dervish and belonged to the súfí community. As soon as he had been informed of the imminent danger that threatened the life of the Báb, Ḥájí

Sulaymán Khán had left Ṭihrán with the object of achieving His deliverance. To his dismay, he arrived too late to carry out his intention. No sooner had his host informed him of the circumstances that had led to the arrest and condemnation of the Báb, and related to him the events of His martyrdom, than he instantly resolved to carry away the bodies of the victims, even at the risk of endangering his own life. The Kalantar advised him to wait and follow his suggestion rather than expose himself to what seemed to him would be inevitable death. He urged him to transfer his residence to another house and to wait for the arrival, that evening, of a certain Ḥájí Alláh-Yár, who, he said, woul be willing to carry out whatever he might wish him to do. At the appointed hour, Ḥájí Sulaymán Khán met Ḥájí Alláh-Yár, who succeeded, in the middle of that same night, in bearing the bodies from the edge of the moat to the silk factory owned by one of the believers of Mílán; laid them, the next day, in a specially constructed wooden case, and transferred them, according to Ḥájí Sulaymán Khán's directions, to a place of safety. Meanwhile the sentinels sought to justify themselves by pretending that, while they slept, wild beasts had carried away the bodies. Their superiors, on their part, unwilling to compromise their own honour, concealed the truth and did not divulge it to the authorities.

Ḥájí Sulaymán Khán immediately reported the matter to Bahá'u'lláh, who was then in Ṭihrán and who instructed Aqáy-i-Kalím to despatch a special messenger to Tabríz for the purpose of transferring the bodies to the capital. This decision was prompted by the wish the Báb Himself had expressed in the *Zíyárat-i-Sháh-'Abdu'l-'Azím*, a Tablet He had revealed while in the neighbourhood of that shrine and which He delivered to a certain Mírzá Sulaymán-i-Khaṭíb, who was instructed by Him to proceed together with a number of believers to that spot and to chant it within its precincts. "Well is it with you," the Báb addressed the buried saint in words such as these, in the concluding passages of that Tablet, "to have found your resting place in Rayy, under the shadow of My Beloved. Would that I might be entombed within the precincts of that holy ground!"

I was myself in Ṭihrán in the company of Mírzá Aḥmad, when the bodies of the Báb and His companion arrived. Bahá'u'lláh had in the meantime departed for Karbilá, in pursuance of the instructions of the Amír-Niẓám. Aqáy-i-Kalím, together with Mírzá Aḥmad, transferred those remains from the Imám-Zádih-Ḥasan, where they were first taken, to a place the site of which remained unknown to anyone excepting themselves. That place remained secret until the departure of Bahá'u'lláh for Adrianople, at which time Aqáy-i-Kalím was charged to inform Munír, one of his fellow-disciples, of the actual site where the bodies had been laid. In spite of his search, he was unable to find it. It was subsequently discovered by Jamál, an old adherent of the Faith, to whom that secret was confided while Bahá'u'lláh was still in Adrianople. That spot is, until now, unknown to the believers, nor can anyone conjecture where the remains will eventually be transferred.[102]

• • •

As to the regiment which, despite the unaccountable failure of Sám Khán and his men to destroy the life of the Báb, had volunteered to renew that attempt, and which eventually riddled His body with its bullets, two hundred and fifty of its members met their death in that same year, together with their officers, in a terrible earthquake. While they were resting on a hot summer day under the shadow of a wall on their way between Ardibíl and Tabríz, absorbed in their games and pleasures, the whole structure suddenly collapsed and fell upon them, leaving not one survivor. The remaining five hundred suffered the same fate as that which their own hands had inflicted upon the Báb. Three years after His martyrdom, that regiment mutinied, and its members were thereupon mercilessly shot by command of Mírzá Ṣádiq Khán-i-Núrí. Not content with a first volley, he ordered that a second one be fired in order to ensure that none of the mutineers had survived. Their bodies were afterwards pierced with spears and lances, and left exposed to the gaze of the people of Tabríz. That day many of the inhabitants of the city, recalling the circumstances of the Báb's martyrdom, wondered at that same fate which had overtaken those who had slain Him. "Could it be, by any chance, the vengeance of God," a few were heard to whisper to one another, "that has brought the whole regiment to so dishonourable and tragic an end? If that youth had been a lying imposter, why should his persecutors have been so severely punished?" These expressed misgivings reached the ears of the leading mujtahids of the city, who were seized with great fear and ordered that all those who entertained such doubts should be severely punished. Some were beaten, others were fined, all were warned to cease such whisperings, which could only revive the memory of a terrible adversary and rekindle enthusiasm for His Cause.

The prime mover of the forces that precipitated the Báb's martyrdom, the Amír-Niẓám, and also his brother, the Vazír-Niẓám, his chief accomplice, were, within two years of that savage act, subjected to a dreadful punishment, which

---

102. Nabíl-i-A'ẓam, *The Dawn Breakers,* pp. 507-22.

ended miserably in their death. The blood of the Amír-Niẓám stains, to this very day, the wall of the bath of Fín, a witness to the atrocities his own hand had wrought.[103]

2.5.6 *The Judgment of God*, from the Writings of Shoghi Effendi

The regiment which, scorning the miracle that warned Sám <u>Kh</u>án and his men to dissociate themselves from any further attempt to destroy the life of the Báb, volunteered to take their place and riddled His body with its bullets, lost, in that same year, no less than two hundred and fifty of its officers and men, in a terrible earthquake between Ardibíl and Tabríz; two years later the remaining five hundred were mercilessly shot in Tabríz for mutiny, and the people, gazing on their exposed and mutilated bodies, recalled their savage act, and indulged in such expressions of condemnation and wonder as to induce the leading mujtahids to chastise and silence them. The head of that regiment, Áqá Jan Big, lost his life, six years after the Báb's martyrdom, during the bombardment of Muḥammarih by the British naval forces.

The judgment of God, so rigorous and unsparing in its visitations on those who took a leading or an active part in the crimes committed against the Báb and His followers, was not less severe in its dealings with the mass of the people—a people more fanatical than the Jews in the days of Jesus—a people notorious for their gross ignorance, their ferocious bigotry, their wilful perversity and savage cruelty, a people mercenary, avaricious, egotistical and cowardly. I can do no better than quote what the Báb Himself has written in the *Dalá'il-i-Sab'ih* (Seven Proofs) during the last days of His ministry: *"Call thou to remembrance the early days of the Revelation. How great the number of those who died of cholera.! That was indeed one of the prodigies of the Revelation, and yet none recognized it! During four years the scourge raged among <u>Sh</u>í'ah Muslims without any one grasping its significance!"* "As to the great mass of its people (Persia)," Nabíl has recorded in his immortal narrative "who watched with sullen indifference the tragedy that was being enacted before their eyes, and who failed to raise a finger in protest against the hideousness of those cruelties, they fell, in their turn, victims to a misery which all the resources of the land and the energy of its statesmen were powerless to alleviate ... From the very day the hand of the assailant was stretched forth against the Báb ... visitation upon visitation crushed the spirit out of that ungrateful people,

---

103. Nabíl-i-A'ẓam, *The Dawn Breakers,* pp. 525-6.

and brought them to the very brink of national bankruptcy. Plagues, the very names of which were almost unknown to them except for a cursory reference in the dust-covered books which few cared to read, fell upon them with a fury that none could escape. That scourge scattered devastation wherever it spread. Prince and peasant alike felt its sting and bowed to its yoke. It held the populace in its grip, and refused to relax its hold upon them. As malignant as the fever which decimated the province of Gílán, these sudden affliction continued to lay waste the land. Grievous as were these calamities, the avenging wrath of God did not stop at the misfortune that befell a perverse and faithless people. It made itself felt in every living being that breathed on the surface of that stricken land. It afflicted the life of plants and animals alike, and made the people feel the magnitude of their distress. Famine added its horrors to the stupendous weight of afflictions under which the people were groaning. The gaunt spectre of starvation stalked abroad amidst them, and the prospect of a slow and painful death haunted their vision... People and government alike sighed with relief which they could nowhere obtain. They drank the cup of woe to its dregs, utterly unregardful of the Hand which had brought it to their lips, and of the Person for Whose sake they were made to suffer.[104]

2.5.7. Entombment of the Báb's Remains on Mount Carmel

'Abdu'l-Bahá's unexpected and dramatic release from His forty-year confinement dealt a blow to the ambitions cherished by the Covenant-breakers as devastating as that which, a decade before, had shattered their hopes of undermining His authority and of ousting Him from His God-given position. Now, on the very morrow of His triumphant liberation a third blow befell them as stunning as those which preceded it and hardly less spectacular than they. Within a few months of the historic decree which set Him free, in the very year that witnessed the downfall of Sulṭán 'Abdu'l-Ḥamíd, that same power from on high which had enabled 'Abdu'l-Bahá to preserve inviolate the rights divinely conferred on Him, to establish His Father's Faith in the North American continent, and to triumph over His royal oppressor, enabled Him to achieve one of the most signal acts of His ministry: the removal of the Báb's remains from the place of concealment in Ṭihrán to Mt. Carmel. He Himself testified, on more than one occasion, that the safe transfer of these remains, the construction of a befitting mausoleum to receive them, and their final interment with His own

104. Shoghi Effendi, *God Passes By*, pp. 84-5.

hands in their permanent resting-place constituted one of the three principal objectives which, ever since the inception of His mission, He had conceived it His paramount duty to achieve. This act indeed deserves to rank as one of the outstanding events in the first Bahá'í century.

As observed in a previous chapter the mangled bodies of the Báb and His fellow-martyr, Mírzá Muḥammad-'Alí, were removed, in the middle of the second night following their execution, through the pious intervention of Ḥájí Sulaymán Khán, from the edge of the moat where they had been cast to a silk factory owned by one of the believers of Mílán, and were laid the next day in a wooden casket, and thence carried to a place of safety. Subsequently, according to Bahá'u'lláh's instructions, they were transported to Ṭihrán and placed in the shrine of Imám-Zádih Ḥasan. They were later removed to the residence of Ḥájí Sulaymán Khán himself in the Sar-Chashmih quarter of the city, and from his house were taken to the shrine of Imám-Zádih Ma'ṣúm, where they remained concealed until the year AH 1284 (1867-1868), when a Tablet, revealed by Bahá'u'lláh in Adrianople, directed Mullá 'Alí-Akbar-i-Sháhmírzádí and Jamál-i-Burújirdí to transfer them without delay to some other spot, an instruction which, in view of the subsequent reconstruction of that shrine, proved to have been providential.

Unable to find a suitable place in the suburb of Sháh 'Abdu'l-'Aẓím, Mullá 'Alí-Akbar and his companion continued their search until, on the road leading to Chashmih-'Alí, they came upon the abandoned and dilapidated Masjid-i-Mashá'u'lláh, where they deposited, within one of its walls, after dark, their precious burden, having first re-wrapped the remains in a silken shroud brought by them for that purpose. Finding the next day to their consternation that the hiding-place had been discovered, they clandestinely carried the casket through the gate of the capital direct to the house of Mírzá Ḥasan-i-Vazír, a believer and son-in-law of Ḥájí Mírzá Siyyid 'Alíy-i-Tafríshi, the Majdu'l-Ashráf, where it remained for no less than fourteen months. The long-guarded secret of its whereabouts becoming known to the believers, they began to visit the house in such numbers that a communication had to be addressed by Mullá 'Alí-Akbar to Bahá'u'lláh, begging for guidance in the matter. Ḥájí Sháh Muḥammad-i-Manshádí, surnamed Amínu'l-Bayán was accordingly commissioned to receive the Trust from him, and bidden to exercise the utmost secrecy as to its disposal.

Assisted by another believer, Ḥájí Sháh Muḥammad buried the casket beneath the floor of the inner sanctuary of the shrine of Imám-Zádih Zayd, where it lay undetected until Mírzá Asadu'lláh-i-Iṣfáhání was informed of its exact location through a chart forwarded to him by Bahá'u'lláh. Instructed by Bahá'u'lláh to conceal it elsewhere, he first removed the remains to his own house in Ṭihrán, after which they were deposited in several other localities such as the house of Ḥusayn-'Alíy-i-Iṣfáhání and that of Muḥammad-Karím-i-Aṭṭár, where they remained hidden until the year AH 1316 (1899), when, in pursuance of directions issued by 'Abdu'l-Bahá, this same Mírzá Asadu'lláh, together with a number of other believers, transported them by way of Iṣfáhán, Kirmánsháh, Baghdád and Damascus, to Beirut and thence by sea to 'Akká, arriving at their destination on the 19th of the month of Ramaḍán AH 1316 (31 January 1899), fifty lunar years after the Báb's execution in Tabríz.

In the same year that this precious Trust reached the shores of the Holy Land and was delivered into the hands of 'Abdu'l-Bahá, He, accompanied by Dr. Ibráhím Khayru'lláh, whom He had already honoured with the titles of *"Bahá's Peter," "The Second Columbus"* and *"Conqueror of America,"* drove to the recently purchased site which had been blessed and selected by Bahá'u'lláh on Mt. Carmel, and there laid, with His own hands, the foundation-stone of the edifice, the construction of which He, a few months later, was to commence. About that same time, the marble sarcophagus, designed to receive the body of the Báb, an offering of love from the Bahá'í's of Rangoon, had, at 'Abdu'l-Bahá's suggestion, been completed and shipped to Haifa.

No need to dwell on the manifold problems and pre-occupations which, for almost a decade, continued to beset 'Abdu'l-Bahá until the victorious hour when He was able to bring to a final consummation the historic task entrusted to Him by His Father. The risks and perils with which Bahá'u'lláh and later His Son had been confronted in their efforts to insure, during half a century, the protection of those remains were but a prelude to the grave dangers which, at a later period, the Centre of the Covenant Himself had to face in the course of the construction of the edifice designed to receive them, and indeed until the hour of His final release from His incarceration.

The long-drawn out negotiations with the shrewd and calculating owner of the building-site of the holy Edifice, who, under the influence of the Covenant-breakers, refused for a long time to sell; the exorbitant price at first demanded for the opening of a road leading to that site and indispensable to the work of construction; the interminable objections raised by officials, high and low, whose easily aroused suspicions had to be allayed by repeated explanations and assurances given by 'Abdu'l-Bahá Himself; the dangerous situation created by the monstrous accusations brought by Mírzá Muḥammad- 'Alí and his associates regarding the character and purpose of that building; the delays and complications caused by 'Abdu'l-Bahá's prolonged and enforced absence from Haifa, and His consequent inability to supervise in person the vast undertaking He had initiated—all these were among the principal obstacles which He, at so critical a period in His ministry, had to face and surmount ere He could execute in its entirety the Plan, the outline of which Bahá'u'lláh had communicated to Him on the occasion of one of His visits to Mt. Carmel.

"Every stone of that building, every stone of the road leading to it," He, many a time was heard to remark, "I have with infinite tears and at tremendous cost, raised and placed in position." "One night," He, according to an eye-witness, once observed, "I was so hemmed in by My anxieties that I had no other recourse than to recite and repeat over and over again a prayer of the Báb which I had in My possession, the recital of which greatly calmed Me. The next morning the owner of the plot himself came to Me, apologized and begged Me to purchase his property."

Finally, in the very year His royal adversary lost his throne, and at the time of the opening of the first American Bahá'í Convention, convened in Chicago for the purpose of creating a permanent national organization for the construction of the Mashriqu'l-Adhkár, 'Abdu'l-Bahá brought His undertaking to a successful conclusion, in spite of the incessant machinations of enemies both within and without. On the 28th of the month of Ṣafar AH 1327, the day of the first Naw-Rúz ([AD]1909), which He celebrated after His release from His confinement, 'Abdu'l-Bahá had the marble sarcophagus transported with great labour to the vault prepared for it, and in the evening, by the light of a single lamp, He laid within it, with His own hands—in the presence of believers from the East and the West and in circumstances at once solemn and moving—the wooden casket containing the sacred remains of the Báb and His companion.

When all was finished, and the earthly remains of the Martyr-Prophet of Shíráz were, at long last, safely deposited for their everlasting rest in the bosom of God's holy mountain, 'Abdu'l-Bahá, Who had cast aside His turban, removed His shoes and thrown off His cloak, bent low over .the still open sarcophagus, His silver hair waving about His head and His face transfigured and luminous, rested His forehead on the border of the wooden casket, and-, sobbing aloud, wept with such a weeping that all those who were present wept with Him. That night He could not sleep, so overwhelmed was He with emotion.[105]

2.5.8 Tablet of 'Abdu'l-Bahá about the Entombment of the Báb's Remains

The most joyful tiding is this, that the holy, the luminous body of the Báb...after having for sixty years been transferred from place to place, by reason of the ascendancy of the enemy, and from fear of the malevolent, and having known neither rest nor tranquillity has, through the mercy of the Abhá' Beauty, been ceremoniously deposited, on the day of Naw-Rúz, within the sacred casket, in the exalted Shrine on Mt. Carmel ... By a strange coincidence, on that same day of Naw-Rúz, a cablegram was received from Chicago, announcing that the believers in each of the American centres had elected a delegate and sent to that city...and definitely decided on the site and construction of the Mashriqu'l-Adhkár[106]

2.5.9 Tablet of Visitation

The praise which hath dawned from Thy most august Self, and the glory which hath shone forth from Thy most effulgent Beauty, rest upon Thee, O Thou Who art the Manifestation of Grandeur, and the King of Eternity, and the Lord of all who are in heaven and on earth! I testify that through Thee the sovereignty of God and His dominion, and the majesty of God and His grandeur, were revealed, and the Day-Stars of ancient splendour have shed their radiance in the heaven of Thine irrevocable decree, and the Beauty of the Unseen hath shone forth above the horizon of creation. I testify moreover, that with but a movement of Thy Pen Thine injunction *'Be Thou'* hath been enforced, and God's hidden Secret hath been divulged, and all created things have been called into being, and all the Revelations have been sent down.

I bear witness, moreover, that through Thy beauty the beauty of the Adored One hath been unveiled, and through Thy face the face of the Desired One hath shone forth, and that through a word from Thee Thou hast decided between all created things, causing them who are devoted to Thee to ascend unto the summit of glory, and the infidels to fall into the lowest abyss.

I bear witness that he who hath known Thee hath known God, and he who hath attained unto Thy presence hath attained unto the presence of God. Great, therefore, is the blessedness of him who hath believed in Thee, and in Thy

---

105. Shoghi Effendi, *God Passes By*, pp. 84-5.
106. 'Abdu'l-Bahá, quoted by Shoghi Effendi in *God Passes By*, p. 276.

signs, and hath humbled himself before Thy sovereignty, and hath been honoured with meeting Thee, and hath attained the good pleasure of Thy will, and circled around Thee, and stood before Thy throne. Woe betide him that hath transgressed against Thee, and hath denied Thee, and repudiated Thy signs, and gainsaid Thy sovereignty, and risen up against Thee, and waxed proud before Thy face, and hath disputed Thy testimonies, and fled from Thy rule and Thy dominion, and been numbered with the infidels whose names have been inscribed by the fingers of Thy behest upon Thy holy Tablets.

Waft, then, unto me, O my God and my Beloved, from the right hand of Thy mercy and Thy loving- kindness, the holy breaths of Thy favours, that they may draw me away from myself end from the world unto the courts of' Thy nearness and Thy presence. Potent art Thou to do what pleaseth Thee. Thou, truly, hast been supreme over all things.

The remembrance of God and His praise, and the glory of God and His splendour, rest upon Thee, O Thou Who art His Beauty! I bear witness that the eye of creation hath never gazed upon one wronged like Thee. 'Thou wast immersed all the days of Thy life beneath an ocean of tribulations. At one time Thou wast in chains and fetters at another Thou wast threatened by the sword of' Thine enemies. Yet, despite all this, Thou didst enjoin upon all men to observe what had been prescribed unto Thee by Him Who is the All-Knowing, the All-Wise.

May my spirit be a sacrifice to the wrongs Thou didst suffer, and my soul be a ransom for the adversities Thou didst sustain. I beseech God, by Thee and by them whose faces have been illumined with the splendours of the light of Thy countenance, and who, for love of Thee, have observed all whereunto they were bidden, to remove the veils that have come in between Thee and Thy creatures, and to supply me with the good of this world and the world to come. Thou art, in truth, the Almighty, the Most Exalted, the All-Glorious, the Ever-Forgiving, the Most Compassionate.

Bless Thou, O Lord my God, the Divine Lote-Tree and its leaves, and its boughs, and its branches, and its stems, and its offshoots, as long as Thy most excellent titles will endure and Thy most august attributes will last. Protect it, then, from the mischief of the aggressor and the hosts of tyranny. Thou art, in truth, the Almighty, the Most Powerful. Bless Thou, also, O Lord my God, Thy servants and Thy handmaidens who have attained unto Thee. Thou, truly, art the All-Bountiful, Whose grace is infinite. No God is there save Thee, the Ever-

Forgiving, the Most Generous. [107]

---

107. Bahá'u'lláh, *Prayers and Meditations*, pp. 310-3.

Tower in which the Báb was first confined.
Máh-kú, Iran

2.6
Birth of the Báb
October 20, 1819

The Báb, the Exalted One, is the Morn of Truth, Whose Light shineth throughout all regions.[108]

Suggested Readings:

2.6.1	Excerpt from a Prayer Revealed by Bahá'u'lláh
2.6.2	A Tablet Revealed by Bahá'u'lláh
2.6.3	Prayer Revealed by the Báb
2.6.4	Another Prayer by the Báb
2.6.5	A Tablet from 'Abdu'l-Bahá
2.6.6	*The Báb*, 'Abdu'l-Bahá's Discourse
2.6.7	The Herald of the Bahá'í Faith
2.6.8	His Place in Religious History
2.6.9	The Báb's Early Life

---

108. 'Abdu'l-Bahá, quoted by Shoghi Effendi in *World Order of Bahá'u'lláh*, p. 127.

2.6.1   Excerpt from a Prayer Revealed by Bahá'u'lláh

Magnify Thou, O Lord my God, Him Who is the Primal Point, the Divine Mystery, the Unseen Essence, the Day-Spring of Divinity, and the Manifestation of Thy lordship, through Whom all the knowledge of the past and all the knowledge of the future were made plain, through Whom the pearls of Thy hidden wisdom were uncovered, and the mystery of Thy treasured name disclosed, Whom Thou hast appointed as the Announcer of the One through Whose name the letter B and the letter E have been joined and united, through Whom Thy majesty, Thy sovereignty and Thy might were made known, through Whom Thy words have been sent down, and Thy laws set forth with clearness, and Thy signs spread abroad, and Thy Word established, through Whom the hearts of Thy chosen ones were laid bare, and all that were in the heavens and all that were on the earth were gathered together, Whom Thou hast called 'Alí Muḥammad in the kingdom of Thy names, and the Spirit of Spirits in the Tablets of Thine irrevocable decree, Whom Thou hast invested with Thine own title, unto Whose name all other names have, at Thy bidding and through the power of Thy might, been made to return, and in Whom Thou hast caused all Thine attributes and titles to attain their final consummation. To Him also belong such names as lay hid within Thy stainless tabernacles, in Thine invisible world and Thy sanctified cities.[109]

2.6.2.   A Tablet Revealed by Bahá'u'lláh

All praise be to Thee, O my God, inasmuch as Thou hast adorned the world with the splendour of the dawn following the night wherein was born the One Who heralded the Manifestation of Thy transcendent sovereignty, the Dayspring of Thy divine Essence and the Revelation of Thy supreme Lordship. I beseech Thee, O Creator of the heavens and Fashioner of names, to graciously aid those who have sheltered beneath the shadow of Thine abounding mercy and have raised their voices amidst the peoples of the world for the glorification of Thy Name.

O my God! Thou beholdest the Lord of all mankind confined in His Most Great Prison, calling aloud Thy Name, gazing upon Thy face, proclaiming that which hath enraptured the denizens of Thy kingdoms of revelation and of creation. O my God! I behold Mine own Self captive in the hands of Thy servants, yet the light of Thy sovereignty and the revelations of Thine invincible

---

109. Bahá'u'lláh, *Prayers and Meditations*, no. LVI, pp. 84-5.

power shine resplendent from His face, enabling all to know of a certainty that Thou art God, and that there is none other God but Thee. Neither can the power of the powerful frustrate Thee, nor the ascendancy of the rulers prevail against Thee. Thou doest whatsoever Thou wiliest by virtue of Thy sovereignty which encompasseth all created things, and ordainest that which Thou pleasest through the potency of Thy behest which pervadeth the entire creation.

I implore Thee by the glory of Thy Manifestation and by the power of Thy might, Thy sovereignty and Thine exaltation to render victorious those who have arisen to serve Thee, who have aided Thy Cause and humbled themselves before the splendour of the light of Thy face. Make them then, O my God, triumphant over Thine enemies and cause them to be steadfast in Thy service, that through them the evidences of Thy dominion may be established throughout Thy realms and the tokens of Thine indomitable power be manifested in Thy lands. Verily Thou art potent to do what Thou willest; no God is there but Thee, the Help in Peril, the Self-Subsisting.

This glorious Tablet hath been revealed on the Anniversary of the Birth [of the Báb] that thou mayest recite it in a spirit of humility and supplication and give thanks unto Thy Lord, the All-Knowing, the All-Informed. Make thou every effort to render service unto God, that from thee may appear that which will immortalize thy memory in His glorious and exalted heaven.

Say: Glorified art Thou, O my God! I implore Thee by the Dawning Place of Thy signs and by the Revealer of Thy clear tokens to grant that I may, under all conditions, hold fast the cord of Thy loving providence and cling tenaciously to the hem of Thy generosity. Reckon me then with those whom the changes and chances of the world have failed to deter from serving Thee and from bearing allegiance unto Thee, whom the onslaught of the people hath been powerless to hinder from magnifying Thy Name and celebrating Thy praise. Graciously assist me, O my Lord, to do whatever Thou lovest and desirest. Enable me then to fulfil that which will exalt Thy Name and will set ablaze the fire of Thy love.

Thou art, in truth, the Forgiving, the Bountiful.[110]

2.6.3 A Prayer Revealed by the Báb

Thou are aware, O My God, that since the day Thou didst call Me into being out of the water of Thy love till I reached fifteen years of age I lived in the land

---

110. Bahá'u'lláh, *Tablets of Bahá'u'lláh*, pp. 233-4.

which witnessed My birth [Shíráz]. Then Thou didst enable Me to go to the seaport [Búshihr] where for five years I was engaged in trading with the goodly gifts of Thy realm and was occupied in that with which Thou hast favoured Me through the wondrous essence of Thy loving-kindness. I proceeded therefrom to the Holy Land [Karbilá] where I sojourned for one year. Then I returned to the place of My birth. There I experienced the revelation of Thy sublime bestowals and the evidences of Thy boundless grace. I yield Thee praise for all Thy goodly gifts and I render Thee thanksgiving for all Thy bounties. Then at the age of twenty-five I proceeded to thy sacred House [Mecca], and by the time I returned to the place where I was born, a year had elapsed. There I tarried patiently in the path of Thy love and beheld the evidences of Thy manifold bounties and of Thy loving-kindness until Thou didst ordain for Me to set out in Thy direction and to migrate to Thy presence. Thus I departed therefrom by Thy leave, spending six months in the land of Ṣád [Iṣfáhán] and seven months in the First Mountain [Má-Kú], where Thou didst rain down upon Me that which beseemeth the glory of Thy heavenly blessings and befitteth the sublimity of Thy gracious gifts and favours. Now, in My thirtieth year, Thou beholdest Me, O My God, in this Grievous Mountain [Chihríq] where I have dwelt for one whole year.

Praise be unto Thee, O My Lord, for all times, heretofore and hereafter; and thanks be unto Thee, O My God, under all conditions, whether of the past or the future. The gifts Thou hast bestowed upon Me have reached their fullest measure and the blessings Thou hast vouchsafed unto Me have attained their consummation. Naught do I now witness but the manifold evidences of Thy grace and loving-kindness, Thy bounty and gracious favours, Thy generosity and loftiness, Thy sovereignty and might, Thy splendour and Thy glory, and that which befitteth the holy court of Thy transcendent dominion and majesty and beseemeth the glorious precincts of Thine eternity and exaltation.[111]

2.6.4 A Prayer Revealed by the Báb

Immeasurably glorified and exalted art Thou. How can I make mention of Thee, O Thou the Beloved of the entire creation; and how can I acknowledge Thy claim, O Thou, before Whom every created thing standeth in awe. The loftiest station to which human perception can soar and the utmost height which the minds and souls of men can scale are but signs created through the potency

---

111. The Báb, *Selections from the Writings of the Báb*, pp. 180-2.

of Thy command and tokens manifested through the power of Thy Revelation. Far be it from Thy glory that anyone other than Thee should make mention of Thee or should attempt to voice Thy praise. The very essence of every reality beareth witness to its debarment from the precincts of the court of Thy nearness, and the quintessence of every being testifieth to its failure to attain Thy holy Presence. Immeasurably glorified and exalted art Thou! That which alone beseemeth Thee is the befitting mention made by Thine Own Self, and that only which is worthy of Thee is the anthem of praise voiced by Thine Own Essence...

Through the revelation of Thy grace, O Lord, Thou didst call Me into being on a night such as this, and lo, I am now lonely and forsaken in a mountain. Praise and thanksgiving be unto Thee for whatever conformeth to Thy pleasure within the empire of heaven and earth. And all sovereignty is Thine, extending beyond the uttermost range of the kingdoms of Revelation and Creation.

Thou didst create Me, O Lord, through Thy gracious favour and didst protect Me through Thy bounty in the darkness of the womb and didst nourish Me, through Thy loving-kindness, with life-giving blood. After having fashioned Me in a most comely form, through Thy tender providence, and having perfected My creation through Thine excellent handiwork and breathed Thy Spirit into My body through Thine infinite mercy and by the revelation of Thy transcendent unity, Thou didst cause Me to issue forth from the world of concealment into the visible world, naked, ignorant of all things, and powerless to achieve aught. Thou didst then nourish Me with refreshing milk and didst rear Me in the arms of My parents with manifest compassion, until Thou didst graciously acquaint Me with the realities of Thy Revelation and apprised Me of the straight path of Thy Faith as set forth in Thy Book. And when I attained full maturity Thou didst cause Me to bear allegiance unto Thine inaccessible Remembrance, and enabled Me to advance towards the designated station, where Thou didst educate Me through the subtle operations of Thy handiwork and didst nurture Me in that land with Thy most gracious gifts. When that which had been preordained in Thy Book came to pass Thou didst cause Me, through Thy kindness, to reach Thy holy precincts and didst suffer Me, through Thy tender mercy, to dwell within the court of fellowship, until I discerned therein that which I witnessed of the clear tokens of Thy mercifulness, the compelling evidences of Thy oneness, the effulgent splendours of Thy majesty, the source of Thy supreme singleness, the heights of Thy transcendent sovereignty, the signs of Thy peerlessness, the manifestations of Thine exalted glory, the retreats of Thy sanctity, and whatsoever is inscrutable to all but Thee.[112]

2.6.5 A Tablet from 'Abdu'l-Bahá

He is God!

O friends and maidservants of the Merciful!

Thanks be to God! that you have been gathered together and celebrated the birthday of the Báb with much joy and amity and were engaged in remembering God.

From the rose-garden of that meeting a beautiful fragrance has reached to the nostrils of these friends, and the light of God's love hath shone; therefore, it was a cause of delighting the hearts of these friends. I ask God, by His infinite mercy, that such meetings may be held often.

Likewise, that the entertainment every nineteen days may become current among you; so that the friends and maidservants of the Merciful may be engaged in praising and remembering God and singing to Him, and may become the cause of guiding the people.

Upon you all be the Glory of the Most Glorious! [113]

2.6.6 *The Báb*, 'Abdu'l-Bahá's Discourse

As for the Báb—may my soul be his sacrifice!—at a youthful age, that is to say when He had reached the twenty-fifth year of His blessed life, He stood forth to proclaim His Cause. It was universally admitted by the Shí'ites that he had never studied in any school, and had not acquired knowledge from any teacher; all the people of Shíráz bear witness to this. Nevertheless, He suddenly appeared before the people, endowed with the most complete erudition. Although He was but a merchant, He confounded all the 'ulamá of Persia. All alone, in a way which is beyond imagination, He upheld the Cause among the Persians, who are renowned for their religious fanaticism. This illustrious soul arose with such power that He shook the supports of the religion, of the morals, the conditions, the habits, and the customs of Persia, and instituted new rules, new laws, and a new religion. Though the great personages of the State, nearly all the clergy, and the public men, arose to destroy and annihilate him, He alone withstood them, and moved the whole of Persia.

Many 'ulamá and public men, as well as other people, joyfully sacrificed their

---

112. The Báb, *Selections from the Writings of the Báb*, pp. 173-4.

113. 'Abdu'l-Bahá, quoted in *Star of the West*, vol II, no. 17, p. 6.

lives in His Cause, and hastened to the plain of martyrdom.

The government, the nation, the doctors of divinity, and the great personages, desired to extinguish His light, but they could not do so. At last His moon arose, His star shone forth, His foundations became firmly established, and his dawning-place became brilliant. He imparted divine education to an unenlightened multitude and produced marvellous results on the thoughts, morals, customs, and conditions of the Persians. He announced the glad tidings of the manifestation of the Sun of Bahá to His followers, and prepared them to believe.

The appearance of such wonderful signs and great results, the effects produced upon the minds of the people, and upon prevailing ideas; the establishment of the foundations of progress, and the organisation of the principles of success and prosperity by a young merchant, constitute the greatest proof that He was a perfect Educator. A just person will never hesitate to believe this.[114]

2.6.7 The Herald of the Bahá'í Faith

The Bahá'í Faith revolves around three central Figures, the first of whom was a youth, a native of Shíráz, named Mírzá 'Ali-Muḥammad, known as the Báb (Gate), who in May 1844, at the age of twenty-five, advanced the claim of being the Herald Who, according to the sacred Scriptures of previous Dispensations, must needs announce and prepare the way for the advent of One greater than Himself, Whose mission would be, according to those same Scriptures, to inaugurate an era of righteousness and peace, an era that would be hailed as the consummation of all previous Dispensations, and initiate a new cycle in the religious history of mankind. Swift and severe persecution, launched by the organized forces of Church and State in His native land, precipitated successively His arrest, His exile to the mountains of Adhirbáyján, His imprisonment in the fortresses of Máh-Kú and Chihríq, and His execution, in July 1850, by a firing squad in the public square of Tabríz. No less than twenty thousand of his followers were put to death with such barbarous cruelty as to evoke the warm sympathy and the unqualified admiration of a number of Western writers, diplomats, travellers, and scholars, some of whom were witnesses of these abominable outrages, and were moved to record them in their books and diaries.[115]

---

114. 'Abdu'l-Bahá, *Some Answered Questions*, pp. 25-26.
115. Shoghi Effendi, *Guidance for Today and Tomorrow*, pp. 4-5.

2.6.8 His Place in Religious History

The Báb, acclaimed by Bahá'u'lláh as the *"Essence of Essences"*, the *"Sea of Seas"*, the *"Point round Whom the realities of the Prophets and Messengers revolve"*, *"from Whom God hath caused to proceed the knowledge of all that was and shall be"*, Whose *"rank excelleth that of all the Prophets"*, and Whose *"Revelation transcendeth the comprehension and understanding of all their chosen ones"*, had delivered His Message and discharged His mission. He Who was, in the words of 'Abdu'l-Bahá, the *"Morn of Truth"* and *"Harbinger of the Most Great Light"*, Whose advent at once signalized the termination of the *"Prophetic Cycle"* and the inception of the *"Cycle of Fulfilment"*, had simultaneously through His Revelation banished the shades of night that had descended upon His country, and proclaimed the impending rise of that Incomparable Orb Whose radiance was to envelop the whole of mankind. He, as affirmed by Himself, *"the Primal Point from which have been generated all created things"* *"one of the sustaining pillars of the Primal Word of God"*, the *"Mystic Fane"*, the *"Great Announcement"*, the *"Flame of that supernal Light that glowed upon Sinai"*, the *"Remembrance of God"* concerning Whom *"a separate Covenant hath been established with each and every Prophet"* had, through His advent, at once fulfilled the promise of all ages and ushered in the consummation of all Revelations. He the *"Qá'im"* (He Who ariseth) promised to the Shí'ihs, the *"Mihdí"* (One Who is guided) awaited by the Sunnís, the *"Return of John the Baptist"* expected by the Christians, the *"Ushídar-Máh"* referred to in the Zoroastrian Scriptures, the *"Return of Elijah"* anticipated by the Jews, Whose Revelation was to show forth *"the signs and tokens of all the Prophets"*, Who was to *"manifest the perfection of Moses, the radiance of Jesus and the patience of Job"* had appeared, proclaimed His Cause, been mercilessly persecuted and died gloriously. The *"Second Woe"*, spoken of in the Apocalypse of St John the Divine, had, at long last, appeared, and the first of the two *"Messengers"*, Whose appearance had been prophesied in the Qur'án, had been sent down. The first *"Trumpet Blast"*, destined to smite the earth with extermination, announced in the latter Book, had finally been sounded. *"The Inevitable"* *"The Catastrophe"* *"The Resurrection"* *"The Earthquake of the Last Hour"* foretold by that same Book, had all come to pass. The *"clear tokens"* had been *"sent down"* and the *"Spirit"* had *"breathed"* and the *"souls"* had *"waked up"*, and the *"heaven"* had been *"cleft"*, and the *"angels"* had *"ranged in order"*, and the *"stars"* had been *"blotted out"*, and the *"earth"* had *"cast forth her burden"*, and *"Paradise"* had been *"brought near"*, and *"hell"* had been *"made to blaze"*, and the *"Book"* had been *"set"*, and the *"Bridge"* had been *"laid out"*, and the *"Balance"* had been *"set up"*, and the *"mountains scattered in dust"*. The *"cleansing of the Sanctuary"*, prophesied by

Daniel and confirmed by Jesus Christ in His reference to *"the abomination of desolation"*, had been accomplished. The *"day whose length shall be a thousand years"*, foretold by the Apostle of God in His Book, had terminated. The *"forty and two months"*, during which the *"Holy City"*, as predicted by St John the Divine, would be trodden underfoot, had elapsed. The *"time of the end"* had been ushered in, and the first of the *"two Witnesses"* into Whom, *"after three days and a half the Spirit of Life from God"* would enter, had arisen and had *"ascended up to heaven in a cloud"*. The *"remaining twenty and five letters to be made manifest"*, according to Islamic tradition, out of the *"twenty and seven letters"* of which Knowledge has been declared to consist, had been revealed. The *"Man Child"*, mentioned in the Book of Revelation, destined to *"rule all nations with a rod of iron"*, had released, through His coming, the creative energies which, reinforced by the effusions of a swiftly succeeding and infinitely mightier Revelation, were to instil into the entire human race the capacity to achieve its organic unification, attain maturity and thereby reach the final stage in its age-long evolution. The clarion-call addressed to the *"concourse of kings and of the sons of kings"*, marking the inception of a process which, accelerated by Bahá'u'lláh's subsequent warnings to the entire company of the monarchs of East and West, was to produce so widespread a revolution in the fortunes of royalty, had been raised in the *Qayyúmu'l-Asmá'*. The *"Order"*, whose foundation the Promised One was to establish in the *Kitáb-i-Aqdas*, and the features of which the Centre of the Covenant was to delineate in His Testament, and whose administrative framework the entire body of His followers are now erecting, had been categorically announced in the Persian Bayán. The laws which were designed, on the one hand, to abolish at a stroke the privileges and ceremonials, the ordinances and institutions of a superannuated Dispensation, and to bridge, on the other, the gap between an obsolete system and the institutions of a world-encompassing Order destined to supersede it, had been clearly formulated and proclaimed. The Covenant which, despite the determined assaults launched against it, succeeded, unlike all previous Dispensations, in preserving the integrity of the Faith of its Author, and in paving the way for the advent of the One Who was to be its Centre and Object, had been firmly and irrevocably established. The light which, throughout successive periods, was to propagate itself gradually from its cradle as far as Vancouver in the West and the China Sea in the East, and to diffuse its radiance as far as Iceland in the North and the Tasman Sea in the South, had broken. The forces of darkness, at first confined to the concerted hostility of the civil and ecclesiastical powers of Shí'ih Persia, gathering momentum, at a later stage, through the avowed and persistent opposition of the Caliph of Islám and the Sunní hierarchy in Turkey, and destined to culminate in the fierce antagonism of the sacerdotal orders associated with other and still more powerful religious systems, had launched their initial assault. The nucleus of the divinely ordained, world-embracing Community—a Community whose infant strength had already plucked asunder the fetters of Shí'ih orthodoxy, and which was, with every expansion in the range of its fellowship, to seek and obtain a wider and still more significant recognition of its claims to be the world religion of the future, had been formed and was slowly crystallizing. And, lastly, the seed, endowed by the Hand of Omnipotence with such vast potentialities, though rudely trampled under foot and seemingly perished from the face of the earth, had, through this very process, been vouchsafed the opportunity to germinate and remanifest itself, in the shape of a still more compelling Revelation—a Revelation destined to blossom forth, in a later period, into the flourishing institutions of a world-wide administrative System, and to ripen, in the Golden Age as yet unborn, into mighty agencies functioning in consonance with the principles of a world-unifying, world-redeeming Order.[116]

2.6.9   The Báb's Early Life

The Báb, whose name was Siyyid 'Alí-Muḥammad, was born in the city of Shíráz, on the first day of Muḥarram, in the year AH 1235.[117] He belonged to a house which was renowned for its nobility and traced its origin to Muḥammad Himself. The date of His birth confirmed the truth of the prophecy traditionally attributed to the Imám 'Alí: "I am two years younger than my Lord." Twenty-five years, four months, and four days had elapsed since the day of His birth, when he declared His Mission. In His early childhood He lost His father, Siyyid Muḥammad-Riḍá, a man who was known throughout the province, of Fárs for his piety and virtue, and was held in high esteem and honour. Both His father and His mother were descendants of the Prophet, both were loved and respected by the people. He was reared by His maternal uncle, Ḥájí Mírzá Siyyid 'Alí, a martyr to the Faith, who placed Him, while still a child, under the care of a tutor named Shaykh 'Abid. The Báb, though not inclined to study, submitted to His uncle's will and directions.

Shaykh 'Abid, known by his pupils as Shaykhuná, was a man of piety and learning. He had been a disciple of both Shaykh Aḥmad and Siyyid Kázim.

116. Shoghi Effendi, *Guidance for Today and Tomorrow*, pp. 30-4.
117. October 20, 1819 AD.

"One day," he related, "I asked the Báb to recite the opening words of the Qur'án: 'Bismi'lláhi'r-Raḥmáni'r-Raḥím.'[118] He hesitated, pleading that unless He were told what these words signified, He would in no wise attempt to pronounce them. I pretended not to know their meaning. 'I know what these words signify,' observed my pupil; 'by your leave, I will explain them.' He spoke with such knowledge and fluency that I was struck with amazement. He expounded the meaning of 'Allah', of 'Raḥmán', end 'Raḥím', in terms such as I had neither read nor heard. The sweetness of His utterance still lingers in my memory. I felt impelled to take Him back to His uncle and to deliver into his hands the Trust he had committed to my care. I determined to tell him how unworthy I felt to teach so remarkable a child. I found His uncle alone in his office. 'I have brought Him back to you,' I said, 'and commit Him to your vigilant protection. He is not to be treated as a mere child, for in Him I can already discern evidences of that mysterious power which the Revelation of the Ṣáḥibu'z-Zamán[119] alone can reveal. It is incumbent upon you to surround Him with your most loving care. Keep Him in your house, for He, verily, stands in no need of teachers such as I'. Ḥájí Mírzá Siyyid 'Alí sternly rebuked the Báb. 'Have You forgotten my instructions?' he said. 'Have I not already admonished You to follow the example of Your fellow-pupils, to observe silence, and to listen attentively to every word spoken by Your teacher?' Having obtained His promise to abide faithfully by his instructions, he bade the Báb return to His school. The soul of that child could not, however, be restrained by the stern admonitions of His uncle. No disciple could repress the flow of His intuitive knowledge. Day after day He continued to manifest such remarkable evidences of superhuman wisdom as I am powerless to recount." At last His uncle was induced to take Him away from the school of Shaykh 'Abid', and to associate Him with himself in his own profession. There, too, He revealed signs of a power and greatness that few could approach and none could rival.

Some years later the Báb was united in wedlock with the sister of Mírzá Siyyid Ḥasan and Mírzá Abu'l-Qásim. The child which resulted from this union, He named Aḥmad. He died in the year AH 1259,[120] the year preceding the declaration of the Faith by the Báb.[121]

---

118. In the name of God, the Compassionate, the Merciful.
119. "The Lord of the Age," one of the titles of the Promised Qá'im.
120. 1843 AD.
121. Nabíl-i-A'ẓam, *The Dawn Breakers, pp. 72-6*

2.7
Birth of Bahá'u'lláh

November 12, 1817

This is the Day whereon the All-Merciful hath come down in the clouds of knowledge, clothed with manifest sovereignty.[122]

Suggested Readings:
2.7.1   Prayer Revealed by Bahá'u'lláh
2.7.2   The Ancestory of Bahá'u'lláh
2.7.3   Childhood and Early Life
2.7.4   *The Blessed Perfection*, A Talk by 'Abdul-Bahá
2.7.5   *The Light of Guidance*, A Talk by 'Abdu'l-Bahá
2.7.6   Bahá'u'lláh's Visit to Núr, Mazindaran

---

122. Bahá'u'lláh, *Gleanings from the Writings of Bahá'u'lláh*, no. XVIII, p. 45.

2.7.1 Prayer Revealed by Bahá'u'lláh

Lauded be Thy name, O Lord my God! How great is Thy might and Thy sovereignty; how vast Thy strength and Thy dominion! Thou hast called into being Him Who speaketh in Thy name before all who are in Thy heaven and on Thy earth, and hast bidden Him cry out amongst Thy creatures.

No sooner had a word gone forth from His lips, however, than the divines among Thy people turned back from Him, and the learned among Thy servants cavilled at His signs. Thereby the fire of oppression was kindled in Thy land, until the kings themselves rose up to put out Thy light, O Thou Who art the King of kings!

Hostility waxed so intense that my kindred and my loved ones were made captives in Thy land, and they that are dear to Thee were hindered from gazing on Thy beauty and from turning in the direction of Thy mercy. This hostility failed to cause the fire that burned within them to subside. The enemy finally carried away as captive Him Who is the Manifestation of Thy beauty and the Revealer of Thy signs, and confined Him in the fortress-town of 'Akká, and sought to hinder Him from remembering Thee and from magnifying Thy name. Thy servant, however, could not be restrained from carrying out what Thou hadst bidden Him fulfil. Above the horizon of tribulation He hath lifted up His voice and He crieth out, summoning all the inmates of heaven and all the inhabitants of the earth to the immensity of Thy mercy and the court of Thy grace. Day and night He sendeth down the signs of Thine omnipotent power and revealeth the clear tokens of Thy majesty, so that the souls of Thy creatures may be drawn towards Thee, that they may forsake themselves and turn unto Thee, and may flee from their misery and seek the tabernacle of Thy riches, and may haste away from their wretchedness into the court of Thy majesty and glory.

This is the Lamp which the light of Thine own Essence hath lit, and whose radiance the winds of discord can never extinguish. This is the Ocean that moveth by the power of Thy sovereign might, and whose waves the influence of the infidels that have disbelieved in the Judgment Day can never still. This is the Sun that shineth in the heaven of Thy will and the splendour of which the veils of the workers of iniquity and the doubts of the evil doers can never cloud.

I yield Thee thanks, O my God, for that Thou hast offered me up as a sacrifice in Thy path, and made me a target for the arrows of afflictions as a token of Thy love for Thy servants, and singled me out for all manner of tribulation for the regeneration of Thy people.

How sweet to my taste is the savour of woes sent by Thee, and how dear to my heart the dispositions of Thy providence! Perish the soul that fleeth from the threats of kings in its attempt to save itself in Thy days! I swear by Thy glory! Whoso hath quaffed the living waters of Thy favours can fear no trouble in Thy path, neither can he be deterred by any tribulation from remembering Thee or from celebrating Thy praise.

I beseech Thee, O Thou Who art my Governor and the Possessor of all names, to protect them that have branched out from me (Afnán), whom Thou hast caused to be related to Thyself, and to whom Thou hast, in this Revelation, shown Thy special favour, and whom Thou hast summoned to draw nigh unto Thee and to turn towards the horizon of Thy Revelation. Withhold not from them, O my Lord, the outpourings of Thy mercy or the effulgence of the Day-Star of Thy grace. Enable them to distinguish themselves amongst Thy people, that they may exalt Thy word and promote Thy Cause. Aid them, O my God, to do Thy will and pleasure.

No God is there but Thee, the All-Powerful, the Most Exalted, the Most High.[123]

2.7.2 The Ancestry of Bahá'u'lláh

Bahá'u'lláh was descended from the pre-Islamic monarchs of Írán. He came from a region of the country, bordering on the Caspian Sea and well protected by the high peaks of the Alburz range, whose dwellers, for scores of years after the victory of Arab arms, continued to defy the invader, refusing to accept the new ordering and new Faith. And when they finally bowed to the inevitable, they submitted not to the system accepted by the generality of Muslims and represented by the Caliphate in Baghdád, but to the Shí'ism of the Zaydí variety. In the succeeding centuries there were a number of dynasties and petty kingdoms which held sway and guarded their autonomy in the fastnesses of mountains and in the depths of thick forests by the Caspian Sea. And strangely enough, when Sháh Ismá'íl united all of Írán in allegiance to the apostolic Imáms of the House of the Prophet, Áqá Rustam-i-Rúzafzún, the last of these proud potentates, refused to recognize his authority, and chose to put his trust in Muḥammad Khán-i-Shaybání (also known as Shaybak Khán), the Sunní Uzbak ruler of Transoxania, to overthrow the Ṣafavid upstart. But fate decreed other-

---

123. Bahá'u'lláh, *Prayers and Meditations*, no. XCI, pp. 152-5.

House of Bahá'u'lláh
Ṭihrán, Iran

wise, and it was Shaybak Khán who met defeat and lost his life. Áqá Rustam, it is said, died of fright when a devotee of Sháh Ismá'íl threw the severed hand of the Uzbak ruler onto his lap.

It is to Yazdigird III, the last Sásánian monarch to occupy the throne of Írán, that the genealogy of Bahá'u'lláh can be traced. Ustád Javánmard, the principal of the Zoroastrian school of Yazd, presented seven queries to Bahá'u'lláh, the seventh of which concerned His ancestry. The Tablet known as *Shír-Mard* (Lion of a Man) —thus called because the recipient was so addressed by Bahá'u'lláh— was sent to him in reply. (This Tablet is also known as *Lawḥ-i-Haft-Pursish*.) Answering his questions one by one, to the seventh query Bahá'u'lláh responded by referring him to the genealogy which Mírzá Abu'l-Faḍl-i-Gulpáygání had gathered and compiled. Many years later; in the year AH 1320 (10 April 1902 - 30 March 1903), Áqá Khusraw Bimán, who was also of Zoroastrian origin, was visiting the Holy Land. He asked resident Bahá'ís for information regarding the ancestry of Bahá'u'lláh. They presented his request to 'Abdu'l-Bahá, who also referred them to Mírzá Abu'l-Faḍl-i-Gulpáygání, then visiting the United States. Mírzá Abu'l-Faḍl's answer to Áqá Khusraw Bimán's letter was published in Bombay, at a later date, as a pamphlet.

Mírzá Abu'l-Faḍl, designated by the Guardian of the Bahá'í Faith as one of the nineteen 'apostles of Bahá'u'lláh', was a man of rare erudition and a degree of scholarship so far unequalled amongst the followers of Bahá'u'lláh, whether in the East or in the West. In his reply to Áqá Khusraw Bimán, he describes how his interest was aroused in the genealogy of Bahá'u'lláh, and how his researches led him to Yazdigird III, the last of the Sásánian monarchs of Írán. He goes on to state, however, that his work, which Bahá'u'lláh had mentioned in the Tablet addressed to the schoolmaster of Yazd, was lost when he and a number of other Bahá'ís were arrested in Ṭihrán in the early months of 1883 by the order of Kámrán Mírzá, the Náyibu's-Salṭanih, son of Náṣiri'd-Dín Sháh.

Mírzá Abu'l-Faḍl writes that he was, in the course of his investigation, particularly impressed by the fact that so severe and unsympathetic a critic of the Bahá'í Faith (and so hostile a commentator) as Riḍá-Qulí Khán-i-Hidáyat, entitled the Amíru'sh-Shu'ara' (The Emir of Poets), had admitted in the Nizhád-Námih (The Book of Ancestry), that the Núrís of Mázindarán are descended from Chosroes I, the renowned Sásánian monarch known as 'Ádil (The Just). And final confirmation came from the Ḥájí Mírzá Riḍá-Qulí, a half-brother of Bahá'u'lláh, who told Mírzá Abu'l-Faḍl categorically, in answer to his query, that the Núrís possessed a genealogical table tracing their line back to Yazdigird the

Sásánian.[124]

2.7.3 Childhood and Early Life

Bahá'u'lláh was born and brought up in Ṭihrán, in a house in the district known as Darvázih Shimrán (Shimrán Gate). In those days this district was on the edge of the city, close to the moat which was filled in during the reign of Náṣiri'd-Dín Sháh. Another moat was dug much further away: that too has now disappeared. But the house of Mírzá Buzurg and its adjuncts still stand today.

The infancy of Bahá'u'lláh was a cause of astonishment to His mother, as 'Abdu'l-Bahá recalled one day. He never cried, never showed restlessness. Mírzá Buzurg had come to realize that amongst all his sons and daughters, this son, Mírzá Ḥusayn-'Alí, was one apart. It will be remembered that Tákur, in the district of Núr, was the home of Mírzá Buzurg and his ancestors. There he had built a palatial house, and Bahá'u'lláh always spent part of the year in Tákur, usually in the summer months. Mírzá Buzurg, in his own masterly calligraphic hand, had written the following lines in a prominent place in that mansion:

When thou reaches the threshold of the Beloved say 'Aye',
For there neither 'salám'['Peace'] nor 'alayk'['upon thee'] can find a way.
This is the vale of Love, hold thy steps;
This is holy ground, shed thy foot-gear.

To this day, those lines written by Mírzá Buzurg have endured.

When Bahá'u'lláh was a child of five or six years, He dreamt that He was in a garden where huge birds were flying overhead and attacking Him, but they could not harm Him; then he went to bathe in the sea, and there he was attacked by fishes, but they too could cause Him no injury. Bahá'u'lláh related this strange dream to His father, and Mírzá Buzurg sent for a man who claimed to interpret dreams. After making his calculations, he told Mírzá Buzurg that the expanse of the sea was this world in its entirety, and the birds and fishes were the peoples of the world assailing his Son, because He would promulgate something of vital importance related to the minds of men. But they would be powerless to harm Him, for He would triumph over them all to achieve a momentous matter.

It is related that one day, when Mírzá Ḥusayn-'Alí was seven years old, as He was walking His parents were watching Him, and His mother remarked that

---

124. H. M. Balyuzi, *Bahá'u'lláh: The King of Glory*, pp. 9-11.

He was a little short in stature. His father replied: 'That matters not. Do you not know how intelligent He is and what a wonderful mind He has!'

The education and instruction which Mírzá Ḥusayn-'Alí received was limited both in nature and extent, as He Himself states in the Tablet addressed to Náṣiri'd-Dín Sháh: 'The learning current amongst men I studied not; their schools I entered not. Ask of the city wherein I dwelt, that thou mayest be well assured that I am not of them who speak falsely.'

In those days, the scions of noble houses were taught such matters as befitted their station in life, such as riding, handling a gun, wielding a sword, calligraphy, acquaintance with the works of the great classical poets of the land, a good reading knowledge of the Holy Book, the Qur'án, and hardly ever anything more. They were given such instruction by tutors, specially engaged by the parents, who were also required to teach them good manners.

But as Mírz Ḥusayn-Alí, the son of the Vazír-i-Núrí, grew up the fame of his keen intelligence, His alert mind, His upright character, His benign, compassionate, benevolent nature, spread.

By the time Mírzá Ḥusayn-'Alí was fourteen, His rare understanding, His complete mastery of argument, and His unparalleled powers of exposition were remarked in all circles. Yet He was never assertive nor argumentative; rather, always courteous and patient. Only one thing aroused His ire, and that was any disrespectful reference to the Messengers of God and His Chosen Ones. Even then He would admonish the offender with kindliness and calm.

In a Tablet addressed to a Bahá'í of Shíráz, Bahá'u'lláh Himself tells of an incident in His childhood, when two hugely-turbaned divines were expounding theological questions to ladies in purdah. One such was whether the angel Gabriel had a higher station than Qanbar, the slave of 'Alí (the first Imám), who was greatly devoted to his master. Another concerned the station of 'Abbás, the brother of Ḥusayn (the third Imám), who suffered a martyr's death with the Imám in Karbilá; had he a rank higher than Salmán the Persian (Salmán-i-Fársí), who was one of the companions of the Prophet Muḥammad? Bahá'u'lláh recalls in that Tablet that he was astonished by this line and tone of argument, for if Gabriel, as stated in the holy Book, was the One by Whom the Holy Spirit descended upon the heart of the Apostle of God, then even the master of Qanbar could have no entry to that sphere.

In Yálrúd there lived a mujtahid, Shaykh Muḥammad-Taqí…, well-famed throughout the land. He had a thousand scholars of divinity around him, whom he taught and, from time to time, presented with a complex question to resolve. Whenever He returned to His home in Tákur, Bahá'u'lláh would usually stop for a while in Yálrúd, and here He would visit the mujtahid, who was distantly related to His family. 'Abdu'l-Bahá has described how His own grand-mother, who lived in Yálrúd, went one day at dawn to the house of the mujtahid to pray. After the morning prayer, Shaykh Muḥammad-Taqí told her that he had some excellent news for her. He had had a dream in which he had found himself outside a house which no one was allowed to enter, because, said the door-keeper, within it the Qá'im of the House of Muḥammad was closeted with Mírzá Ḥusayn-'Alí of Núr. At first the mujtahid had expressed his surprise that the son of a vizier should be so privileged; but on remembering their distant kinship, he had ascribed the privilege to this fact.

During a visit to Yálrúd, when Mírzá Ḥusayn-'Alí was sitting in the company of Shaykh Muḥammad-Taqí and other scholars and divines, He was asked to resolve a question they had been unable to answer to the mujtahid's satisfaction The problem was this: an Islamic tradition states that 'Fáṭimih is the best of the women of this world, but for the one born of Mary'. But since Mary had no daughter, what did this conundrum mean? Bahá'u'lláh replied that the initial statement emphasized the impossibility of its alternative, since there could be no other woman comparable to Fáṭimih. It was like saying that a certain mon-arch is the greatest of the kings of this world, except for the one who comes down from Heaven; since no king has or will come down from heaven, the uniqueness of that one monarch is stressed. Bahá'u'lláh's explanation left the great mujtahid silent, but next day he upbraided his disciples for having let him down badly. 'I have taught and trained you for years on end,' he complained, 'but when the need arises, I find you wanting in understanding, whereas an unturbaned youth has brilliantly explained the problem I had presented to you.'

At another time, Shaykh Muḥammad-Taqí had a dream of coming upon a room filled with trunks, which, he was told, belonged to Bahá'u'lláh. On open-ing one of them, he found it packed with books, and all the lines of those books studded with gems, the brilliance of which awakened him, he said.

Mírzá Abu'l-Faḍl-i-Gulpáygání relates in one of his works what he himself heard from a divine. In a gathering where Bahá'u'lláh was present, Mírzá Naẓar'Alí of Qazvín..., the celebrated Súfí murshid who was highly esteemed by Muḥammad Sháh, was holding forth on the station that a human being can attain. Referring to himself, he said, 'Should my servant come to me and say that Jesus the Christ was at the door, asking for me, my detachment is such that I would express no wish to see Him.' Some of those present kept silent, while others out of flattery murmured assent. Only Mírzá Ḥusayn-'Alí spoke up. He turned to the Qazvíní braggart, who had expressed such disrespect for a Manifestation of God, and said: 'You are very close to the person of the sovereign and he is very devoted to you, but if the chief executioner with ten of his men were to come to this door and tell you that the monarch wanted to see you, would you take it calmly or would you be perturbed?' Mírzá Naẓar-'Alí paused for a while before replying, 'In truth, I would feel anxious." 'In that case,' said Bahá'u'lláh, 'you should not make such an assertion.' Bahá'u'lláh's authoritative statement, according to Mírzá Abu'l-Faḍl, left them all speechless.

When Bahá'u'lláh was nearly fifteen years old, His elder sister Sárih Khánum and Mírzá Maḥmúd, the son of Mírzá Ismá'íl-i-Vazír of Yálrúd, were married. This Mírzá Maḥmúd, who never espoused the new Faith, had a younger sister, Ásíyih Khánum: winsome, vivacious and exceedingly beautiful. As soon as she came of age, and Bahá'u'lláh was nearly eighteen, Sárih Khánum requested her father, Mírzá Buzurg, to ask the hand of this sister-in-law for her Brother, Mírzá Ḥusayn-'Alí. Their marriage took place, in Jamádi´yu'l-Ukhrá (Jamádíyu'th-Thání) AH 1251 (about October 1835). Ásíyih Khánum was the mother of 'Abdu'l-Bahá.

Even those who were inimical towards His father, held Bahá'u'lláh in high esteem. One such was the Grand Vizier, Ḥájí Mírzá Áqásí.[125]

2.7.4 *The Blessed Perfection*, A Talk by 'Abdu'l-Bahá

The Blessed Perfection, Bahá'u'lláh, belonged to the nobility of Persia. From earliest childhood He was distinguished among His relatives and friends. They said: "This child has extraordinary power." In wisdom, intelligence and as a source of new knowledge, He was advanced beyond His age and superior to His surroundings. All who knew Him were astonished at his precocity. It was usual for them to say, "Such a child will not live," for it is commonly believed that precocious children do not reach maturity. During the period of youth the Blessed Perfection did not enter school. He was not willing to be taught. This fact is well established among the Persians of Ṭihrán. Nevertheless He was capable of solving the difficult problems of all who came to Him. In whatever meeting, scientific assembly or theological discussion He was found, He became the authority of explanation upon intricate and abstruse questions presented.

Until His father passed away Bahá'u'lláh did not seek position or political

---

125. H. M. Balyuzi, *Bahá'u'lláh: The King of Glory*, pp. 19-23.

station notwithstanding His connection with the government. This occasioned surprise and comment. It was frequently said, "How is it that a young man of such keen intelligence and subtle perception does not seek lucrative appointments? As a matter of fact every position is open to him." This is a historical statement fully attested by the people of Persia.

He was most generous, giving abundantly to the poor. None who came to Him were turned away. The doors of His house were open to all. He always had many guests. This unbounded generosity was conducive to greater astonishment from the fact that He sought neither position nor prominence. In commenting upon this His friends said He would become impoverished, for His expenses were many and His wealth becoming more and more limited. "Why is he not thinking of his own affairs?" they inquired of each other; but some who were wise declared, "This personage is connected with another world; he has something sublime within him that is not evident now; the day is coming when it will be manifested." In truth, the Blessed Perfection was a refuge for every weak one, a shelter for every fearing one, kind to every indigent one, lenient and loving to all creatures.

He became well-known in regard to these qualities before the Báb appeared. Then Bahá'u'lláh declared the Báb's mission to be true and promulgated His teachings. The Báb announced that the greater Manifestation would take place after Him and called the Promised One "Him Whom God would manifest," saying that nine years later the reality of His own mission would become apparent. In His writings He stated that in the ninth year this expected One would be known; in the ninth year they would attain to all glory and felicity; in the ninth year they would advance rapidly. Between Bahá'u'lláh and the Báb there was communication privately. The Báb wrote a letter containing three hundred and sixty derivatives of the root *"Bahá."* The Báb was martyred in Tabríz, and Bahá'u'lláh exiled into 'Iráq in 1852, announced Himself in Baghdad. For the Persian Government had decided that as long as He remained in Persia the peace of the country would be disturbed; therefore He was exiled in the expectation that Persia would become quiet. His banishment, however, produced the opposite effect. New tumult arose and the mention of His greatness and influence spread everywhere throughout the country. The proclamation of His manifestation and mission was made in Baghdad. He called his friends together there and spoke to them of God.

At one point, He left the city and went alone into the mountains of Kurdistán where He made His abode in caves and grottoes. A part of this time He lived in the city of Sulimáníyyih. Two years passed during which neither His friends nor family knew just where He was.

Although Bahá'u'lláh was solitary, secluded and unknown in His retirement, the report spread throughout Kurdistan that this was a most remarkable and learned personage gifted with a wonderful power of attraction. In a short time Kurdistán was magnetized with His love. During this period Bahá'u'lláh lived in poverty. His garments were those of the poor and needy. His food was that of the indigent and lowly. An atmosphere of majesty haloed Him as the sun at midday. Everywhere He was greatly revered and beloved.

After two years He returned to Baghdád. Friends He had known in Sulimáníyyih came to visit Him. They found Him in His accustomed environment of ease and affluence and were astonished at the appointments of One who had lived in seclusion under such frugal conditions in Kurdistán.

The Persian government believed the banishment of the Blessed Perfection from Persia would be the extermination of His Cause in that country. These rulers now realized that it spread more rapidly. His prestige increased; His teachings became more widely circulated. The chiefs of Persia then used their influence to have Bahá'u'lláh exiled from Baghdád. He was summoned to Constantinople by the Turkish authorities. While in Constantinople He ignored every restriction, especially the hostility of ministers of state and clergy. The official representatives of Persia again brought their influence to bear upon the Turkish authorities and succeeded in having Bahá'u'lláh banished from Constantinople to Adrianople, the object being to keep Him as far away as possible from Persia and render His communication with that country more difficult. Nevertheless the Cause still spread and strengthened.

Finally, they consulted together and said: "We have banished Bahá'u'lláh from place to place but each time he is exiled his cause is more widely extended, his proclamation increases in power and day by day his lamp is becoming brighter. This is due to the fact that we have exiled him to large cities and populous centres. Therefore we will send him to a penal colony as a prisoner so that all may know he is the associate of murderers, robbers and criminals; in a short time he and his followers will perish." The Sulṭan of Turkey then banished Him to the prison of 'Akká in Syria.

When Bahá'u'lláh arrived at 'Akká, through the power of God He was able to hoist His banner. His light at first had been a star; now it became a mighty sun and the illumination of His Cause expanded from the East to the West. Inside prison walls He wrote Epistles to all the kings and rulers of nations summoning them to arbitration and universal peace. Some of the kings received His words with disdain and contempt. One of these was the Sultán of the Ottoman kingdom. Napoleon III of France did not reply. A second Epistle was addressed to him. It stated, "I have written you an Epistle before this, summoning you to the Cause of God but you are of the heedless. You have proclaimed that you were the defender of the oppressed; now it hath become evident that you are not. Nor are you kind to your own suffering and oppressed people. Your actions are contrary to your own interests, and your kingly pride must fall. Because of your arrogance God shortly will destroy your sovereignty. France will flee away from you, and you will be overwhelmed by a great conquest. There will be lamentation and mourning, women bemoaning the loss of their sons." This arraignment of Napoleon III was published and spread.

Read it and consider: One prisoner, single and solitary, without assistant or defender, a foreigner and stranger imprisoned in the fortress of 'Akká writing such letters to the Emperor of France and Sultan of Turkey. Reflect upon this how Bahá'u'lláh upraised the standard of His Cause in prison. Refer to history. It is without parallel. No such thing has happened before that time nor since, a prisoner and an exile advancing His Cause and spreading His teachings broadcast so that eventually He became powerful enough to conquer the very king who banished Him.

His Cause spread more and more. The Blessed Perfection was a prisoner twenty-five years. During all this time He was subjected to the indignities and revilement of the people. He was persecuted, mocked and put in chains. In Persia His properties were pillaged and His possessions confiscated. First, banishment from Persia to Baghdád, then to Constantinople; then Adrianople; finally from Rumelia to the prison fortress of 'Akká.

During His lifetime He was intensely active. His energy was unlimited. Scarcely one night was passed in restful sleep. He bore these ordeals, suffered these calamities and difficulties in order that a manifestation of selflessness and service might become apparent in the world of humanity; that the Most Great Peace should become a reality; that human souls might appear as the angels of heaven; that heavenly miracles would be wrought among men; that human faith should be strengthened and perfected; that the precious, priceless bestowal of God—the human mind—might be developed to its fullest capacity in the temple of the body; and that man become the reflection and likeness of God, even as it hath been revealed in the Bible, "Let us make man in our image."

Briefly, the Blessed Perfection bore all these ordeals and calamities in order that our hearts might become enkindled and radiant, our spirits be glorified, our faults become virtues, our ignorance transformed into knowledge; in order that we might attain the real fruits of humanity and acquire heavenly graces; in order that, although pilgrims upon earth, we should travel the road of the heavenly kingdom, and, although needy and poor, we might receive the treasures of eternal life. For this has He borne these difficulties and sorrows.

Trust all to God. The lights of God are resplendent. The blessed Epistles are spreading. The blessed teachings are promulgated throughout the East and West. Soon you will see that the heavenly Words have established the oneness of the world of humanity. The banner of the Most Great Peace has been unfurled, and the great community is appearing. [126]

2.7.5 *The Light of Guidance*, A Talk by 'Abdu'l-Bahá

He brought the light of guidance to the world; He kindled the fire of love and revealed the great reality of the True Beloved...

...His mission was to change ignorant fanaticism into Universal love, to establish in the minds of His followers the basis of the unity of humanity and to bring about in practice the equality of mankind...

Yet the whole of Bahá'u'lláh's life was spent in the midst of great trial and cruel tyranny. In Persia He was thrown into prison, put into chains, and lived constantly under the menace of the sword. He was scorned and scourged.[127]

• • •

As the East and the West are illumined by one sun, so all races, nations, and creeds shall be seen as the servants of the One God. The whole earth is one home, and all peoples, did they but know it, are bathed in the oneness of God's mercy. God created all. He gives sustenance to all. He guides and trains all under the shadow of His bounty. We must follow the example God Himself gives us, and do away with all disputations and quarrels.

...In the future untrue reports will be spread regarding Bahá'u'lláh in order to hinder the spread of Truth. I tell you this, that you may be awake and prepared.

I leave you with prayer that all the beauty of the Kingdom may be yours. In deep regret at our separation, I bid you good-bye. [128]

---

126. 'Abdu'l-Bahá, *Promulgation of Universal Peace*, pp. 25-29.

127. 'Abdu'l-Bahá, *'Abdu'l-Bahá in London*, pp. 37.

128. Ibid., pp. 38-9.

2.7.6   Bahá'u'lláh's Visit to Núr, Mázindarán

Bahá'u'lláh's visit to Núr had produced the most far-reaching results, and had lent a remarkable impetus to the spread of the new-born Revelation. By His magnetic eloquence, by the purity of His life, by the dignity of His bearing, by the unanswerable logic of His argument, and by the many evidences of His loving-kindness, Bahá'u'lláh had won the hearts of the people of Núr, had stirred their souls, and had enrolled them under the standard of the Faith. Such was the effect of His words and deeds, as He went about preaching the Cause and revealing its glory to His countrymen in Núr, that the very stones and trees of that district seemed to have been quickened by the waves of spiritual power which emanated from His person. All things seemed to be endowed with a new and more abundant life, all things seemed to be proclaiming aloud: "Behold, the Beauty of God has been made manifest! Arise, for He has come in all His glory." The people of Núr, when Bahá'u'lláh had departed from out their midst, continued to propagate the Cause and to consolidate its foundations. A number of them endured the severest afflictions for His sake; others quaffed with gladness the cup of martyrdom in His path. Mázindarán in general, and Núr in particular, were thus distinguished from the other provinces and districts of Persia, as being the first to have eagerly embraced the Divine Message. The district of Núr, literally meaning "light," which lay embedded within the mountains of Mázindarán, was the first to catch the rays of the Sun that had arisen in Shíráz, the first to proclaim to the rest of Persia, which still lay enveloped in the shadow of the vale of heedlessness, that the Day-Star of heavenly guidance had at length arisen to warm and illuminate the whole land.

When Bahá'u'lláh was still a child, the Vazír, His father, dreamed a dream. Bahá'u'lláh appeared to him swimming in a vast, limitless ocean. His body shone upon the waters with a radiance that illumined the sea. Around His head, which could distinctly be seen above the waters, there radiated, in all directions, His long, jet-black locks, floating in great profusion above the waves. As he dreamed, a multitude of fishes gathered round Him, each holding fast to the extremity of one hair. Fascinated by the effulgence of His face, they followed Him in whatever direction He swam. Great as was their number, and however firmly they clung to His locks, not one single hair seemed to have been detached from His head, nor did the least injury affect His person. Free and unrestrained, He moved above the waters and they all followed Him.

The Vazír, greatly impressed by this dream, summoned a soothsayer, who had achieved fame in that region, and asked him to interpret it for him. This man, as if inspired by a premonition of the future glory of Bahá'u'lláh, declared: "The limitless ocean that you have seen in your dream, O Vazír, is none other than the world of being. Single-handed and alone, your son will achieve supreme ascendancy over it. Wherever He may please, He will proceed unhindered. No one will resist His march, no one will hinder His progress. The multitude of fishes signifies the turmoil which He will arouse amidst the peoples and kindreds of the earth. Around Him will they gather, and to Him will they cling. Assured of the unfailing protection of the Almighty, this tumult will never harm His person, nor will His loneliness upon the sea of life endanger His safety."

That soothsayer was subsequently taken to see Bahá'u'lláh. He looked intently upon His face, and examined carefully His features. He was charmed by His appearance, and extolled every trait of His countenance. Every expression in that face revealed to his eyes a sign of His concealed glory. So great was his admiration, and so profuse his praise of Bahá'u'lláh, that the Vazír, from that day, became even more passionately devoted to his son. The words spoken by that soothsayer served to fortify his hopes and confidence in Him. Like Jacob, he desired only to ensure the welfare of his beloved Joseph, and to surround Him with his loving protection. [129]

---

129. Nabíl-i-A'ẓam, *The Dawn Breakers,* pp. 118-20.

PART THREE

Suggested Readings for Celebration or
Commemoration of Bahá'í Holy Days and
Anniversaries on Which Suspension of Work is
not Obligatory

Bahá'í Holy Days and Anniversaries on Which Suspension of Work is not Obligatory

3.1
Ascension of 'Abdu'l-Bahá

November 28, 1921

. . . I am with you always, whether living or dead, I am with you to the end.
130

Suggested Readings:

3.1.1   Excerpts from the Writings of Bahá'u'lláh
3.1.2   Excerpts from the Writings of 'Abdu'l-Bahá
3.1.3   Excerpts from the Will and Testament of 'Abdu'l-Bahá
3.1.4   *His Last Wish,* from the Writings of 'Abdu'l-Bahá
3.1.5   A Survey of the Outstanding Features of the Ministry of
        'Abdu'l-Bahá
3.1.6   Station of 'Abdu'l-Bahá
3.1.7   The Passing of 'Abdul-Bahá
3.1.8   Prayer of Visitation of 'Abdu'l-Bahá
3.1.9   Prayer of Shoghi Effendi,

---

130. `Abdu'l-Bahá, quoted in *Star of the West*, vol. XII, no. 16, p. 250.

3.1.1 Excerpts from the Writings of Bahá'u'lláh

O thou Who art the apple of Mine eye! My glory, the ocean of My loving-kindness, the sun of My bounty, the heaven of My mercy rest upon Thee. We pray God to illumine the world through Thy knowledge and wisdom, to ordain for Thee that which will gladden Thine heart and impart consolation to Thine eyes. [131]

• • •

We have made Thee a shelter for all mankind, a shield unto all who are in heaven and on earth, a stronghold for whosoever hath believed in God, the Incomparable, the All-knowing. God grant that through Thee He may protect them, may enrich and sustain them, that He may inspire Thee with that which shall be a wellspring of wealth unto all created things, an ocean of bounty unto all men, and the dayspring of mercy unto all peoples. [132]

• • •

O Thou My Greatest Branch!... Verily, We have ordained Thee the Guardian of all the creatures, and a Protection to all those in the heavens and earths, and a Fortress to those who believe in God, the One, the Omniscient!...

I beg of Him to water the earth and all that is in it by Thee.... [133]

• • •

All the atoms of the earth have announced unto all created things that from behind the gate of the Prison- city there hath appeared and above its horizon there hath shone forth the Orb of the beauty of the great, the Most Mighty Branch of God—His ancient and immutable Mystery—proceeding on its way to another land. Sorrow, thereby, hath enveloped this Prison-city, whilst another land rejoiceth ...

Blessed, doubly blessed, is the ground which His footsteps have trodden, the eye that hath been cheered by the beauty of His countenance, the ear that hath been honoured by hearkening to His call, the heart that hath tasted the sweetness of His love, the breast that hath dilated through His remembrance' the pen that hath voiced His praise, the scroll that hath borne the testimony of His writings.[134]

---

131. Bahá'u'lláh, quoted by Shoghi Effendi in *World Order of Bahá'u'lláh*, p. 135.

132. Ibid., p. 135.

133. Bahá'u'lláh, quoted in *Star of the West*, vol. IV, no. 14, p. 239.

134. Bahá'u'lláh, *Tablets of Bahá'u'lláh*, pp. 227-8.

3.1.2 Excerpts from the Writings of 'Abdu'l-Bahá

The Blessed Beauty is the Sun of Truth, and His light the light of truth. The Báb is likewise the Sun of Truth, and His light the light of truth … My station is the station of servitude—a servitude which is complete, pure and real, firmly established, enduring, obvious, explicitly revealed and subject to no interpretation whatever … I am the Interpreter of the Word of God; such is my interpretation. [135]

• • •

I affirm that the true meaning, the real significance, the innermost secret of these verses, of these very words, is my own servitude to the sacred Threshold of the Abhá Beauty, my complete self-effacement, my utter nothingness before Him. This is my resplendent crown, my most precious adorning. On this I pride myself in the kingdom of earth and heaven. Therein I glory among the company of the well-favoured!

No one is permitted to give these verses any other interpretation. I am according to the explicit texts of the *Kitáb-i-Aqdas* and the *Kitáb-i-'Ahd* the manifest Interpreter of the Word of God … Whoso deviates from my interpretation is a victim of his own fancy. [136]

• • •

But if any soul asks concerning the station of the servant the answer is— 'Abdu'l-Bahá. If he inquires after the meaning of The Branch, the answer is— 'Abdu'l-Bahá. If he desires to know the significance of the verse regarding The Branch, the answer is—'Abdu'l-Bahá. If he insists upon the explanation of the meaning of the "Branch extended from the Ancient Root", the answer is— 'Abdu'l-Bahá. [137]

• • •

My name is 'Abdu'l-Bahá. My qualification is 'Abdu'l-Bahá. My reality is 'Abdu'l-Bahá. My praise is 'Abdu'l-Bahá. Thraldom to the Blessed Perfection is my glorious and refulgent diadem, and servitude to all human race my perpetual religion…. No name, no title, no mention, no commendation have I, nor will ever have, except 'Abdu'l-Bahá. This is my longing. This is my greatest yearning. This is my eternal life. This is my everlasting glory. [138]

---

135. 'Abdu'l-Bahá, quoted by Shoghi Effendi in *World Order of Bahá'u'lláh*, p. 133.

136. Ibid., p. 138.

137. 'Abdu'l-Bahá, quoted in *Star of the West*, Vol. VIII, no. 14, p. 186.

138. 'Abdu'l-Baha, quoted by Shoghi Effendi in *World Order of Bahá'u'lláh*, p. 139.

3.1.3   Excerpts from *The Will and Testament of 'Abdu'l-Bahá*

O ye that stand fast in the Covenant! When the hour cometh that this wronged and broken-winged bird will have taken its flight into the Celestial Concourse, when it will have hastened to the Realm of the Unseen and its mortal frame will have been either lost or hidden neath the dust, it is incumbent upon the Afnán, that are steadfast in the Covenant of God and have branched from the Tree of Holiness; the Hands, (pillars) of the Cause of God (the glory of the Lord rest upon them), and all the friends and loved ones, one and all to bestir themselves and arise with heart and soul and in one accord, to diffuse the sweet savours of God, to teach His Cause and to promote His Faith. It behooveth them not to rest for a moment, neither to seek repose. They must disperse themselves in every land, pass by every clime, and travel throughout all regions. Bestirred without rest and steadfast to the end they must raise in every land the triumphal cry "Yá Bahá'u'l-Abhá!" (O Thou the Glory of Glories!), must achieve renown in the world wherever they go, must burn brightly even as a candle in every meeting and must kindle the flame of Divine love in every assembly; that the light of truth may rise resplendent in the midmost heart of the world, that throughout the East and throughout the West a vast concourse may gather under the shadow of the Word of God, that the sweet savours of holiness may be diffused, that faces may shine radiantly, hearts be filled with the Divine spirit and souls be made heavenly.

In these days, the most important of all things is the guidance of the nations and peoples of the world. Teaching the Cause is of utmost importance for it is the head corner-stone of the foundation itself. This wronged servant has spent his days and nights in promoting the Cause and urging the peoples to service. He rested not a moment, till the fame of the Cause of God was noised abroad in the world and the celestial strains from the Abhá Kingdom roused the East and the West. The beloved of God must also follow the same example. This is the secret of faithfulness, this is the requirement of servitude to the Threshold of Bahá!

The disciples of Christ forgot themselves and all earthly things forsook all their cares and belongings, purged themselves of self and passion, and with absolute detachment scattered far and wide and engaged in calling the peoples of the world to the Divine Guidance, till at last they made the world another world, illumined the surface of the earth and even to their last hour proved self-sacrificing in the pathway of that Beloved One of God. Finally in various lands they suffered glorious martyrdom. Let them that are men of action follow in their footsteps!

O my loving friends! After the passing away of this wronged one, it is incumbent upon the Aghṣán (Branches), the Afnán (Twigs) of the Sacred Lote-Tree, the Hands (pillars) of the Cause of God and the loved ones of the Abhá Beauty to turn unto Shoghi Effendi—the youthful branch branched from the two hallowed and sacred Lote-Trees and the fruit grown from the union of the two offshoots of the Tree of Holiness,—as he is the sign of God, the chosen branch, the Guardian of the Cause of God, he unto whom all the Aghṣán, the Afnán, the Hands of the Cause of God and His loved ones must turn. He is the Interpreter of the Word of God and after him will succeed the first-born of his lineal descendants.

The sacred and youthful branch, the Guardian of the Cause of God as well as the Universal House of Justice, to be universally elected and established, are both under the care and protection of the Abhá Beauty, under the shelter and unerring guidance of the Exalted One (may my life be offered up for them both). Who ever they decide is of God. Whoso obeyeth him not, neither obeyeth them, hath not obeyed God; whoso rebelleth against him and against them hath rebelled against God, whoso opposeth him hath opposed God; whoso contendeth with them hath contended with God; whoso disputeth with him hath disputed with God; whoso denieth him hath denied God; whoso disbelieveth in him hath disbelieved in God; whoso deviateth, separateth himself and turneth aside from him hath in truth deviated, separated himself and turned aside from God. May the wrath, the fierce indignation, the vengeance of God rest upon him! The mighty stronghold shall remain impregnable and safe through obedience to him who is the gurdian of the Cause of God. It is incumbent upon the members of the House of Justice, upon all the Aghṣán, the Afnán, the Hands of the Cause of God to show their obedience, submissiveness and subordination unto the Guardian of the Cause of God, to turn unto him and be lowly before him. He that opposeth him hath opposed the True One, will make a breach in the Cause of God, will subvert His Word and will become a manifestation of the Centre of Sedition. Beware, beware, lest the days after the ascension (of Bahá'u'lláh) be repeated when the Centre of Sedition waxed haughty and rebellious and with Divine Unity for his excuse deprived himself and perturbed and poisoned others. No doubt every vain-glorious one that purposeth dissension and discord will not openly declare his evil purposes, nay rather, even as impure gold, will he seize upon divers measures and various pretexts that he may separate the gathering of the people of Bahá. My object is to show that the Hands of the Cause of God must be ever watchful and so soon as they find anyone beginning to oppose and protest against the Guardian of the Cause of God, cast him out from the congregation of the people of Bahá and in no wise accept any excuse from him. How often hath grievous error been disguised in the garb of truth, that it might sow the seeds of doubt in the hearts of men! [139]

• • •

And now, concerning the House of Justice which God hath ordained as the source of all good and freed from all error, it must be elected by universal suffrage, that is, by the believers. Its members must be manifestations of the fear of God and daysprings of knowledge and understanding, must be steadfast in God's faith and the well-wishers of all mankind. By this House is meant the Universal House of Justice, that is, in all countries a secondary House of Justice must be instituted, and these secondary Houses of Justice must elect the members of the Universal one. Unto this body all things must be referred. It enacteth all ordinances and regulations that are not to be found in the explicit Holy Text. By this body all the difficult problems are to be resolved and the Guardian of the Cause of God is its sacred head and the distinguished member for life of that body. Should he not attend in person its deliberations, he must appoint one to represent him. Should any of the members commit a sin, injurious to the common weal, the Guardian of the Cause of God hath at his own discretion the right to expel him, whereupon the people must elect another one in his stead. This House of Justice enacteth the laws and the government enforceth them. The legislative body must reinforce the executive, the executive must aid and assist the legislative body so that through the close union and harmony of these two forces, the foundation of fairness and justice may become firm and strong, that all the regions of the world may become even as Paradise itself.[140]

• • •

O dearly beloved friends! I am now in very great danger and the hope of even an hour's life is lost to me. I am thus constrained to write these lines for the protection of the Cause of God, the preservation of His Law, the safeguarding of His Word and the safety of His Teachings. By the Ancient Beauty! This

---

139. `Abdu'l-Bahá, *Will and Testament of `Abdu'l-Bahá*, pp. 10-12.
140. Ibid., pp. 14-15.

wronged one hath in no wise borne nor doth he bear a grudge against any one; towards none doth he entertain any ill-feeling and uttereth no word save for the good of the world. My supreme obligation, however, of necessity, prompteth me to guard and preserve the Cause of God. Thus, with the greatest regret, I counsel you saying: Guard ye the Cause of God, protect His law and have the utmost fear of discord. This is the foundation of the belief of the people of Bahá (may my life be offered up for them): "His Holiness, the Exalted One (the Báb), is the Manifestation of the Unity and Oneness of God and the Forerunner of the Ancient Beauty. His Holiness the Abhá Beauty (may my life be a sacrifice for His steadfast friends) is the Supreme Manifestation of God and the Dayspring of His Most Divine Essence. All others are servants unto Him and do His bidding." Unto the Most Holy Book every one must turn and all that is not expressly recorded therein must be referred to the Universal House of Justice. That which this body, whether unanimously or by a majority doth carry, that is verily the truth and the purpose of God Himself. Whoso doth deviate therefrom is verily of them that love discord, hath shown forth malice, and turned away from the Lord of the Covenant. By this House is meant that Universal House of Justice which is to be elected from all countries, that is from those parts in the East and West where the loved ones are to be found, after the manner of the customary elections in Western countries such as those of England.

It is incumbent upon these members (of the Universal House of Justice) to gather in a certain place and deliberate upon all problems which have caused difference, questions that are obscure and matters that are not expressly recorded in the Book. Whatsoever they decide has the same effect as the Text itself. Inasmuch as the House of Justice hath power to enact laws that are not expressly recorded in the Book and bear upon daily transactions, so also it hath power to repeal the same. Thus for example, the House of Justice enacteth today a certain law and enforceth it, and a hundred years hence, circumstances having profoundly changed and the conditions having altered, another House of Justice will then have power, according to the exigencies of the time, to alter that law. This it can do because that law formeth no part of the divine explicit Text. The House of Justice is both the initiator and the abrogator of its own laws. [141]

---

141. `Abdu'l-Bahá, *Will and Testament of `Abdu'l-Bahá*, pp. 19-20.

3.1.4 *His Last Wish*, from the Writings of 'Abdu'l-Bahá

O ye beloved of God, these are days for steadfastness, for firmness and perseverance in the Cause of God. Ye must not focus your attention upon the person of 'Abdu'l-Bahá, for ere long he will bid you farewell. Rather must ye fix your gaze upon the Word of God. If the Word of God is being promoted, rejoice and be happy and thankful, though 'Abdu'l-Bahá himself be threatened by the sword or burdened by the weight of chains and fetters. For the Holy Temple of the Cause of God is important, not the physical body of 'Abdu'l-Bahá. The friends of God must arise with such steadfastness that if, at any moment, a hundred souls like 'Abdu'l-Bahá become the target for the arrows of affliction, they will not shift or waver in their resolve, their determination, their enkindlement, their devotion and service in the Cause of God. 'Abdu'l-Bahá is himself a servant at the Threshold of the Blessed Beauty and a manifestation of pure and utter servitude at the Threshold of the Almighty. He hath no other station or tide, no other rank or power. This is my ultimate Purpose, my eternal Paradise, my holiest Temple and my Sadratu'l-Muntahá. With the Abhá Blessed Beauty and the Exalted One, His Herald—may my life be a sacrifice for Them both—hath ended the appearance of God's independent and universal Manifestation. And for a thousand years all shall be illumined by His lights and be sustained by the ocean of His favours.

O ye lovers of God! This, verily, is my last wish and my admonition unto you. Blessed, therefore, is he who is aided by God to follow that which is inscribed upon this scroll whose words are sanctified from the symbols current amongst men. [142]

3.1.5 A Survey of the Outstanding Features of the Ministry of 'Abdu'l-Bahá

Thus was brought to a close the ministry of One Who was the incarnation, by virtue of the rank bestowed upon Him by His Father, of an institution that has no parallel in the entire field of religious history, a ministry that marks the final stage in the Apostolic, the Heroic and most glorious Age of the Dispensation of Bahá'u'lláh. Through Him the Covenant, that "excellent and priceless Heritage" bequeathed by the Author of the Bahá'í Revelation, had been proclaimed, championed and vindicated. Through the power which that Divine

---

142. 'Abdu'-Bahá, *Selections from the Writings of 'Abdu'l-Bahá*, pp. 294-5.

Instrument had conferred upon Him the light of God's infant Faith had penetrated the West, had diffused itself as far as the Islands of the Pacific, and illumined the fringes of the Australian continent. Through His personal intervention the Message, Whose Bearer had tasted the bitterness of a life-long captivity, had been noised abroad, and its character and purpose disclosed, for the first time in its history, before enthusiastic and representative audiences in the chief cities of Europe and of the North American continent. Through His unrelaxing vigilance the holy remains of the Bab, brought forth at long last from their fifty-year concealment, had been safely transported to the Holy Land and permanently and befittingly enshrined in the very spot which Bahá'u'lláh Himself had designated for them and had blessed with His presence. Through His bold initiative the first Mashriqu'l-Adhkár of the Bahá'í world had been reared in Central Asia, in Russian Turkistan, whilst through His unfailing encouragement a similar enterprise, of still vaster proportions, had been undertaken, and its land dedicated by Himself in the heart of the North American continent. Through the sustaining grace overshadowing Him since the inception of His ministry His royal adversary had been humbled to the dust, the arch-breaker of His Father's Covenant had been utterly routed, and the danger which, ever since Bahá'u'lláh had been banished to Turkish soil, had been threatening the heart of the Faith, definitely removed. In pursuance of His instructions, and in conformity with the principles enunciated and the laws ordained by His Father, the rudimentary institutions, heralding the formal inauguration of the Administrative Order to be founded after His passing, had taken shape and been established. Through His unremitting labours, as reflected in the treatises He composed, the thousands of Tablets He revealed, the discourses He delivered, the prayers, poems and commentaries He left to posterity, mostly in Persian, some in Arabic and a few in Turkish, the laws and principles, constituting the warp and woof of His Father's Revelation, had been elucidated, its fundamentals restated and interpreted, its tenets given detailed application and the validity and indispensability of its verities fully and publicly demonstrated. Through the warnings He sounded, an unheeding humanity, steeped in materialism and forgetful of its God, had been apprized of the perils threatening to disrupt its ordered life, and made, in consequence of its persistent perversity, to sustain the initial shocks of that world upheaval which continues, until the present day, to rock the foundations of human society. And lastly, through the mandate He had issued to a valiant community, the concerted achievements of whose members had shed so great a lustre on the annals of His own ministry, He had set in motion a Plan which, soon after its formal inauguration, achieved the opening of the Australian continent, which, in a later period, was to be instrumental in winning over the heart of a royal convert to His Father's Cause, and which, today, through the irresistible unfoldment of its potentialities, is so marvellously quickening the spiritual life of all the Republics of Latin America as to constitute a befitting conclusion to the records of an entire century.

Nor should a survey of the outstanding features of so blessed and fruitful a ministry omit mention of the prophecies which the unerring pen of the appointed Centre of Bahá'u'lláh's Covenant has recorded. These foreshadow the fierceness of the onslaught that the resistless march of the Faith must provoke in the West, in India and in the Far East when it meets the time-honoured sacerdotal orders of the Christian, the Buddhist and Hindu religions. They foreshadow the turmoil which its emancipation from the fetters of religious orthodoxy will cast in the American, the European, the Asiatic and African continents. They foreshadow the gathering of the children of Israel in their ancient homeland; the erection of the banner of Bahá'u'lláh in the Egyptian citadel of Sunní Islam; the extinction of the powerful influence wielded by the Shí'ah ecclesiastics in Persia; the load of misery which must needs oppress the pitiful remnants of the breakers of Bahá'u'lláh's Covenant at the world centre of His Faith; the splendour of the institutions which that triumphant Faith must erect on the slopes of a mountain, destined to be so linked with the city of 'Akká that a single grand metropolis will be formed to enshrine the spiritual as well as the administrative seats of the future Bahá'í Commonwealth; the conspicuous honour which the inhabitants of Bahá'u'lláh's native land in general, and its government in particular, must enjoy in a distant future; the unique and enviable position which the community of the Most Great Name in the North American continent must occupy, as a direct consequence of the execution of the world mission which He entrusted to them: finally they foreshadow, as the sum and summit of all, the "hoisting of the standard of God among all nations" and the unification of the entire human race, when "all men will adhere to one religion ... will be blended into one race, and become a single people."

Nor can the revolutionary changes in the great world which that ministry has witnessed be allowed to pass unnoticed—most of them flowing directly from the warnings which were uttered by the Báb, in the first chapter of His *Qayyúmu'l-Asmá'*, on the very night of the Declaration of His Mission in Shíraz, and which were later reinforced by the pregnant passages addressed by Bahá'u'lláh to the kings of the earth and the world's religious leaders, in both the *Súriy-i-Múlúk* and the *Kitáb-i-Aqdas*. The conversion of the Portuguese monarchy and the Chinese empire into republics; the collapse of the Russian, the German and Austrian empires, and the ignominious fate which befell their rulers; the assassination of Náṣiri'd-Dín Sháh, the fall of Sulṭán 'Abdu'l-Ḥamíd—these may be said to have marked further stages in the operation of that catastrophic process the inception of which was signalized in the lifetime of Bahá'u'lláh by the murder of Sulṭán 'Abdu'l-'Azíz, by the dramatic downfall of Napoleon III, and the extinction of the Third Empire, and by the self-imposed imprisonment and virtual termination of the temporal sovereignty of the Pope himself. Later, after 'Abdu'l-Bahá's passing, the same process was to be accelerated by the demise of the Qájár dynasty in Persia, by the overthrow of the Spanish monarchy, by the collapse of both the Sulṭanate and the Caliphate in Turkey, by a swift decline in the fortunes of Shí'ah Islám and of the Christian Missions in the East, and by the cruel fate that is now overtaking so many of the crowned heads of Europe.

Nor can this subject be dismissed without special reference to the names of those men of eminence and learning who were moved, at various stages of 'Abdu'l-Bahá's ministry, to pay tribute not only to 'Abdu'l-Bahá Himself but also to the Faith of Bahá'u'lláh. Such names as Count Leo Tolstoy, Prof. Arminius Vambery, Prof. Auguste Forel, Dr. David Starr Jordan, the Venerable Archdeacon Wilberforce, Prof Jowett of Balliol, Dr. T. K. Cheyne, Dr. Estlin Carpenter of Oxford University, Viscount Samuel of Carmel, Lord Lamington, Sir Valentine Chirol, Rabbi Stephen Wise, Prince Muḥammad-'Alí of Egypt, Shaykh Muḥammad 'Abdu, Midḥat Páshá, and Khurshíd Páshá attest, by virtue of the tributes associated with them, the great progress made by the Faith of Bahá'u'lláh under the brilliant leadership of His exalted Son—tributes whose impressiveness was, in later years, to be heightened by the historic, the repeated and written testimonies which a famous Queen, a grand-daughter of Queen Victoria, was impelled to bequeath to posterity as a witness of her recognition of the prophetic mission of Bahá'u'lláh.[143]

---

143. Shoghi Effendi, *God Passes By*, pp. 314-7.

House of 'Abdu'l-Bahá in Haifa

3.1.6   Station of 'Abdu'l-Bahá

An attempt I strongly feel should now be made to clarify our minds regarding the station occupied by 'Abdu'l-Bahá and the significance of His position in this holy Dispensation. It would be indeed difficult for us, who stand so close to such a tremendous figure and are drawn by the mysterious power of so magnetic a personality, to obtain a clear and exact understanding of the role and character of One Who, not only in the Dispensation of Bahá'u'lláh but in the entire field of religious history, fulfils a unique function. Though moving in a sphere of His own and holding a rank radically different from that of the Author and the Forerunner of the Bahá'í Revelation, He, by virtue of the station ordained for Him through the Covenant of Bahá'u'lláh, forms together with them what may be termed the Three Central Figures of a Faith that stands unapproached in the world's spiritual history. He towers, in conjunction with them, above the destinies of this infant Faith of God from a level to which no individual or body ministering to its needs after Him, and for no less a period than a full thousand years, can ever hope to rise. To degrade His lofty rank by identifying His station with or by regarding it as roughly equivalent to, the position of those on whom the mantle of His authority has fallen would be an act of impiety as grave as the no less heretical belief that inclines to exalt Him to a state of absolute equality with either the central Figure or Forerunner of our Faith. For wide as is the gulf that separates 'Abdu'l-Bahá from Him Who is the Source of an independent Revelation, it can never be regarded as commensurate with the greater distance that stands between Him Who is the Centre of the Covenant and His ministers who are to carry on His work, whatever be their name, their rank, their functions or their future achievements. Let those who have known 'Abdu'l-Bahá, who through their contact with His magnetic personality have come to cherish for Him so fervent an admiration, reflect, in the light of this statement, on the greatness of One Who is so far above Him in station.

That 'Abdu'l-Bahá is not a Manifestation of God, that, though the successor of His Father, He does not occupy a cognate station, that no one else except the Báb and Bahá'u'lláh can ever lay claim to such a station before the expiration of a full thousand years—are verities which lie embedded in the specific utterances of both the Founder of our Faith and the Interpreter of His teachings.

"Whoso layeth claim to a Revelation direct from God," is the express warning uttered in the *Kitáb-i-Aqdas*, *"ere the expiration of a full thousand years, such a man is assuredly a lying imposter. We pray God that He may graciously assist him to retract and*

187

repudiate such claim. Should he repent, God will no doubt forgive him. If, however, he persists in his error, God will assuredly send down one who will deal mercilessly with him. Terrible indeed is God in punishing!" "*Whosoever,*" He adds as a further emphasis, *"interpreteth this verse otherwise than its obvious meaning is deprived of the Spirit of God and of His mercy which encompasseth all created things."* "*Should a man appear,*" is yet another conclusive statement, *"ere the lapse of a full thousand years—each year consisting of twelve months according to the Qur'án, and of nineteen months of nineteen days each, according to the Bayán—and if such a man reveal to your eyes all the signs of God, unhesitatingly reject him!"*

'Abdu'l-Bahá's own statements, in confirmation of this warning, are no less emphatic and binding: *"This is,"* He declares, *"my firm, my unshakeable conviction, the essence of my unconcealed and explicit belief—a conviction and belief which the denizens of the Abhá Kingdom fully share: The Blessed Beauty is the Sun of Truth, and His light the light of truth. The Báb is likewise the Sun of Truth, and His light the light of truth... . My station is the station of servitude—a servitude which is complete, pure and real, firmly established, enduring, obvious, explicitly revealed and subject to no interpretation whatever... . I am the Interpreter of the Word of God; such is my interpretation."*

Does not 'Abdu'l-Bahá in His own Will—in a tone and language that might well confound the most inveterate among the breakers of His Father's Covenant— rob of their chief weapon those who so long and so persistently had striven to impute to Him the charge of having tacitly claimed a station equal, if not superior to that of Bahá'u'lláh? *"The foundation of the belief of the people of Bahá' is this,"* thus proclaims one of the weightiest passages of that last document left to voice in perpetuity the directions and wishes of a departed Master, *"His Holiness the Exalted One (the Báb) is the Manifestation of the unity and oneness of God and the Forerunner of the Ancient Beauty. His Holiness the Abhá' Beauty (Bahá'u'lláh) (may my life be a sacrifice for His steadfast friends) is the supreme Manifestation of God and the Day-Spring of His most divine Essence. All others are servants unto Him and do His bidding."*

From such clear and formally laid down statements, incompatible as they are with any assertion of a claim to Prophethood, we should not by any means infer that 'Abdu'l-Bahá is merely one of the servants of the Blessed Beauty, or at best one whose function is to be confined to that of an authorized interpreter of His Father's teachings. Far be it from me to entertain such a notion or to wish to instil such sentiments. To regard Him in such a light is a manifest betrayal of the priceless heritage bequeathed by Bahá'u'lláh to mankind. Immeasurably exalted is the station conferred upon Him by the supreme Pen above and beyond the implications of these, His own written statements Whether in the *Kitáb-i-Aqdas*, the most weighty and sacred of all the works of Bahá'u'lláh, or in the *Kitáb-i-'Ahd*, the *Book of His Covenant*, or in the *Súriy-i-Ghuṣn* (*Tablet of the Branch*), such references as have been recorded by the pen of Bahá'u'lláh— references which the Tablets of His Father addressed to Him mightily reinforce—invest 'Abdu'l-Bahá with a power, and surround Him with a halo, which the present generation can never adequately appreciate.

He is, and should for all time be regarded, first and foremost, as the Centre and Pivot of Bahá'u'lláh's peerless and all-enfolding Covenant, His most exalted handiwork, the stainless Mirror of His light, the perfect Exemplar of His teachings, the unerring Interpreter of His Word, the embodiment of every Bahá'í ideal, the incarnation of every Bahá'í virtue, the Most Mighty Branch sprung from the Ancient Root, the Limb of the Law of God, the Being *"round Whom all names revolve,"* the Mainspring of the Oneness of Humanity, the Ensign of the Most Great Peace, the Moon of the Central Orb of this most holy Dispensation—styles and titles that are implicit and find their truest, their highest and fairest expression in the magic name 'Abdu'l-Bahá. He is, above and beyond these appellations, the *"Mystery of God"*—an expression by which Bahá'u'lláh Himself has chosen to designate Him, and which, while it does not by any means justify us to assign to Him the station of Prophethood, indicates how in the person of 'Abdu'l-Bahá the incompatible characteristics of a human nature and superhuman knowledge and perfection have been blended and are completely harmonized.

"When the ocean of My presence hath ebbed and the Book of My Revelation is ended," proclaims the *Kitáb-i-Aqdas*, *"turn your faces towards Him Whom God hath purposed, Who hath branched from this Ancient Root."* And again, *"When the Mystic Dove will have winged its flight from its Sanctuary of Praise and sought its far-off goal, its hidden habitation, refer ye whatsoever ye understand not in the Book to Him Who hath branched from this mighty Stock."*

In the *Kitáb-i-'Ahd*, moreover, Bahá'u'lláh solemnly and explicitly declares: *"It is incumbent upon the Aghṣán, the Afnán and My kindred to turn, one and all, their faces towards the Most Mighty Branch. Consider that which We have revealed in Our Most Holy Book. 'When the ocean of My presence hath ebbed and the Book of My Revelation is ended, turn your faces toward Him Whom God hath purposed, Who hath branched from this Ancient Root.' The object of this sacred verse is none except the Most Mighty Branch ('Abdu'l-Bahá). Thus have We graciously revealed unto you our potent Will, and I am verily the Gracious, the All-Powerful."*

In the *Súriy-i-Ghuṣn* (*Tablet of the Branch*) the following verses have been re-corded: *"There hath branched from the Sadratu'l-Muntahá' this sacred and glorious Being, this Branch of Holiness; well is it with him that hath sought His shelter and abideth beneath His shadow. Verily the Limb of the Law of God hath sprung forth from this Root which God hath firmly implanted in the Ground of His Will, and Whose Branch hath been so uplifted as to encompass the whole of creation. Magnified be He, therefore, for this sublime, this blessed, this mighty, this exalted Handiwork! ... A Word hash, as a token of Our grace, gone forth from the Most Great Tablet— a Word which God hath adorned with the ornament of His own Self, and made it sovereign over the earth and all that is therein, and a sign of His greatness and power among its people ...Render thanks unto God, O people, for His appearance; for verily He is the most great Favour unto you, the most perfect bounty upon you; and through Him every mouldering bone is quickened. Whoso turneth towards Him hath turned towards God, and whoso turneth away from Him hath turned away from My Beauty, hath repudiated My Proof, and transgressed against Me. He is the Trust of God amongst you, His charge within you, His manifestation unto you and His appearance among His favoured servants ...We have sent Him down in the form of a human temple. Blest and sanctified be God Who createth whatsoever He willeth through His inviolable, His infallible decree. They who deprive themselves of the shadow of the Branch, are lost in the wilderness of error, are consumed by the heat of worldly desires, and are of those who will assuredy perish."*[144]

• • •

'Abdu'l-Bahá, writing in confirmation of the authority conferred upon Him by Bahá'u'lláh, makes the following statement: *"In accordance with the explicit text of the Kitáb-i-Aqdas Bahá'u'lláh hath made the Centre of the Covenant the Interpreter of His Word—a Covenant so firm and mighty that from the beginning of time until the present day no religious Dispensation hath produced its like."*

Exalted as is the rank of 'Abdu'l-Bahá, and however profuse the praises with which in these sacred Books and Tablets Bahá'u'lláh has glorified His son, so unique a distinction must never be construed as conferring upon its recipient a station identical with, or equivalent to, that of His Father, the Manifestation Himself. To give such an interpretation to any of these quoted passages would at once, and for obvious reasons, bring it into conflict with the no less clear and authentic assertions and warnings to which I have already referred. Indeed, as I have already stated, those who overestimate 'Abdu'l-Bahá's station are just as

---

144. Shoghi Effendi, *World Order of Bahá'u'lláh,* pp. 131-5.

reprehensible and have done just as much harm as those who underestimate it. And this for no other reason except that by insisting upon an altogether unwarranted inference from Bahá'u'lláh's writings they are inadvertently justifying and continuously furnishing the enemy with proofs for his false accusations and misleading statements.

I feel it necessary, therefore, to state without any equivocation or hesitation that neither in the *Kitáb-i-Aqdas* nor in the Book of Bahá'u'lláh's Covenant, nor even in the *Tablet of the Branch*, nor in any other Tablet, whether revealed by Bahá'u'lláh or 'Abdu'l-Bahá, is there any authority whatever for the opinion that inclines to uphold the so-called "mystic unity" of Bahá'u'lláh and 'Abdu'l-Bahá, or to establish the identity of the latter with His Father or with any preceding Manifestation. This erroneous conception may, in part, be ascribed to an altogether extravagant interpretation of certain terms and passages in the *Tablet of the Branch*, to the introduction into its English translation of certain words that are either non-existent, misleading, or ambiguous in their connotation. It is, no doubt, chiefly based upon an altogether unjustified inference from the opening passages of a Tablet of Bahá'u'lláh, extracts of which, as reproduced in the *Bahá'í Scriptures,* immediately precede, but form no part of, the said *Tablet of the Branch.* It should be made clear to every one reading those extracts that by the phrase *"the Tongue of the Ancient"* no one else is meant but God, and that the Term *"the Greatest Name"* is an obvious reference to Bahá'u'lláh, and that *"the Covenant"* referred to is not the specific Covenant of which Bahá'u'lláh is the immediate Author and 'Abdu'l-Bahá the Centre but that general Covenant which, as inculcated by the Bahá'í teaching, God Himself invariably establishes with mankind when He inaugurates a new Dispensation. *"The Tongue"* that *"gives,"* as stated in those extracts, the *"glad-tidings"* is none other than the Voice of God referring to Bahá'u'lláh, and not Bahá'u'lláh referring to 'Abdu'l-Bahá.

Moreover, to maintain that the assertion *"He is Myself,"* instead of denoting the mystic unity of God and His Manifestations, as explained in the Kitáb-i-Íqán, establishes the identity of Bahá'u'lláh with 'Abdu'l-Bahá, would constitute a direct violation of the oft-repeated principle of the oneness of God's Manifestations— a principle which the Author of these same extracts is seeking by implication to emphasize.

It would also amount to a reversion to those irrational and superstitious beliefs which have insensibly crept, in the first century of the Christian era, into the teachings of Jesus Christ, and by crystallizing into accepted dogmas have impaired the effectiveness and obscured the purpose of the Christian Faith.

"I affirm," is 'Abdu'l-Bahá's own written comment on the *Tablet of the Branch,* *"that the true meaning, the real significance, the innermost secret of these verses, of these very words, is my own servitude to the sacred Threshold of the Abhá Beauty, my complete self-effacement, my utter nothingness before Him. This is my resplendent crown, my most precious adorning. On this I pride myself in the kingdom of earth and heaven. Therein I glory among the company of the well-favoured!"* *"No one is permitted,"* He warns us in the passage which immediately follows, *"to give these verses any other interpretation."* *"I am,"* He, in this same connection, affirms, *"according to the explicit texts of the Kitáb-i-Aqdas and the Kitáb-i-'Ahd the manifest Interpreter of the Word of God.... . Whoso deviates from my interpretation is a victim of his own fancy."*

Furthermore, the inescapable inference from the belief in the identity of the Author of our Faith with Him Who is the Centre of His Covenant would be to place 'Abdu'l-Bahá in a position superior to that of the Báb, the reverse of which is the fundamental, though not as yet universally recognized, principle of this Revelation. It would also justify the charge with which, all throughout 'Abdu'l-Bahá's ministry, the Covenant-Breakers have striven to poison the minds and pervert the understanding of Bahá'u'lláh's loyal followers. [145]

• • •

That 'Abdu'l-Bahá is not a Manifestation of God, that He gets His light, His inspiration and sustenance direct from the Fountainhead of the Bahá'í Revelation; that He reflects even as a clear and perfect Mirror the rays of Bahá'u'lláh's glory, and does not inherently possess that indefinable yet all-pervading reality the exclusive possession of which is the hallmark of Prophethood; that His words are not equal in rank, though they possess an equal validity with the utterances of Bahá'u'lláh; that He is not to be acclaimed as the return of Jesus Christ, the Son Who will come "in the glory of the Father"—these truths find added justification, and are further reinforced, by the following statement of 'Abdu'l-Bahá, addressed to some believers in America, with which I may well conclude this section: *"You have written that there is a difference among the believers concerning the 'Second Coming of Christ.' Gracious God! Time and again this question hath arisen, and its answer hath emanated in a clear and irrefutable statement from the pen of 'Abdu'l-Bahá, that what is meant in the prophecies by the 'Lord of Hosts' and the 'Promised Christ' is the Blessed Perfection* (Bahá'u'lláh) *and His holiness the Exalted One* (the Báb). *My name is 'Abdu'l-Bahá'. My qualification is 'Abdu'l-Bahá'. My reality is 'Abdu'l-Bahá'.*

---

145. Shoghi Effendi, *The World Order of Bahá'u'lláh,* pp. 136-8.

192

My praise is Abdu'l-Bahá'. Thraldom to the Blessed Perfection is my glorious and refulgent diadem, and servitude to all the human race my perpetual religion …No name, no title, no mention, no commendation have I, nor will ever have, except Abdu'l-Bahá. This is my longing. This is my greatest yearning. This is my eternal life. This is my everlasting glory." [146]

3.1.7   The Passing of 'Abdu'l-Bahá

'Abdu'l-Bahá's great work was now ended. The historic Mission with which His Father had, twenty-nine years previously, invested Him had been gloriously consummated. A memorable chapter in the history of the first Bahá'í century had been written. The Heroic Age of the Bahá'í Dispensation, in which He had participated since its inception, and played so unique a role, had drawn to a close. He had suffered as no disciple of the Faith, who had drained the cup of martyrdom, had suffered, He had laboured as none of its greatest heroes had laboured. He had witnessed triumphs such as neither the Herald of the Faith nor its Author had ever witnessed.

At the close of His strenuous Western tours, which had called forth the last ounce of His ebbing strength, He had written: *"Friends, the time is coming when I shall be no longer with you. I have done all that could be done. I have served the Cause of Bahá'u'lláh to the utmost of My ability. I have laboured night and day all the years of My life. O how I long to see the believers shouldering the responsibilities of the Cause! …My days are numbered, and save this there remains none other joy for me."* Several years before He had thus alluded to His passing: *"O ye My faithful loved ones! Should at any time afflicting events come to pass in the Holy Land, never feel disturbed or agitated. Fear not, neither grieve. For whatsoever thing happeneth will cause the Word of God to be exalted, and His Divine fragrances to be diffused."* And again: *"Remember, whether or not I be on earth, My presence will be with you always."* *"Regard not the person of Abdu'l-Bahá,"* He thus counselled His friends in one of His last Tablets, *"for He will eventually take His leave of you all, nay, fix you gaze upon the Word of God …The loved ones of God must arise with such steadfastness that should, in one moment, hundreds of souls even as 'Abdu'l-Bahá Himself be made a target for the darts of woe, nothing whatsoever shall affect or lessen their …service to the Cause of God."*

In a Tablet addressed to the American believers, a few days before He passed away, He thus vented His pent-up longing to depart from this world: *"I have renounced the world and the people thereof . . . In the cage of this world I flutter even as a*

---

146. Shoghi Effendi, *The World Order of Bahá'u'lláh*, pp. 131-5.

frightened bird, and yearn every day to take My flight unto Thy Kingdom. Yá Bahá'u'l-Abhá! Make Me drink of the cup of sacrifice, and set Me free." He revealed a prayer less than six months before His ascension in honour of a kinsman of the Báb, and in it wrote: *"O Lord! My bones are weakened, and the hoar hairs glisten on My head …and I have now reached old age, failing in My powers.' …No strength is there left in Me wherewith to arise and serve Thy loved ones …O Lord, My Lord! Hasten My ascension unto Thy sublime Threshold …and My arrival at the Door of Thy grace beneath the shadow of Thy most great mercy…"*

Through the dreams He dreamed, through the conversations He held, through the Tablets He revealed, it became increasingly evident that His end was fast approaching. Two months before His passing He told His family of a dream He had had. *"I seemed,"* He said, *"to be standing within a great mosque, in the inmost shrine, facing the Qiblih, in the place of the Imám himself. I became aware that a large number of people were flocking into the mosque. More and yet more crowded in, taking their places in rows behind Me, until there was a vast multitude. As I stood I raised loudly the call to prayer. Suddenly the thought came to Me to go forth from the mosque. When I found Myself outside I said within Myself: 'For what reason came I forth, not having led the prayer? But it matters not; now that I have uttered the Call to prayer, the vast multitude will of themselves chant the prayer.'"* A few weeks later, whilst occupying a solitary room in the garden of His house, He recounted another dream to those around Him. *"I dreamed a dream,"* He said, *"and behold, the Blessed Beauty (Bahá'u'lláh) came and said to Me. 'Destroy this room.'"* None of those present comprehended the significance of this dream until He Himself had soon after passed away, when it became clear to them all that by the *"room"* was meant the temple of His body.

A month before His death (which occurred in the 78th year of His age, in the early hours of the 28th of November, 1921) He had referred expressly to it in some words of cheer and comfort that He addressed to a believer who was mourning the loss of His brother. And about two weeks before His passing He had spoken to His faithful gardener in a manner that clearly indicated He knew His end to be nigh. *"I am so fatigued,"* He observed to him, *"the hour is come when I must leave everything and take My flight. I am too weary to walk."* He added: *"It was during the closing days of the Blessed Beauty, when I was engaged in gathering together His papers which were strewn over the sofa in His writing chamber in Bahjí, that He turned to Me and said. 'It is of no use to gather them, I must leave them and flee away.' I also have finished My work. I can do nothing more. Therefore must I leave it, kind take My departure."*

Till the very last day of His earthly life 'Abdu'l-Bahá continued to shower

194

that same love upon high and low alike, to extend that same assistance to the poor and the down-trodden, and to carry out those same duties in the service of His Father's Faith, as had been His wont from the days of His boyhood. On the Friday before His passing, despite great fatigue, He attended the noonday prayer at the mosque, and distributed afterwards alms, as was His custom, among the poor; dictated some Tablets—the last ones He revealed—; blessed the marriage of a trusted servant, which He had insisted should take place that day; attended the usual meeting of the friends in His home; felt feverish the next day, and being unable to leave the house on the following Sunday, sent all the believers to the Tomb of the Báb to attend a feast which a Parsí pilgrim was offering on the occasion of the anniversary of the Declaration of the Covenant; received with His unfailing courtesy and kindness that same afternoon, and despite growing weariness, the Muftí of Haifa, the Mayor and the Head of the Police; and inquired that night—the last of His life—before He retired after the health of every member of His household, of the pilgrims and of the friends in Haifa.

At 1.15 A.M. He arose, and, walking to a table in His room, drank some water, and returned to bed. Later on, He asked one of His two daughters who had remained awake to care for Him, to lift up the net curtains, complaining that He had difficulty in breathing Some rose-water was brought to Him, of which He drank, after which He again lay down, and when offered food, distinctly remarked: *"You wish Me to take some food, and I am going?"* A minute later His spirit had winged its flight to its eternal abode, to be gathered, at long last, to the glory of His beloved Father, and taste the joy of everlasting reunion with Him.

The news of His passing, so sudden, so unexpected, spread like wildfire throughout the town, and was flashed instantly over the wires to distant parts of the globe, stunning with grief the community of the followers of Bahá'u'lláh in East and West. Messages from far and near, from high and low alike, through cablegrams and letters, poured in conveying to the members of a sorrow-stricken and disconsolate family expressions of praise, of devotion, of anguish and of sympathy. [147]

• • •

The coffin containing the remains of 'Abdu'l-Bahá was borne to its last resting-place on the shoulders of His loved ones. The cortege which preceded it

147. Shoghi Effendi, *God Passes By*, pp. 309-11.

was led by the City Constabulary Force, acting as a Guard of Honour, behind which followed in order the Boy Scouts of the Muslim and Christian communities holding aloft their banners, a company of Muslim choristers chanting their verses from the Qur'án, the chiefs of the Muslim community headed by the Muftí, and a number of Christian priests, Latin, Greek and Anglican. Behind the coffin walked the members of His family, the British High Commissioner, Sir Herbert Samuel, the Governor of Jerusalem, Sir Ronald Storrs, the Governor of Phoenicia, Sir Stewart Symes, officials of the government, consuls of various countries resident in Haifa, notables of Palestine, Muslim, Jewish, Christian and Druze, Egyptians, Greeks, Turks, Arabs, Kurds, Europeans and Americans, men, women and children. The long train of mourners, amid the sobs and moans of many a grief-stricken heart, wended its slow way up the slopes of Mt. Carmel to the Mausoleum of the Bab.

Close to the eastern entrance of the Shrine, the sacred casket was placed upon a plain table, and, in the presence of that vast concourse, nine speakers, who represented the Muslim, the Jewish and Christian Faiths, and who included the Muftí of Haifa, delivered their several funeral orations. These concluded, the High Commissioner drew close to the casket, and, with bowed head fronting the Shrine, paid his last homage of farewell to 'Abdu'l-Bahá: the other officials of the Government followed his example. The coffin was then removed to one of the chambers of the Shrine, and there lowered, sadly and reverently, to its last resting-place in a vault adjoining that in which were laid the remains of the Báb.

During the week following His passing, from fifty to a hundred of the poor of Haifa were daily fed at His house, whilst on the seventh day corn was distributed in His memory to about a thousand of them irrespective of creed or race. On the fortieth day an impressive memorial feast was held in His memory, to which over six hundred of the people of Haifa, 'Akká and the surrounding parts of Palestine and Syria, including officials and notables of various religions and races, were invited. More than one hundred of the poor were also fed on that day.

One of the assembled guests, the Governor of Phoenicia, paid a last tribute to the memory of 'Abdu'l- Bahá in the following words: "Most of us here have, I think a clear picture of Sir 'Abdu'l-Bahá 'Abbás, of His dignified figure walking thoughtfully in our streets, of His courteous and gracious manner, of His kindness, of His love for little children and flowers, of His generosity and care for the poor and suffering. So gentle was He, and so simple, that in His presence one almost forgot that He was also a great teacher, and that His writings and His conversations have been a solace and an inspiration to hundreds and thousands of people in the East and in the West."

Thus was brought to a close the ministry of One Who was the incarnation, by virtue of the rank bestowed upon Him by His Father, of an institution that has no parallel in the entire field of religious history, a ministry that marks the final stage in the Apostolic, the Heroic and most glorious Age of the Dispensation of Bahá'u'lláh. [148]

3.1.8   Prayer of Visitation of 'Abdu'l-Bahá

This prayer is read at the Shrine of 'Abdu'l-Bahá. It is also used in private prayer. 'Abdu'l-Bahá says:

Whoso reciteth this prayer with lowliness and fervour will bring gladness and joy to the heart of this Servant, it will be even as meeting Him face to face.'

The Prayer was revealed by 'Abdu'l-Bahá.

He is the All-Glorious!

O God, my God! Lowly and tearful, I raise my suppliant hands to Thee and cover my face in the dust of that Threshold of Thine, exalted above the knowledge of the learned, and the praise of all that glorify Thee. Graciously look upon Thy servant, humble and lowly at Thy door, with the glances of the eye of Thy mercy, and immerse him in the Ocean of Thine eternal grace.

Lord! He is a poor and lowly servant of Thine, enthralled and imploring Thee, captive in Thy hand, praying fervently to Thee, trusting in Thee, in tears before Thy face, calling to Thee and beseeching Thee, saying:

O Lord, my God! Give me Thy grace to serve Thy loved ones, strengthen me in my servitude to Thee, illumine my brow with the light of adoration in Thy court of holiness, and of prayer to Thy Kingdom of grandeur. Help me to be selfless at the heavenly entrance of Thy gate, and aid me to be detached from all things within Thy holy precincts. Lord! Give me to drink from the chalice of selflessness; with its robe clothe me, and in its ocean immerse me. Make me as dust in the pathway of Thy loved ones, and grant that I may offer up my soul for the earth ennobled by the footsteps of Thy chosen ones in Thy path, O Lord of Glory in the Highest.

With this prayer doth Thy servant call Thee, at dawn-tide and in the night-season. Fulfil his heart's desire, O Lord! Illumine his heart, gladden his bosom,

148. Shoghi Effendi, *God Passes By*, pp. 313-4.

kindle his light, that he may serve Thy Cause and Thy servants.

Thou art the Bestower, the Pitiful, the Most Bountiful, the Gracious, the Merciful, the Compassionate! [149]

3.1.9 Prayer of Shoghi Effendi

He is God

O Mighty Lord! Thou seest what hath befallen Thy helpless lovers in this darkest of long nights; Thou knowest how, in all these years of separation from Thy Beauty, the confidants of Thy mysteries have ever been acquainted with burning grief.

O Powerful Master! Suffer not Thy wayfarers to be abased and brought low; succour this handful of feeble creatures with the potency of Thy might. Exalt Thy loved ones before the assemblage of man, and grant them strength. Allow those broken-winged beings to raise their heads and glory in the fulfilment of their hopes, that we in these brief days of life may gaze with our physical eyes on the elevation and exaltation of Thy Faith, and soar up to Thee with gladdened souls and blissful hearts.

Thou knowest that, since Thy ascension, we seek no name or fame, that in this swiftly passing world we wish henceforth no joy, no delight and no good fortune.

Then keep Thy word, and exhilarate once more the lives of these, Thy sick at heart. Bring light to our expectant eyes, balm to our stricken breasts. Lead Thou the caravans of the city of Thy love swiftly to their intended goal. Draw those who sorrow after Thee into the high court of reunion with Thee. For in this world below we ask for nothing but the triumph of Thy Cause. And within the precincts of Thy boundless mercy we hope for nothing but Thy presence.

Thou art the Witness, the Haven, the Refuge; Thou art He who rendereth victorious this band of the innocent. [150]

---

149. `Abdu'l-Bahá, *Selections from the Writings of `Abdu'l-Bahá*, pp. 319-20.
150. Shoghi Effendi, quoted in *The Bahá'í World*, vol. XVIII, pp. 35-6.

3.2
The Day of the Covenant
November 26

As to the most great characteristic of the revelation of Bahá'u'lláh—a specific teaching not given by any of the prophets of the past—It is the ordination and appointment of the Centre of the Covenant.[151]

Readings:
3.2.1 *The Day of the Covenant* Suggested by 'Abdu'l-Bahá
3.2.2 Tablet of the Branch
3.2.3 Excerpts from the Writings of Bahá'u'lláh on the Covenant
3.2.4 Prayer Revealed by 'Abdu'l-Bahá
3.2.5 One of the Tablets of 'Abdu'l-Bahá on the Covenant

---

151. 'Abdu'l-Bahá, *Promulgation of Universal Peace*, p. 455.

3.2.1   The Day of the Covenant Suggested by 'Abdu'l-Bahá

Abdu'l-Bahá told the Bahá'ís that this day[152] was not, under any circumstances, to be celebrated as His day of birth. It was the day of the Declaration of the Báb, exclusively associated with Him. But as the Bahá'ís begged for a day to be celebrated as His, He gave them 26 November, to be observed as the day of the appointment of the Centre of the Covenant. It was known as Jashn-i-A'ẓam (The Greatest Festival), because He was Ghuṣn-i-A'ẓam—the Greatest Branch. In the West it is known as the Day of the Covenant.[153]

3.2.2   Tablet of the Branch

He is Eternal in His Abhá Horizon!

Verily, the Cause of God hath come upon the clouds of utterances and the polytheists are in this day in great torment! Verily, the hosts of revelation have descended with banners of inspiration from the heaven of the Tablet in the name of God, the Powerful, the Mighty! At this time the monotheists all rejoice in the victory of God and His dominion, and the deniers will then be in manifest perplexity.

O ye people! Do ye flee from the mercy of God after it has encompassed the existent things created between the heavens and earths? Beware lest ye prefer your own selves before the mercy of God, and deprive not yourselves thereof! Verily, whosoever turneth away therefrom will be in great loss. Verily, mercy is like unto verses which have descended from the one heaven, and from them the monotheists drink the choice wine of life, whilst the polytheists drink from the fiery water; and when the verses of God are read unto them, the fire of hatred is enkindled within their breasts. Thus have they preferred their own selves before the mercy of God, and are of those who are heedless.

Enter, O people, beneath the shelter of the Word! Then drink therefrom the choice wine of inner significances and utterances; for therein is hidden the Kawthar of the glorious One—and it hath appeared from the horizon of the Will of your Lord, the merciful, with wonderful lights.

Say: Verily, the ocean of pre-existence hath branched forth from this most great Ocean. Blessed, therefore, is he who abides upon Its shores, and is of those who are established thereon. Verily, this most sacred temple of Abhá—

---

152. 23 May 1844.

153. H.M. Balyuzi, '*Abdu'l-Bahá*, p. 523, Note no. 9.

the branch of Holiness—hath branched forth from the Sadratu'l-Muntahá. Blessed is whosoever sought shelter beneath it and is of those who rest therein.

Say: Verily, the branch of command hath sprung forth from this root which God hath firmly planted in the ground of the will the limb of which has been elevated to a station which encompasses all existence. Therefore, exalted be He for this creation, the Lofty, the Blessed, the Inaccessible, the Mighty.

O ye people! Draw nigh unto It, and taste the fruits of its knowledge and wisdom on the part of the mighty, the knowing One. Whosoever will not taste thereof shall be deprived of the bounty, even though he hath partaken of all that is in the earth—were ye of those who know.

Say: Verily, a word hath gone forth in favour from the most great Tablet and God has adorned It with the mantle of Himself, and made it sovereign over all in the earth and a sign of His grandeur and omnipotence among the creatures, in order that through it, the people shall praise their Lord, the Mighty, the Powerful, the Wise; and that, through it, they shall glorify their creator and sanctify the self of God which standeth within all things. Verily, this is naught but a Revelation upon the part of the Wise, the Ancient One!

Say: O people, praise ye God, for its Manifestation, for verily it is the most great favour upon you and the most perfect blessing upon you; and through Him every mouldering bone is quickened. Whosoever turns to Him hath surely turned unto God, and whosoever turneth away from Him hath turned away from My beauty, denied My proof, and is of those who transgress. Verily, He is the remembrance of God amongst you and His trust within you, and His manifestation unto you and His appearance among the servants who are nigh. Thus have I been commanded to convey to you the message of God, your Creator; and I have delivered to you that of which I was commanded. Whereupon, thereunto testifieth God, then His angels, then His messengers, and then His holy servants.

Inhale the fragrances of the Riḍván from His roses and be not of those who are deprived. Appreciate the bounty of God upon you and be not veiled therefrom—and, verily, We have sent Him forth in the temple of man. Thus praise ye the Lord, the Originator of whatsoever He willeth through His wise and inviolable Command!

Verily, those who withhold themselves from the shelter of the Branch are indeed lost in the wilderness of perplexity; and are consumed by the heat of self-desire, and are of those who perish.

Hasten, O people, unto the shelter of God, in order that He may protect you from the heat of the Day whereon none shall find for himself any refuge or shelter except beneath the shelter of His Name, the Clement, the Forgiving! Clothe yourselves, O people, with the garment of assurance, in order that He may protect you from the dart of doubts and superstitions, and that ye may be of those who are assured in those days wherein none shall ever be assured and none shall be firmly established in the Cause, except by severing himself from all that is possessed by the people and turning unto the holy and radiant Outlook.

O ye people! Do ye take unto yourselves the Jebt as a helper other than God, and do ye seek the Tághút as a Lord besides your Lord, the Almighty, the Omnipotent? Forsake, O people, their mention, then hold the chalice of life in the Name of your Lord, the Merciful. Verily, by God, the existent world is quickened through a drop thereof, were ye of those who know.

Say: In that Day there is no refuge for any one save the command of God, and no salvation for any soul but God. Verily, this is the truth and there is naught after truth but manifest error.

Verily, God hath made it incumbent upon every soul to deliver His Cause according to his ability. Thus hath the command been recorded by the finger of might and power upon the Tablet of majesty and greatness.

Whosoever quickens one soul in this Cause is like unto one quickening all the servants and the Lord shall bring him forth in the day of resurrection into the Riḍván of oneness, adorned with the Mantle of Himself, the Protector, the Mighty, the Generous! Thus will ye assist your Lord, and naught else save this shall ever be mentioned in this day before God, your Lord and the Lord of your forefathers.

As to thee, O servant, hearken unto the admonition given unto thee in the Tablet; then seek the grace of thy Lord at all times. Then spread the Tablet among those who believe in God and in His verses; so that they may follow that which is contained therein, and be of those who are praiseworthy.

Say: O people, cause no corruption in the earth and dispute not with men; for, verily, this is not worthy of those who have chosen in the shelter of their Lord a station which shall indeed remain secure.

If ye find one athirst, give him to drink from the chalice of Kawthar and Tasnín; and if ye find one endowed with an attentive ear, read unto him the verses of God, the Mighty, the Merciful, the Compassionate! Unloose the tongue with excellent utterance, then admonish the people if ye find them advancing unto the sanctuary of God; otherwise abandon them unto themselves and forsake them in the abyss of hell. Beware lest ye scatter the pearls of inner significance before every barren, dumb one. Verily, the blind are deprived of witnessing the lights and are unable to distinguish between the stone and the holy, precious pearl.

Verily, wert thou to read the most mighty, wonderful verses to the stone for a thousand years, will it understand, or will they take any effect therein? No! by the Lord, the Merciful, the Clement. If thou readest all the verses of God unto the deaf, will he hear a single letter? No! Verily, by the Beauty, the mighty, the Ancient.

Thus have We delivered unto thee some of the jewels of wisdom and utterance, in order that thou mayest gaze unto the direction of thy Lord and be severed from all the creatures. May the spirit and glory rest upon thee, and upon those who dwell upon the plain of holiness and who remain in the Cause of their Lord in manifest steadfastness.[154]

3.2.3 Excerpts from the Writings of Bahá'u'lláh on the Covenant

When the ocean of My presence hath ebbed and the Book of My Revelation is ended, turn your faces towards Him Whom God hath purposed, Who hath branched from this Ancient Root.[155]

• • •

When the Mystic Dove will have winged its flight from its Sanctuary of Praise and sought its far-off goal, its hidden habitation, refer ye whatsoever ye understand not in the Book, to Him Who hath branched from this mighty Stock.[156]

• • •

There hath branched from the Sadratu'l-Muntahá this sacred and glorious Being, this Branch of Holiness; well is it with him that hath sought His shelter and abideth beneath His shadow. Verily the Limb of the Law of God hath sprung forth from this Root which God hath firmly implanted in the Ground of His Will, and Whose Branch hath been so uplifted as to encompass the whole of creation. Magnified be He, therefore, for this sublime, this blessed,

---

154. Bahá'u'lláh, *The Bahá'í World Faith*, pp. 204-7.
155. Bahá'u'lláh, *The Kitáb-i-Aqdas*, p. 63.
156. Bahá'u'lláh, *The Kitáb-i-Aqdas*, p.82.

this mighty, this exalted Handiwork!... A Word hath, as a token of Our grace, gone forth from the Most Great Tablet—a Word which God hath adorned with the ornament of His own Self, and made it sovereign over the earth and all that is therein, and a sign of His greatness and power among its people... [157]

3.2.4 Prayer Revealed by 'Abdu'l-Bahá

O God, my God! Shield Thy trusted servants from the evils of self and passion, protect them with the watchful eye of Thy loving kindness from all rancour, hate and envy, shelter them in the impregnable stronghold of Thy care and, safe from the darts of doubtfulness, make them the manifestations of Thy glorious signs, illumine their faces with the effulgent rays shed from the Dayspring of Thy Divine Unity, gladden their hearts with the verses revealed from Thy Holy Kingdom, strengthen their loins by Thy all-swaying power that cometh from Thy Realm of Glory. Thou art the All-Bountiful, the Protector, the Almighty, the Gracious! [158]

3.2.5 One of the Tablets of 'Abdu'l-Bahá on the Covenant

O thou who art firm in the Covenant! Three consecutive letters have been received from thee. From their contents it became known that in Cleveland the hearts are afflicted by the murky breaths of the Covenant-breakers and harmony hath decreased among the friends. Gracious God! A hundred times it hath been foretold that the violators are lying in ambush and by every means desire to. cause dissension among the friends so that this dissension may end in violation of the Covenant. How is it that, notwithstanding this warning, the friends have neglected this explicit statement?

The point at issue is clear, direct and of utmost brevity. Either Bahá'u'lláh was wise, omniscient and aware of what would ensue, or was ignorant and in error. He entered, by His supreme pen, into such a firm Covenant and Testament with all the Bahá'ís, first with the Aghṣán, the Afnán and His kindred, and commanded them to obey and turn toward Him. By His supreme pen He hath explicitly declared that the object of the following verse of the *Kitáb-i-Aqdas* is the Most Great Branch:

When the ocean of My presence hath ebbed and the Book of My Revelation is ended, turn your faces toward Him Whom God hath purposed, Who hath branched from this Ancient

---

157. Bahá'u'lláh, quoted by Shoghi Effendi in *The World Order of Bahá'u'lláh*, p. 135.
158. 'Abdu'l-Bahá, *The Will and Testament of 'Abdu'l-Bahá*, p. 9.

Root.' Its meaning briefly is this: that after My ascension it is incumbent upon the Aghṣán, the Afnán and the kindred, and all the friends of God, to turn their faces to Him Who hath branched from the Ancient Root.

He also plainly saith in the *Kitáb-i-Aqdas*: '*O ye people of the world! When the Mystic Dove will have winged its flight from its Sanctuary of Praise and sought its far-off goal, its hidden habitation, refer ye whatsoever ye understand not in the Book to Him Who hath branched from this mighty Stock.'* Addressing all the people of the world He saith: When the Mystic Dove flieth away from the orchard of praise to the Most Supreme and Invisible Station—that is, when the Blessed Beauty turneth away from the contingent world towards the invisible realm—refer whatever ye do not understand in the Book to Him Who hath branched from the Ancient Root. That is, whatever He saith is the very truth.

And in the Book of the Covenant He explicitly saith that the object of this verse 'Who hath branched from this Ancient Root' is the Most Mighty Branch. And He commandeth all the Aghṣán, the Afnán, the kindred and the Bahá'ís to turn toward Him. Now, either one must say that the Blessed Beauty hath made a mistake, or He must be obeyed. 'Abdu'l-Bahá hath no command for the people to obey save the diffusion of the fragrances of God, the exaltation of His Word, the promulgation of the oneness of the world of humanity, the establishment of universal peace, and other of the commands of God. These are divine commands and have nothing to do with 'Abdu'l-Bahá. Whoever wisheth may accept them, and anyone who rejecteth them may do as he pleaseth.

Now some of the mischief-makers, with many stratagems, are seeking leadership, and in order to reach this position they instil doubts among the friends that they may cause differences, and that these differences may result in their drawing a party to themselves. But the friends of God must be awake and must know that the scattering of these doubts hath as its motive personal desires and the achievement of leadership.

Do not disrupt Bahá'í unity, and know that this unity cannot be maintained save through faith in the Covenant of God.

Thou hast the desire to travel that thou mayest spread the fragrances of God. This is highly suitable. Assuredly divine confirmations will assist thee and the power of the Covenant and Testament will secure for thee triumph and victory.[159]

---

159. 'Abdu'l-Bahá, *Selections from the Writings of 'Abdu'l-Bahá*, no. 186, p. 213-215.

Bibliography

'Abdu'-Bahá, *'Abdu'l-Bahá in London*, Bahá'í Publishing Trust, London, 1982.

'Abdu'l-Bahá, *Paris Talks*, Bahá'í Publishing Trust, London, 1972.

'Abdu'l-Bahá, *The Promulgation of Universal Peace*, 2nd ed., Bahá'í Publishing Trust, Wilmette, 1982.

'Abdu'l-Bahá, *Selections from the Writings of 'Abdu'l-Bahá*, Bahá'í World Centre, Haifa, 1978.

'Abdu'l-Bahá, *Some Answered Questions*, Bahá'í Publishing Trust, Wilmette, 1982.

'Abdu'l-Bahá, *The Will and Testament of 'Abdu'l-Bahá*, Bahá'í Publishing Trust, Wilmette, 1971.

Báb, The, *Selections from the Writings of the Báb*, Bahá'í World Centre, Haifa, 1978.

Bahá'í World: An International Record, The, 1954-1963, Vol. XIII, Bahá'í World Centre, Haifa, 1970.

Bahá'í World: An International Record, The, 1968-1973, Vol. XV, Bahá'í World Centre, Haifa, 1976.

Bahá'í World: An International Record, The, 1979-83, Vol. XVIII, Bahá'í World Centre, Haifa..

Bahá'u'lláh and 'Abdu'l-Bahá, *Bahá'í World Faith: Selected Writings of Bahá'u'lláh and 'Abdu'l-Bahá*, Bahá'í Publishing Trust, Wilmette, 1971.

Bahá'u'lláh, *Gleanings from the Writings of Bahá'u'lláh*, 2nd ed., Bahá'í Publishing Trust, Wilmette, 1982.

Bahá'u'lláh, *The Kitáb-i-Aqdas*, Bahá'í Publications Australia, Sydney, 1992.

Bahá'u'lláh, *The Kitáb-i-Íqan*, Bahá'í Publishing Trust, Wilmette, 1981.

Bahá'u'lláh, *Prayers and Meditations of Bahá'u'lláh*, 8th ed., Bahá'í Publishing Trust, Wilmette, 1987.

Bahá'u'lláh, *The Proclamation of Bahá'u'lláh*, Bahá'í World Centre, Haifa, 1978.

Bahá'u'lláh, *Tablets of Bahá'u'lláh*, Bahá'í World Centre, Haifa, 1978.

Balyuzi, H. M., *Bahá'u'lláh: The King of Glory*, 2nd ed., George Ronald Publisher, Oxford, 1991.

Balyuzi, H. M., *Muhammad and the Course of Islám*, George Ronald Publisher, Oxford, 1976.

Hornby, Helen (Comp.), *Lights of Guidance*, 4rd rev. ed., Bahá'í Publishing Trust, New Delhi, 1996.

Principles of Bahá'í Administration, Bahá'í Publishing Trust, London, 1973.

Shoghi Effendi, *Dawn of a New Day: Messages to India 1923-1957*, Bahá'í Publishing Trust, New Delhi, 1970.

Shoghi Effendi (Ed.), *The Dawn-Breakers: Nabil's Narrative of the Early Days of the Bahá'í Revelation*, Bahá'í Publishing Trust, Wilmette, 1974.

Star of the West, Bahá'í Publishing Society, Chicago, 1910.

Shoghi Effendi, *Directives from the Guardian*, Bahá'í Publishing Trust, New Delhi, 1973.

Shoghi Effendi, *God Passes By*, Bahá'í Publishing Trust, Wilmette, 1974.

Shoghi Effendi, *Guidance for Today and Tomorrow*, Bahá'í Publishing Trust, London, 1973.

Shoghi Effendi, *Letters to Australia and New Zealand*, Bahá'í Publishing Trust, Fiji,

Shoghi Effendi, *Unfolding Destiny of the British Bahá'í Community*, Bahá'í Publishing Trust, London, 1981.

Shoghi Effendi, *The World Order of Bahá'u'lláh*, 2nd rev. ed., Bahá'í Publishing Trust, Wilmette, 1974.

Taherzadeh, Adib, *The Revelation of Bahá'u'lláh*, Vols 1-4, George Ronald Publisher, Oxford, 1974.

Universal House of Justice, *Messages from the Universal House of Justice 1963-86*, Bahá'í Publishing Trust, Wilmette, 1996.

Other Books about Bahá'í Holy Days and Anniversaries

Ascension of Bahá'u'lláh

Birth of the Báb

Birth of Bahá'u'lláh

Days of Riḍván

Declaration of the Báb

The Martyrdom of the Báb

The Passing of `Abdu'l-Bahá

Available from

Bahá'í Publications Australia
173 Mona Vale Road
Mona Vale NSW 2101
Australia

Telephone: 61 2 9913 1554

Fax: 61 2 9970 6710

Email: bpa@bahai.org.au

For more information on these and other titles, please visit our website

www.bahaibooks.com